FAN MAIL

A GUIDE TO WHAT WE LOVE, LOATHE, AND MOURN

Jason Guriel

Véhicule Press

Published with the generous assistance of the Canada Council for the Arts and the Canada Book Fund of the Department of Canadian Heritage.

Cover design by David Drummond
Set in Minion and Futura by Simon Garamond
Printed by Marquis Imprimeur

Copyright © Jason Guriel 2025
All rights reserved.

Dépôt légal, Library and Archives Canada and the Bibliothèque national du Québec, third trimester 2025

Library and Archives Canada Cataloguing in Publication
Title: Fan mail : a guide to what we love, loathe, and mourn / Jason Guriel.
Names: Guriel, Jason, 1978- author
Identifiers: Canadiana (print) 20250205572 | Canadiana (ebook) 20250205637 | ISBN 9781550656923 (softcover) | ISBN 9781550656954 (EPUB)
Subjects: LCSH: Fans (Persons) | LCSH: Popular culture. | LCSH: Criticism. | LCSH: Mass media—Audiences. | LCSH: Arts audiences.
Classification: LCC P94.5.F36 G87 2025 | DDC 306—dc23

Published by Véhicule Press, Montréal, Québec, Canada
www.vehiculepress.com

Distribution by LitDistCo
www.litdistco.ca

Printed in Canada on FSC certified paper.

Praise for Jason Guriel's Recent Books

THE FULL-MOON WHALING CHRONICLES

"Jason Guriel is a Canadian poet of gobsmacking originality."
—*Washington Post*

"Without question this is the most imaginative piece of young-adult-adjacent fiction I have ever read. It's a big wolfy huff-and-puff of fresh air in a genre swamped with tired plots and love triangles."
—*Wall Street Journal*

"The first thing to know about Guriel's 2023 book is that it's a novel written in rhyming couplets. The second is that it's about whalers who are also werewolves. Guriel has completely nailed his own ambitious brief; it's imaginative, innovative and unlike anything else published this year."
—*Globe and Mail*

"[D]izzyingly interesting . . . there is something utterly new and exciting here."
—*Toronto Star*

"If Guriel's fiction debut about a musical scavenger hunt was 1970s-era space rock, this book is full-on *Lord of the Rings* via Ralph Bakshi with a scattering of cyberpunk tropes to keep things spicy . . ."
—*Kirkus Reviews*

FORGOTTEN WORK

"A futuristic dystopian rock novel in rhymed couplets, this rollicking book is as unlikely, audacious and ingenious as the premise suggests."
—New York Times

"A wondrous novel written entirely in heroic couplets."
—Washington Post

"Strange and affectionate, like *Almost Famous* penned by Shakespeare. A love letter to music in all its myriad iterations."
—Kirkus Reviews

"Guriel's bountiful celebration of connections between art finds an inspiring, infectious groove."
—Publishers Weekly

ON BROWSING

"Why don't you reminisce with Jason Guriel about the vanishing art of browsing?"
—New York Times

"We need the voices of those like Guriel in our midst."
—Literary Matters

"'Our choices are chisels,' says Jason Guriel. This moving book will fill you with a good kind of sadness and help you understand your own nostalgias."
—Nicholson Baker

To Christie, Henry, and Annie,
from your number one fan

Contents

LETTER TO THE READER 13

LOVE

Patrick Leigh Fermor's Walk Across Europe 23
Peter Bogdanovich's Fandom for Golden Age Hollywood 28
Clive James's *Poetry Notebook* 32
Brian De Palma's *Dressed to Kill* 37
Randall Jarrell's Pigheaded Soul 41
Orson Welles's *Mr. Arkadin* 43
Simon Callow's Biography of Orson Welles 47
Whit Stillman's Yuppie Trilogy 53
J.G. Ballard's *Concrete Island* 57
Brian Wilson's *Pet Sounds* 61
Charles Bruce's Poems 65
Christian Wiman's *Poetry* and Poetry 67
Kingsley Amis's *The Alteration* 72
Vladimir Nabokov's Heroic Couplets 77
Dave Sim's *Cerebus* 83
Kay Ryan's Essays 89
Howard Hawks's *Bringing Up Baby* 100
Jake Tapper's Joke 103
Byron's Poetical Commandments 106
Truman Capote's Blurb for *A Separate Peace* 108
Christopher Lehmann-Haupt's Blurb for *Gravity's Rainbow* 113
William Gibson's Realism 116

J.G. Ballard's *The Drowned World* 123
Monte Hellman's *Two-Lane Blacktop* 126
A.E. Stallings's Poems 129
Tom Scioli's Graphic Biography of Stan Lee 132
Jason Guriel's Guilty Pleasure 135
Jason Guriel's Childhood Comic Store 138
Holiday Shopping IRL 141
Brief Recommendations 146

LOATHE

Carl Wilson's Case for Celine Dion 155
Michael Robbins's Shtick 160
The *Best American* Anthologies' Boosterism 165
Kenneth Goldsmith's Stunts 170
Jonathan Galassi's First Novel 175
Jeffrey Eugenides's *The Virgin Suicides* 180
David Foster Wallace's Criticism 184
Criticism's Selfie Habit 190
Bob Dylan's Nobel Prize 196
Literary Community's Pitfalls 197
Alan Moore and Brian Bolland's *The Killing Joke* 203
Toni Morrison's Assertion that "All Good Art is Political!" 207
Criticism's Overinvestment in Fanboy Concerns 212
Criticism's Overanalysis of Pop Culture 217
Authors' Injunctions to Read Widely 223
Seth Abramson's Very, Very, Very Long Bio 227
Prose Poetry's Pitfalls 232
Lyric Poetry's Pitfalls 240

MOURN

Fandom Before the Internet 247
Bygone Phenomena Like Innate Talent, Quiet Ambition, and Deference to Authority 254
My Academic Hopes 258
Elise Partridge (1958-2015) 261
Rishma Dunlop (1956-2016) 264
Harold Bloom (1930-2019) 265
Phil Spector (1939-2021) 268
Peter Van Toorn (1944-2021) 272
Ed Piskor (1982-2024) 274
Peter Bogdanovich (1939-2022) 279

ACKNOWLEDGMENTS 287
INDEX 289

Garbo never answered a single fan letter in her whole Hollywood career. She ordered them destroyed before they reached her. The few that did reach her she threw into the fire. She was acting on the defensible assumption that they had already done their work simply through having been sent.

—Clive James, *Cultural Amnesia*

Letter to the Reader

The other night in the kitchen, I half-whispered to my wife, "Our son is obsessively drawing Scrooge characters again."

The previous Christmas, Henry had fallen for an illustrated seek-and-find version of *A Christmas Carol*—and here he was, a year later at the dining room table, duly copying Dickens's characters on printer paper, the beloved seek-and-find propped open.

Henry, who has gotten quite good at drawing, overheard my "obsessive" comment—and said as much. The eight-year-old seemed to assume it was a slight, a parental *faux pas*. He thought he'd caught me out.

But I was delighted. I'd just been reading about David Lynch's struggle to make his debut feature, *Eraserhead*. The cult classic (and favourite film of another obsessive, Stanley Kubrick) started as a student project. With a small crew of true believers, the young Lynch filmed at night for five years, whenever he could cobble together the funds. (The production would pause in the early morning so that Lynch could deliver his paper route.) The process was painstaking. Piecemeal. "There was one shot," said Lynch in an interview, "where [the movie's main character] walks down the hall, turns the doorknob, and a year and a half later he comes through the door!"

Anyway, obsession, I told Henry, is a good thing. All the best artists are obsessive. All the best athletes, too. You get great when you get obsessive.

I've been an obsessive fan since as far back as Henry's age, perhaps farther. I loved to reread the same comic over and over—then draw my favourite characters at the kitchen table for hours on end. At one point in the mid-eighties, I required a championship title belt to properly express my enthusiasm for professional wrestling. So, I began saving the gold foil wrappers from Caramilk bars. When I'd accumulated enough foil, I glued sections of it onto a wide strip of cardboard. Next, I blackened out portions of the cardboard with a permanent marker (an attempt to render six-pack-girding leather) and presto: I'd fashioned a title belt of my own.

Video games were another obsession. Thanks to the Nintendo Entertainment System, my grades briefly dipped in Grade Six—like 8-bit Mario failing to clear a chasm. But while maneuvering Mario was fun, lingering on stills of unreleased games in gaming magazines was even better. (Does fussing over screenshots in physical periodicals count as screen time?) I still remember the first photographs I saw of *Super Mario Bros. 4* in the November 1990 issue of *Electronic Gaming Monthly*, likely purchased at the World's Biggest Bookstore in Toronto. I remember those photographs as if they were the Zapruder stills in *LIFE* magazine.

Enchanted by images of unattainable games, I folded sheets of paper and founded my own trade publications. I drew the sample stills for imaginary games, including an off-model entry in the Super Mario franchise. I even came up with a gaming system! The comically unplayable controller, I recall, had dozens of buttons, each corresponding to a discrete move your avatar might make: a jab, an uppercut, and so on. (It hadn't occurred to me that fewer buttons, in combination, would be more efficient.)

The impulse to create carried over into secondary school. I got into William Gibson and, one summer, banged out a sci-fi novella on the Macintosh Classic in my basement. I think this lost masterpiece—something to do with people puppeteering the bodies of other people—came to about 150 pages, and I think I sent a copy of it to myself through registered mail. (They used to call this the "poor man's copyright," a workaround the internet assures me doesn't protect IP.) The unopened envelope is likely in a storage bin, lying in wait to horrify my heirs.

Around the same time, I also got into Dave Sim's black-and-white comic *Cerebus*, about an anthropomorphic aardvark who gigs as a barbarian, then becomes prime minister, then pope, then—well, you have to read it (or read my essay about it in this book). I especially loved Sim's background artist, Gerhard. Working in ink, Gerhard supplied photorealistic clouds, cobblestones, and buildings: miracles of analogue mark-making. I decided I needed to make my own comic—and my own such marks. My book, though, would focus on an anthropomorphic *eggplant*. (No one else had called the vegetable, I guess.) Thus, for a fleeting, Edenic moment in the late 1990s, a photocopied comic called *Mote* (read: "Man of the Eggplant") was available in downtown Toronto's finer comic stores, alongside masterworks by my friends, sold on consignment.

Still later, as a music snob in my twenties, I fetishized liner notes, pored over reviews in magazines, and, once again, created something: in this case, a fictional five-piece band called "Pomme." They became a kind of musical ideal, embodying the purest version of every genre that mattered to me. (The band's name was an allusion to Apple, the Beatles' label—but fancier, Frenchified.) A storehouse of styles, Pomme could do no wrong, earn nothing but five-star raves. Indeed, I never talked or wrote about them. This is the first mention of Pomme in print.

Nevertheless, the crater Pomme left in the culture had a comically long radius. In its early years, the band's "angular" guitars (amateur critics love that adjective) inspired Sonic Youth, My Bloody Valentine, and Pavement, among others. But in time, Pomme swapped guitars for samplers, inspiring a generation to go, as was said, "techno." Soon enough, Pomme ditched the digital and brought back analogue tape and artisanal beards. The band broke up, recorded solo albums, and reformed: a river crashing against my whims. The Strokes reverse-engineered their first album from Pomme's example. Taylor selfied herself wearing a Pomme tee. Kanye trashed-talked the band.

Only after reading Roberto Bolaño, who filled his novels with fictional writers, did I understand that in dreaming up Pomme's corpus and its sudden swerves of style, I wasn't just tracking my own ever-evolving tastes back here on Earth One; I was writing fanfic.

The homemade title belt, the counterfeit gaming mags, the off-model Marios, the novice novella, the crudely crosshatched egg-plant—these were forms of fanfic, too. I didn't have that word back then in the dark ages before dial-up. There were no fan pages, no online forums. You might've attended the occasional *Star Trek* or comic convention, as I did, but these were exceptional events that required a lift from dad. For the most part, to be a fan was to be wowed in isolation—and, for some of us, to be wowed into making our *own* works.

Put another way: fandom kindles creativity. As a teenage dilettante, in between ruling panel borders and writing dubious sci-fi, I fell hard for figurative language. Similes and metaphors that drew original (but precise) connections between unlike things made me swoon—and made me want to draw my own connections. Novelist E. Annie Proulx's description of an acne-scarred face "like cottage cheese clawed with a fork," David Foster Wallace's description of the "rickety alphabets of exposed plumbing" under old-fashioned sinks—these were envy-inducing incitements to attempt my own figurative feats. To play matchmaker between a previously unpaired tenor ("exposed plumbing") and vehicle ("rickety alphabets"). To make metaphors. Poems.

Work backwards toward the steamy, frond-obscured origin of any artistic career and you will find a fan. (All artists start out as *homofanicus*.) "I just want to be Muddy Waters," said a blues enthusiast named Keith Richards once. Fan begets artist, and artist begets fan.

I just want to be Kay Ryan—or wanted to be. I don't read Ryan as much as I used to. But there was a time in my early thirties when I couldn't shake her shadow and some (okay, many) of my poems sounded like hers. In fact, the editor and poet Christian Wiman once rejected a piece I'd sent to *Poetry* magazine because he judged it too close an approximation of Ryan's work, even as he suggested that he didn't feel good about the rejection. I took this to mean I'd written a real poem—a publishable poem!—while simultaneously perfecting the art of fanfic (or fanpo?). Years before ChatGPT, I had assimilated another entity's style.

In time, I stopped writing like Ryan. I abandoned poetry for a few years and wrote quite a few of the pieces that make up this book. And then, fired by my fandom for Vladimir Nabokov's heroic couplets in *Pale Fire*, I started composing couplets of my own in 2017. The resulting verse novel, called *Forgotten Work*, came to be about, well, fandom: a cult following searching for a lost band.

But the novel was an *expression* of fandom, too. It fused many of my enthusiasms, including obscure artists, William Gibson, poetry, and music criticism. (Alas, I couldn't find a way to work wrestling in.) A sequel, *The Full-Moon Whaling Chronicles*, concerned the quest for a reclusive writer and incorporated chapters of fanfic. Still *another* book of mine, a monograph-cum-pamphlet called *On Browsing*, offered a longform love letter to the bygone ritual of combing brick-and-mortar shops for physical media.

Fandom, I came to realize, had been my beat for years.

The essays in this book, written over the course of more than a decade, include reviews, criticism, personal essays, comic-strips, brief recommendations, parodic stanzas, and obituaries. They dwell on things I love, loathe, and mourn: the three primal functions of the fan. The things I love comprise the book's first, biggest section, but it's important to mark one's objections, too. (Love everything and you love nothing.) The elegies make up the smallest section, which is probably for the best since they tend to require bodies.

Sometimes, the essays are *about* fans and fandom. Peter Bogdanovich is a presiding spirit. Two pieces about the filmmaker-cum-critic bookend this book. The first was written for *The New Republic* in 2015 and occasioned by the release of Bogdanovich's last picture; the second, for *The Yale Review* and filed after he died, seven years later. His name pops up in other pieces throughout *Fan Mail*, too.

Why Bogdanovich? It was his irresistibly distressed voice: a wizened wagon that hauled both enthusiasm and authority. His DVD commentary tracks—recorded for *Citizen Kane*, *The Searchers*, and other classics—beguiled me when I was younger. You didn't need to be a filmmaker to find Bogdanovich's eye for craft inspiring. There was a sense that he'd been steeped in this stuff for years and that he was sharing treasure (a film, an approach to editing, an ethos) that the rest of the world had taken a pass on. He took you in, entrusted you with secret knowledge. Really, he was the consummate fan-artist: a model for how to swoon in the face of art and then mint some of your own.

"I am very susceptible to other people's enthusiasms, at times actually courting them," says Kay Ryan in her great essay "I Go to AWP." "I like to sit among people who feel strongly about a basketball team, say, and get excited with them. I love to love ouzo with ouzo lovers." Bogdanovich's enthusiasm for John Ford, Ryan's for Stevie Smith, Clive James's for Frost, Brian De Palma's for Hitchcock, Brian Wilson's for Phil Spector, Harold Bloom's for the Western Canon, Ed Piskor's for *Love and Rockets*—these acts of fandom, cited in the pages that follow, energize me.

The *object* of obsessive passion is often beside the point; it's the example of an exceptional writer (or musician or filmmaker) *being bowled over* that thrills. What impressed such an impressive talent? What have they valued that I, too, should prize? Many of the pieces in this book—covering film, fiction, comics, poetry, criticism, travel writing, and more—aspire to convey enthusiasm and, hopefully, deliver a jolt.

In other pieces, I contend that the internet ruined fandom; attempt to rehabilitate the supposedly loathsome figure of the fanboy; take a razor, like a De Palma heavy, to inflated reputations; lambast worrisome trends in criticism; mourn the loss of sundry talents; and contradict myself. Each piece is date stamped at the end; these expressions of fandom happened at specific moments. A few of them even roiled Twitter and sundered relationships. *Fan Mail* is a partisan book about passions, not a sociological study. I chase my whims, and I don't check boxes.

This is also an aesthetically minded book. I try to avoid the clichés of contemporary criticism—the "problematizing" of artists who fail to conform to the moral code of the moment. Appraising metaphors, not pointing out missteps, tends to be my province.

I don't expect readers to agree with all or even most of my opinions, though I hope they detect conductive material in these essays. I hope they find something to obsess over, to quarrel with, to join me in mourning.

And I welcome their mail.

Jason Guriel
Toronto, 2025

Love

Patrick Leigh Fermor's Walk Across Europe

IN 1933, A NINETEEN-YEAR-OLD Englishman, finding himself booted from school for holding hands with a local, decided to cross Europe on foot. He had a mind to make it from the Hook of Holland down to Constantinople—unpurple "Istanbul" would never do. Even more romantic than the goal was the gear: used rucksack (its previous owner had tramped about with the travel writer Robert Byron), Oxford Book of English Verse, and ace sidekick (Horace). He slept outdoors, but in castles, too, as freshly minted friends—an ever-expanding network of social capital—reached ahead of the young traveler, by post, to ensure he would be received by the next available count or baron.

But it wasn't until the 1970s, over four decades later, that Patrick Leigh Fermor—by then, an established author and war hero—turned his full attention to writing up the European walk. *A Time of Gifts* appeared in 1977, followed by *Between the Woods and the Water* in 1986. By the end of the first book, Leigh Fermor's younger self had reached the edge of Hungary; by the end of the second, Bulgaria. There he waited, stalled in 1934, for decades.

A cult began to fire up after the publication of these books. Blame the affable character Leigh Fermor cuts in the first two: ravenous for knowledge but willing to risk expulsion for the girl. He's charming, too; he tries to pay his way ("...I would make a frantic flourish with two thousand-lei notes..."), but others wave him off ("These two bits of paper sank to the symbolic role of stage currency"). In contrast to the angry, quirky misfits who often populate memoirs and novels, Leigh Fermor's charming young man—the Ur-backpacker—would've seemed crisp. (Today, we would bloody him with the word "privileged.")

It's unsurprising that a cult came to be transfixed; after the walk across Europe, Leigh Fermor helped carry out the kidnapping of a German general, spent time among monks, traveled in the Caribbean, erected a house in Greece (the setting for the Richard Linklater film *Before Midnight*)—his life was so colourful it seemed to stream from a prism. But he had chops, too. Vision. His prose was the slow output of an eye committed to registering exact contours, but only in original terms. "Blown askew, the Trafalgar Square fountains twirled like mops," he writes near the start of *A Time of Gifts*. "[B]ristling regiments of lancers moved about like counter-marching cornfields," he writes at another point. If you're tasked with putting over a windblown fountain or marching lancers, there are no better solutions than these. At a time when plenty of upstarts have already committed to print their formative years—when trauma is trumpeted, and meta-memoir, over-Eggered—Leigh Fermor's patient approach to prose is positively alien.

His patience may have left him stuck, though. In 2011, when Leigh Fermor finally died, his younger self was still stranded at the edge of Bulgaria. But there was a manuscript. The intervention of editors, and the publication of *The Broken Road*, the final book of the trilogy—holiest of those systems by which we mete out the franchise—gets the younger self moving again.

In a slightly more just universe, people would have lined up for *The Broken Road* with all the enthusiasm they bring to the subject of adolescent life in dystopias. On this side of the wormhole, however, *The Broken Road* was published earlier this year by NYRB Classics and is coming out in paperback next month. (John Murray brought it out in England in 2013.) NYRB Classics is to literature what the Criterion Collection is to film: a prestige imprint that, by issuing niche titles in handsome editions, attempts to rescue titles from niche. We long ago ceded the useful word "curate" to artisanal butchers and Pinterest, but NYRB Classics curates in the best sense. (*Mary Oliver: A Life*, by May Sinclair! *On Being Blue*, by William Gass!) Over the last few years, it has restored much of Leigh Fermor's catalogue to the bookstore and done a public good.

The Broken Road, however, is far from the fully realized book Leigh Fermor's fans were hoping for. It covers the last leg of his journey, from Bulgaria to Constantinople, but as editors Colin Thubron and Artemis Cooper explain, the new book was composed before its predecessors, in the early 1960s, when a magazine invited 5,000 words from Leigh Fermor on "The Pleasures of Walking." Leigh Fermor, then in his forties, finally began to set down the European journey of his youth and came to focus on the final stretch. But in the mid-1960s, he abandoned the manuscript. When he resolved to return to the subject of his European travels in the 1970s, he started over, repositioning his narrator in London, the day of departure. The rest we know: Leigh Fermor's renewed effort produced the two best works of travel writing of the twentieth century.

But for the next two decades, he was unable to make headway on a book that would bring the trilogy to an end. The editors describe a "long ice age": the "loyal and long-suffering" publisher was lost in 1993, the wife, ten years later. Leigh Fermor consulted a psychiatrist, but his energy had been flagging for some time. "The whole subject was beginning to feel stale, barren, written out, and he feared he no longer had the strength to bring it back to life," is how Cooper puts it, darkly, in her recent biography of Leigh Fermor.

Then, in 2008, the biographer turned up a copy of the sixties manuscript, and the writer, in his nineties, began to fuss with it. Not too long after, Leigh Fermor passed away. The forty-year-old text breaks off before reaching Constantinople—breaks off in the middle of a sentence, in fact, a rough edge the editors have respected. (No ellipsis sands it down.) They have supplemented the manuscript with fragments from a diary he kept, but the impressions of Constantinople are partial, and the diary firms up and expands only when Leigh Fermor finds himself among monasteries in Greece.

And that's where *The Broken Road* ends. The legendary

destination of Constantinople, then, remains mostly unremarked upon: a rip in space around which the book, like sparkling debris, swirls. The poignant title is an imposition of the editors; the sacred text, a salvage job: recovered by apostles from the late author's leavings and pieced together.

What's really absent, of course, isn't so much an account of Constantinople, as a third book written by the mature author of the first two. Thubron and Cooper are clear about the lack of polish, but it's not until you start in on *The Broken Road* that you realize how crucial to his prose was the mature writer's patient, if unsustainable, perfectionism. Generic adjectives function as placeholders for yet-to-be realized images ("amazing colours," "amazing robes," "amazing sunset"), or serve to reel off a character quickly ("She was so pretty, kind, funny, intelligent, and good").

When he does write well, it's often too well: a "sweep" of land "climbs and coils and leapfrogs clean across Northern Bulgaria from Serbia to the Black Sea"—a metaphor that sounds good (listen to that alliteration) but lacks the precision of Fermor's better prose (land doesn't have legs). "Plumed with poplars and mulberries," on the very first page, is lovely enough, but the plume-idea comes to be plumed again and again.

He is more original elsewhere. "The dome and the walls were almost intact," he writes of a mosque, "but most of the plaster had fallen away and the minaret was broken diagonally near its base, exposing to the moon the twist of the stairs round their central pillar like the volutes of a smashed ammonite's fossil." That's enough to keep you going; fans of *A Time of Gifts*, who will have already sought out the hardcover, will push forward on principle.

The Broken Road, after all, belongs to a class of aesthetic object that includes The Beach Boys' *Smile*, Orson Welles's *The Other Side of the Wind*, and Nabokov's *The Original of Laura*—works that benefit from their incompleteness because they spark speculation, devotion, delusion. Reviewers certainly seemed to be reassuring themselves. "Friends and fans, acolytes, devotees and disciples can all rest easy," declared one. "In some respects this book is even more satisfying than its predecessors...", hazarded another. Why don't they recognize that Leigh Fermor's failure to bring off a third book—and it is a failure, let's not pretend otherwise—only buttresses his legend? The line that weighs down the last page of *Between the Woods and the Water*, "TO BE CONCLUDED," gains great poignancy now that we know a proper conclusion cannot be provided.

Had it been provided, and promptly, we might be slightly less romantic about the author. He might strike us as less tortured, less remote. Perhaps the release of recent long-gestating albums by Guns N' Roses and My Bloody Valentine has dissolved some of the legend that once occluded the very real humans behind those bands. Perhaps David Foster Wallace's estate should've kept back *The Pale King*, his unfinished novel, for a generation or two. (Sure, *The Pale King*, in its partial form, still tantalizes, still dangles the counterfactual of what could've been. But some of its mystery has dispersed.) Let the corpse of work cool. Let the cult heat up.

In Fermor's case, *The Broken Road* is a carefully presented box of brilliant bits: a kit for keeping up one's enthusiasm for one of the great travel writers of the previous century. It's also part-emptied skull, part-time capsule: like its publisher, it extracts voice from void, paper from ashbin, expertly. ("Nearly all the people in this book..." Leigh Fermor observes, "were attached to trails of powder which were already invisibly burning.") But *The Broken Road* is no place to begin—as Leigh Fermor himself may have sensed when he turned away from it more than four decades ago. Those wishing to fire up an enthusiasm would do well to search out any of the other books, including especially *A Time of Silence*: a slim, quick account of time spent among monks, whom Fermor's fans, in their extreme, cultish devotion, can start to resemble.

(*The New Republic*, 2014)

Peter Bogdanovich's Fandom for Golden Age Hollywood

SHE'S FUNNY THAT WAY is the first film Peter Bogdanovich has directed in fourteen years. He used to churn them out; in the early 1970s alone, Bogdanovich dispatched a run of classics that included *The Last Picture Show*, *What's Up, Doc?* and *Paper Moon*. But in recent years, productions have been hard to come by, and memories have faded like filmstock. Today, those who care to inspect the special features on their DVDs experience the bescarved Bogdanovich primarily as a pundit. To most of the rest of the known universe, he plays the therapist's therapist on *The Sopranos*.

But what Peter Bogdanovich really is—what he's been for more than fifty-five years—is something like Hollywood's conscience: part-repository, part-angel, perched on the industry's epaulette and pointing out, with a sigh, that they no longer make 'em like they used to. ("You have to watch this stuff," he reminds us on the audio commentary for *The Searchers*, when John Wayne glances briefly but meaningfully at another character, unaided by close-up.) *She's Funny That Way*, featuring Owen Wilson and Imogen Poots, is merely the conscience's latest expression: a screwball comedy about a Broadway director who casts a call girl in his latest production.

The angel, however, is also a dinosaur who needed some help. Younger, hipper directors—Wes Anderson and Noah Baumbach—had to intervene to get *She's Funny That Way* made. (They signed on as executive producers.) This, after all, is the age when CGI-engorged franchises walk the earth, the desired target audience is still reckoning with puberty, and opening weekend is everything. It's hard, then, not to root for Bogdanovich's small curiosity, lurking in the shadows of August—a modestly-scaled movie for adults that's short on superhero spandex. And it's hard not to root for the craftsman who made it.

"I like movies where I feel the director, the storyteller, is taking me somewhere," Bogdanovich told Anderson in an interview a few years ago. "I have faith that he's got a strong grip on me, and he's taking me somewhere." Their exchange continued a tradition; as a young man in the 1960s, Bogdanovich himself interviewed many of his touchstones: directors like John Ford, Howard Hawks, Alfred Hitchcock, and Orson Welles. Back then, Bogdanovich wrote essays for *Esquire*. A critic and journalist, he was enthralled by the Golden Age of Hollywood, which had already come to an end by the time he got to LA.

He was especially in awe of its directors, who thrived within strict limits. Scrappy, unpretentious craftsmen, they could hold a shot for minutes, but never shot more footage than they needed, and sometimes even "cut in the camera," throwing a hand in front of the lens when they felt they'd nailed the scene. They weren't interested in "coverage," in amassing alternate takes from different angles; more film in the can would only give the editor options, and the studio, ideas. Bogdanovich's mentors (only later were they called "auteurs") knew exactly how they wanted to get a story across.

Eventually, B-movie producer Roger Corman offered the dogged enthusiast a picture to direct—but there was a catch. Corman had twenty minutes of footage of aging horror actor Boris Karloff. Bogdanovich was to go off and shoot more footage with Karloff, who owed Corman two days of work, and then an additional forty minutes to fatten the material to feature length. (This is your movie, should you choose to accept it.)

But like his director-heroes, Bogdanovich would have the best kind of freedom: all the elbow room the studio straitjacket allowed. He cast Karloff as a fading movie star and solved the problem of what to do with the pre-existing footage by displaying it on the screen of a drive-in theatre: one of the key settings Bogdanovich dreamed up. He then contrived for Karloff's character, the fading movie star, to make an appearance at this drive-in, while an unstable young man on a shooting spree heads toward the same location. The resulting movie—*Targets*, released in 1968—proved Bogdanovich's resourcefulness and served as a love letter to the suave monsters of Golden Age Hollywood, played by actors like Karloff, who'd been made obsolete by more modern terrors.

Bogdanovich would go on to helm bigger productions. Some of them would be about movies and moviemaking. All, like *Targets*, would reboot the bygone values and techniques of Hollywood. Bogdanovich sometimes shot in black and white, preferred long takes, favoured deep focus, resuscitated dead genres like the screwball comedy, and used close-ups frugally, the better to ensure their impact. (He was nearly fired from *The Last Picture Show* for cutting in the camera.) There was something both honourable and hopeless about his efforts; as he noted in 1972, the medium had, "for twenty years, been steadily losing its sense of craft." While filmmakers like Steven Spielberg invented the summer blockbuster, Bogdanovich worked to preserve the best of what had come before.

But by the late 1970s, he had directed some duds—for example, the well-meaning homage to thirties musicals *At Long Last Love*, which not only employed the singing voices of Cybil Shepherd and Burt Reynolds but recorded them live. Tragedy also took the wind out of the wunderkind: his charming 1981 comedy *They All Laughed* was overshadowed on its initial release by the murder of one of its actresses, Dorothy Stratten, with whom Bogdanovich had been starting to build a life.

As he directed less, however, Bogdanovich returned to writing about film. ("Bogdanovich, though he might never be allowed to direct another movie, looks admirably determined to keep at least one side of his best gift well tended and fruitful," observed the critic Clive James.) The digital age found a place for him, too. On DVDs for classics like *Citizen Kane*, *The Searchers*, and *Bringing Up Baby*, Bogdanovich's warm, weary voice supplied commentary tracks and a sense of history. Younger filmmakers, like Anderson and Baumbach, took to calling him "Pop." (Bogdanovich reciprocated with "Son Wes" and "Son Noah.") He has spoken out against movie violence and the "general numbing of the audience." Lately, he has been working on getting Orson Welles's unfinished final film, *The Other Side of the Wind*, edited. This isn't reinvention—merely the extension of a life's work devoted to remembering the way the dream factory once manufactured its dreams.

That said, I don't have high hopes for *She's Funny That Way*, at least in commercial terms; Bogdanovich's last few films haven't been big successes, and anyway, screwball comedies are an acquired taste. (He may be a national treasure, but he's not money in the bank.) Still, I'm cheered by the picture's very existence, and by the fact that Bogdanovich—who once made a habit of pestering his idols—has attracted his own protégés. It's certainly hard to imagine a better living repository of knowledge about movies, moviemaking, and Hollywood's golden age.

Such precious data will need its monk-like defenders as the shadows cast by Marvel reboots and other hulking blockbusters throw the industry into greater darkness. Am I being reactionary? Let's call it "nostalgic." I got that from Pop.

(*The New Republic*, 2015)

Clive James's *Poetry Notebook*

F̲o̲r̲ ̲a̲ ̲c̲e̲r̲t̲a̲i̲n̲ ̲d̲e̲m̲o̲g̲r̲a̲p̲h̲i̲c̲ in September 2014, the breaking news was all about five stanzas. News outlets, from the *Guardian* to *Slate*, were reporting the existence of a poem on the subject of death, called "Japanese Maple." You might've thought you were living in a Martin Amis story, the one where poets have agents and screenwriters have to endure rejection slips from little magazines. A poet occupied with his mortality is hardly wire-worthy. The market for morbid poems is so flooded it could float an ark.

But "Japanese Maple," which appeared in *The New Yorker*, wasn't your typical poem, nor its author your typical poet. Clive James was one of the preeminent culture critics of the last forty years—and a celebrity, to boot. Born in 1939, he left Sydney for London in the early sixties. He made a name writing for publications like the *Times Literary Supplement*, back when the byline was often redacted. (An unsigned essay on Edmund Wilson made James infamous the old-fashioned, germy way: it went viral by word of mouth.) James became a TV critic in the seventies, and eventually wound up on TV screens, interviewing celebrities and hosting documentaries. (Princess Diana was a lunch companion.) He has filed on auto-racing, Larkin, musicals, and *The Da Vinci Code*. Nevermind Žižek; James's beat ranges from Benjamin to Bogdanovich.

After being diagnosed with emphysema and leukemia, however, the main event for James became the poems. In his final years, they materialized steadily in magazines, and some parts of the media duly took up a deathwatch, the ghoulishness only augmented by a voyeuristic interest in his love life: in 2012, it came out that

James had been cheating on his wife with a former model. ("Is this devastating poem Clive James's farewell to his family...and apology for his eight-year affair?" asked *The Daily Mail*, after the TLS printed a poem called "Holding Court" in February 2013.) Stories about the affair tended to identify James as "broadcaster"—in addition to some variation of writer, *raconteur,* or critic. But North Americans, less familiar with James's TV work, found themselves transfixed by an alternate universe in which the sins of a translator of the *Inferno* can fire up the tabloids.

James's late poems, of course, are so much more than fuel for Grub Street; they represent the very best work James has ever done in verse. Here are the final, moving stanzas of "Japanese Maple":

> My daughter's choice, the maple tree is new.
> Come autumn and its leaves will turn to flame.
> What I must do
> Is live to see that. That will end the game
> For me, though life continues all the same:
>
> Filling the double doors to bathe my eyes,
> A final flood of colors will live on
> As my mind dies,
> Burned by my vision of a world that shone
> So brightly at the last, and then was gone.

The old-school rhyme scheme ("shone"/ "gone"), the flush and fitted iambs ("What I must do"), the simple, almost elemental nouns ("leaves," "flame," "world")—unlike many contemporary poems, which tend toward opacity and fragmentation, James's is apprehensible and self-contained. Minor but masterful moments, like the break after "What I must do," or the doubling up of "that," project a sense of control and provide just enough jolt. "Japanese Maple" lowers roots into the reader's mind.

Many of James's artistic heroes and touchstones were good at beguiling an audience. "Whole generations of Jewish literati were denied the opportunity of wasting their energies on compiling abstruse doctoral theses," James wrote in his great book of essays, *Cultural Amnesia*. "They were driven instead to journalism, plain speech, direct observation and the necessity to entertain."

A compulsion to compel drives many of James's other subjects. Whether they work in Viennese coffeehouses, the music business, or Hollywood, James's heroes (another man's hacks or hams) strive for clarity and economy, precisely because they don't have the luxury to be opaque. They assume that their audience is restless, demanding, and frugal with its disposable income. From their example, James seems to have extracted the sort of practical tip the typical poet tends to resent: the person who means to reach his reader had better intensify the message, especially if he's running short on time.

James's book of essays, *Poetry Notebook: Reflections on the Intensity of Language*, makes plain at the outset a desire to "keep things terse and particular." Many of these pieces are short essays that address a general reader and conduct close readings of particular poems, even particular lines; many were commissioned by Christian Wiman, the former editor of *Poetry* magazine (to whom James dedicated a recent collection of poems). "I was getting old," James observes in the introduction, "and the concentration necessary for writing a long piece seemed better reserved for writing poems, when they came."

The essays may be compact and entertaining, but they have a subtle way of encouraging self-scrutiny. James often makes generous assumptions about the reader of *Poetry Notebook*; offhand sentences casually suggest she balances a *Norton*'s worth of verse on the tip of her skull. "Read [Robert Lowell's poem] 'A Quaker Graveyard in Nantucket' again," he encourages at one point, "or merely recall the bits of it that you have in your memory." Elsewhere, he tosses off lines like, "most of us would not have much trouble in compiling a list of well-separated poems that we keep complete, or almost complete, in our heads."

One hardly has the heart to point out that sixty-plus years of MFA workshops have ensured that if canonical poems are to reside anywhere, it's not between the ears of "most of us," who would rather labour at our own poems than consume the ones that already exist.

But James's mode is deliberate, even strategic. His confidence in the capacities of contemporary readers is in fact a shrewd, inoffensive way of campaigning for the heavies in the culture wars. "Everyone knows the first line [of Hopkins's 'Spring'] because everyone knows the poem," translates to, "It wouldn't hurt to have some Hopkins by heart, whatever your walk of life." This is James's general approach to prescription: pretending the reader already has an interest in antibiotics.

In *Cultural Amnesia*, he's always commending to us the one book that will serve as the ideal doorway into some foreign language. The underlying, cavalier assumption—that his reader has the time, desire, and wherewithal to tackle the language in the first place—is less a sign of an out-of-touch expert, than of a scrappy, self-made scholar who can't bear to depend on translations and can't imagine his reader choosing to be any different.

The true object of James's devotion, however, is something he calls, channeling Frost, "the choppily well-separated thing." He means a poem with internal integrity, its every word pertinent and poised—a product that has come to be a curio in our age of overproduction. "On both sides of the Atlantic, and in Australia," James recounts, "the creative writing schools churned forth slim volumes by the thousand, all of them supposedly full of poetry but few of them with even a single real poem in them." Of course, the recently matriculated would pick at James's adjective: "real" according to whom? They would turn the table of contents upside down and shake out a patriarchy.

Real readers—the few who don't aspire to tenure—know what James means and will forgive him his apparent chauvinism; he cops to as much in the book itself when he worries that he "might not have done enough" on behalf of women writers. It's a fair self-criticism. And yet: "Will I get myself off the hook just by saying that I ended up with almost as many lines by Elizabeth Bishop in my head as by Robert Lowell?" It's a fair question; I'd bet my Beauvoir Reader that James has internalized more lines by women than almost of any of us.

At bottom, James is loyal to poems, not poets. He's concerned with the question of why some stretches of verse stick with the reader and why others don't. It's clear he has spent years white-boarding problems that contemporary poets no longer think about. For example, most of us dabblers would delight to be able to manage a brilliant line or two of poetry per poem. But James is preoccupied not just with how to generate brilliance—feat enough—but how to muffle it slightly so that it serves a larger light show. As he says of Frost,

> His easy-seeming, usually iambic, conversational forward flow is a deception, a way of not just bringing show-stopping moments to your attention but of moving them *past* your attention, so that you will form the correct impression that he has wealth to spare and does not want the show stopped for such a secondary consideration as brilliance.

Brilliance as a "secondary consideration" is, well, brilliant—a counterintuitive point at a time when the practitioners who tend to trend, like Frederick Seidel and Patricia Lockwood, specialize in show-stopping lines. Elsewhere, James reminds us that poets once taught readers how to pronounce a word simply by its placement in a pattern of stresses. He can talk couplets, alliteration, nuts, bolts. It's not that *Poetry Notebook* is perversely arcane; it's rather as if a ballet textbook had readmitted to its pages, after years of doing without, the pirouette.

Readers who make the mistake of finding James's taste for canonical poems "conservative" should still get a charge from his bloody-minded drive. "Reading his absurdly confident critical prose," James writes of Ezra Pound, "I could scarcely catch my breath when he talked about poetry as if it were the most exciting thing in the world, which indeed it is." You could say much the same about *Poetry Notebook*, a breathtaking book by an old master running out of breaths.

(*The New Republic*, 2015)

Brian De Palma's *Dressed to Kill*

ONE OF THE MORE POPULAR functions of contemporary criticism is quality control. From off-colour craft beer labels to that colonialist Taylor Swift video, hardly a cultural product goes by that isn't seized upon and inspected for trace elements of racism, misogyny, and the like. This is fine and noble work, I suppose; somebody's got to keep an eye on the assembly line. But at their most finger-waggy, critics risk becoming "hall monitors," to borrow a phrase from James Wolcott. "Gender studies/cultural studies grads, who have set up camp on the pop-cult left, can be a prickly lot," says Wolcott, "ready to pounce on any doctrinal deviation, language-code violation, or reckless disregard of intersectionality."

It's hard to imagine a more pounce-ready, politically incorrect work of pop culture than Brian De Palma's 1980 thriller *Dressed to Kill*, which turns thirty-five this year, and is now out in a new edition from the Criterion Collection. *Dressed to Kill* is a slasher film about a call girl, played by Nancy Allen, who teams up with a teenager to solve a murder. It's also what graduate students like to call "problematic." (A "minefield of potential offense" is how the new edition's liner notes put it.) There's the cross-dressing killer, played by Michael Caine; fuzzily soft-core close-ups of Angie Dickinson's pubic hair, played by *Penthouse* body double; and plenty of violence against women wearing concealed blood packs.

But although it's tempting to fire up the hot take, *Dressed to Kill* is also a slasher film *about* slasher films. Clever references to Alfred Hitchcock's *Psycho* (1960) suggest a tongue half-sheathed in its cheek. De Palma's film is also lushly aesthetic and a lot of fun: a truly guilty pleasure that, if it came with trigger warnings, would wear them proudly on its sleeve.

De Palma is not much thought about anymore. It's easy to forget he directed *Carrie*, which brought blood-soused Sissy Spacek to public consciousness, and *Scarface*, which continues to supply dorm rooms with a poster, and their occupants, a quotable line.

But in the seventies and eighties, De Palma was something like Quentin Tarantino: American cinema's most notorious purveyor of pastiche and violence. Tarantino tended to repurpose pulpy matter, squeezed from the B-genres it's become hip to admire, but which only a video clerk could love. De Palma looked higher, usually to Hitchcock. His early thrillers weren't so much thinly-veiled as shower-curtain-thin covers of *Rear Window*, *Vertigo*, and *Psycho*—replete with women in trouble, split personalities, uncanny doublings, and moody scores. For 1973's *Sisters*, De Palma went so far as to employ the composer Bernard Herrmann, who worked on Hitchcock classics like *Psycho*. (Hermann did the strings for the shower scene that does in Janet Leigh.) This wasn't plagiarism so much as pathological fandom.

Dressed to Kill is De Palma's most shameless and loving remix of *Psycho*, replacing shower with elevator, and Janet Leigh with Angie Dickinson. While Leigh plays a secretary who makes off with funds from work to finance an affair, Dickinson plays an unsatisfied housewife who cheats on her husband. Both actresses are snuffed out early in their films' running times, the better to startle their audiences. Star power usually guarantees more screen time.

But if De Palma repurposes Hitchcock's shock tactics, he also carries forward his mid-century moralism—or appears to. After consummating the affair, Dickinson quietly slips out of her lover's bed and resolves to compose a goodbye note. As she riffles around in his desk, however, she discovers paperwork that suggests her lover has a venereal disease. In a panic, Dickinson grabs her stuff and flees to the elevator. Naturally, she forgets her wedding ring and must go back. But a young girl and her mother briefly get on, the girl fixing

Dickinson in her glare before being pulled off the elevator. When the doors finally open on her lover's floor, Dickinson is attacked by a cross-dresser wielding a straight razor.

Various women's groups rallied against *Dressed to Kill* when it was released. Movie screens were attacked with red spray paint, and Allen, Caine, and De Palma all received Razzie nominations, the award that celebrates motion picture mediocrity. De Palma's *Body Double*, which came out a few years later, also rankled. In that movie's most infamous scene, a woman is run through with a two-foot drill bit. "I do a lot of murder mysteries," De Palma told *People* magazine in 1984, "and after a while you get tired of the usual instruments." When his interviewer pressed him—"But why a drill? Why one that big?"—De Palma pointed out that the tool had to be big enough for the main character to spot through a window. "It was not my intention to create a sexual image with the drill, although it could be construed that way." *Body Double*'s fan base includes the fictional yuppie Patrick Bateman from Brett Easton Ellis's novel *American Psycho*, who is given to masturbating to the drill bit.

But over three decades later, *Dressed to Kill*, which once drew red paint, now looks like an innocuous artifact of Culture War 1.0—and the hot takes that originally greeted it seem overheated. Of course, it helps that De Palma's thriller has received the Criterion treatment, the film buff's version of an expensive, authoritative, scholarly edition. The Criterion Collection, a kind of canon, can confer dignity, even prestige, on the politically incorrect work of art. The new edition of *Dressed to Kill* comes with a smart, spirited essay by Michael Koresky. The movie doesn't simply perpetuate the gender politics of the slasher film, suggests Koresky, it critiques them, too. For instance, the various stones De Palma hurls at Dickinson only earn the adulteress our sympathy.

But does De Palma's work anticipate the feminist critique of the male gaze, as Koresky suggests? That seems a stretch. De Palma's use of soft-focus photography, syrupy strings, and that *Penthouse* body double might be ironic—but it's clear his lushly aesthetic movies like to linger on imperiled female bodies at various degrees of undress.

(The director wants to have his objectification and critique it, too.) Moreover, De Palma's depiction of a murderous "transsexual" is cartoonishly stigmatizing. Caine's cross-dressing killer, we're told, corrals opposing sexes in the same body. (When the "male side" acquires an erection, in response to a Dickinson, the female side takes over and produces a straight razor.)

Still, as meta-slashers go, De Palma's has great fun exposing our expectations. The movie's two shower scenes turn out to be audience-baiting dreams. Allen's character is a hooker with a heart of gold plate. (She strips her Park Avenue johns of stock tips and invests in works of art, innocently expressing the fiscally-sound preference for the artists to die.) De Palma also pokes fun at the inevitable scene of exposition, of *de rigueur* DSMing; at the end of the film, Allen and a police detective, played by Dennis Franz, occupy school desks, as a psychiatrist, standing before them, explains Caine's warring identities.

Thirty-five years after its release, *Dressed to Kill* looks like a lavishly filmed, if slightly out-of-date, postmodern thriller. (Think *Scream* for aesthetes.) De Palma deploys slow tracking shots, split screens, obsessive craft, and a sense of humour. An early, wordless scene, in which Dickinson and her lover give chase to each other in an art gallery, is a marvel of visual storytelling, the sort of thing Hitchcock, who got his start in the silent era, used to call, "pure cinema."

Perhaps there's no such thing as pure cinema; movies tend to carry trace elements of the beliefs of their moment. But *Dressed to Kill* mostly transcends its dated, politically incorrect impurities. If anything, the movie's changing fortunes suggest we ought to be wary of our indignant other self—that inner, joyless critic.

(*The New Republic*, 2015)

RANDALL JARRELL'S PIGHEADED SOUL

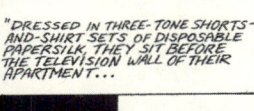

Orson Welles's *Mr. Arkadin*

Orson welles's 1955 picture *Mr. Arkadin*, which turns sixty this year, rarely makes lists of classic Christmas movies. Sometimes called *Confidential Report* (the title it went by in England), *Mr. Arkadin* isn't typically regarded as holiday fare, and isn't even one of Welles's better-known efforts. It lacks the iconic status of his first feature *Citizen Kane* (which tends to top lists of best movies) and the infamy of his *War of the Worlds* radio broadcast (which convinced many voting-age Americans that Martian spacecraft had put down in Grover's Mill, New Jersey). It's certainly not as memorable as *The Third Man*, which Welles didn't direct, but which contains his turn as the charismatic Harry Lime, a cameo so brilliant it throws all surrounding performances into chiaroscuro.

In fact, *Mr. Arkadin*, shot throughout Europe during Welles's nomadic exile from Hollywood, wasn't even really finished. It was wrested away from the director after he took too long editing it. The result was different rogue cuts and no definitive version. The movie posits a mystery, but is itself a puzzle, a completist's nightmare that has busied film scholars. And yet it's also a great, dark Christmas movie, with gorgeous shots of snow-blanketed Munich and the saddest version of "Silent Night" ever recorded.

Mr. Arkadin follows a petty smuggler named Guy Van Stratten, played by Robert Arden, who comes into the employ of Gregory Arkadin, a wealthy tycoon. Modeled after an actual arms dealer, Arkadin has acquired a fortune, a daughter to dote upon, and a case of MacGuffin-grade amnesia; he can't remember his past before the winter of 1927, when he found himself on the streets of Zurich. All he had was a suit and, inside the suit's wallet, 200,000 Swiss francs, the capital with which he would eventually build his empire. So, Arkadin assigns Van Stratten a job: see if anything incriminating can be discovered about his life pre-1927. The movie is a kind of Cold War *Kane*, a low-budget reboot of Welles's debut, in which a journalist attempts to piece together the life of a newspaper magnate.

Arkadin, we discover, is a front for a dark criminal past, but also for Welles, who plays the tycoon, Wizard of Oz-like, behind a false nose and arras-thick accent. (Welles had a weakness for melodrama and makeup.) It turns out Arkadin doesn't have amnesia; he puts Van Stratten on the trail of his former associates so that he can flush them out and kill them off, thus insulating his daughter against his earlier misdeeds.

When the movie starts, Van Stratten has just figured out his boss's murderous motives and tracked the last surviving member of Arkadin's one-time gang, Jakob Zuk, to an apartment in Munich. It's Christmas Eve, and Zuk has just been released from prison. Van Stratten is desperate to save Zuk, his only living proof of Arkadin's malevolence. Zuk, for his part, couldn't care less if he's rubbed out. A plate of goose liver, however, might persuade him to stay alive—it's the only thing the existentially indifferent ex-con dreamed about while locked up. Thus, Van Stratten takes to the streets of Munich: a last-minute shopper looking for the insurance that will keep Zuk (and himself) alive.

There's a lot more that's deeply odd about *Mr. Arkadin*: a visit to a flea circus, a set piece on a tilting yacht that sends the actors pitching across the frame, a near-orgiastic Christmas party in which Arkadin wears a ghoulish Santa mask, and so on. Much of the movie is explained in flashback, as Van Stratten brings Zuk up to speed, the picture toggling between present and past. Adding additional torque to the vertigo: Welles sometimes dubbed his actors' voices, which don't always sync perfectly with the corresponding pairs of lips. At times, he even swapped in his own baritone, and in the case of Arkadin's daughter, an entirely different actress's voice. As a filmmaker, he stubbornly refused to be hemmed in by the images he committed to film, even if the audience couldn't help but notice the soundtrack meandering ever so slightly away from the actors' mouths.

But it's the scenes of Christmas that give this weird movie a heartbeat, however irregular. Welles films winter with a lot of warmth. He frames beautiful, snow-speckled shots of Van Stratten trudging through Munich. Elsewhere, he shoots a Salvation Army band from a characteristically Wellesian angle—low—inflating the musicians with weight as they blow "Silent Night" up into the sky, a pathos-plump rendition that manages to reach the hopeless Zuk. ("I ain't heard that piece in fourteen years," he sighs.) Akim Tamiroff, who would later become a Welles regular, is magnificent as the ex-con, especially in closeup. He wears a bowler, a stratum of semi-permanent stubble, and a scarf so threadbare it could be a gnawed-off noose. He's one part Tiny Tim (if Tiny Tim had done hard time), one part tramp from *Waiting for Godot*.

For all its charm, however, *Mr. Arkadin* is an acquired taste, rarely acquired. In 1956, the magazine *Cahiers du Cinema* named it one of the top ten movies of the year, and in 1958, one of the twelve greatest movies ever, which was received more as provocation than endorsement. More recently, in 2012, Japanese director Shinji Aoyama made a point of preferring *Mr. Arkadin* to any other movie by Welles, placing it among his top films of all time. (This was for the decennial *Sight and Sound* list, a cinephile's comet that streaks by once a decade, when the magazine polls critics and filmmakers.) For super fans like Aoyama, a feast of a box set stuffed with three different versions—including a comprehensive edit that attempts to honour Welles's intentions—came out in 2006.

As one of the super fans, I can't help but revisit *Mr. Arkadin* every winter—for Tamiroff's tragicomic turn as Zuk, for that sluggishly beautiful "Silent Night," and for the movie's many memorable set pieces. Welles, who would've turned one hundred this year, couldn't help but call *Mr. Arkadin* his "biggest disaster"—when he could stand talking about it at all. Like *The Magnificent Ambersons* or *The Lady from Shanghai*, it represented yet another production he'd lost control of. Especially poignant, then, is the shot of Arkadin's small plane flying empty on Christmas morning. His secrets revealed, the tycoon has hurled himself out of the cockpit, into oblivion. What's left is a sort of Santa-less sled, flying solo—out of control, yes, but buoyed, like Welles's movie, by its own wonderfully imperfect wavelength.

(*The New Republic*, 2015)

Simon Callow's Biography
of Orson Welles

ONE-MAN BAND, THE THIRD installment in Simon Callow's biography of Orson Welles, arrives nearly a decade after the last, 2007's *Hello Americans*, and nearly twenty years after the first, 1997's *The Road to Xanadu*. This isn't unusual; multipart biographies tend to be the product of tectonic plates, their individual volumes mountaining up after much research, soul-searching, and rumbling. But the dazzling entries in Callow's life of Welles, which he began in 1989, are closer to comets, the sort that fanboys track and log. In other words, *One-Man Band* is a cultural event. It's like getting a new installment of *Star Wars*, except better, and we already know what happens.

Or do we? The romantic view is that Welles was a prodigy who singlehandedly revolutionized whichever medium was at hand. After mastering theatre and radio in the 1930s, he addressed himself to motion pictures and immediately produced a masterpiece, 1941's *Citizen Kane*. But Welles shorted out relationships almost as quickly as he electrified audiences. For the rest of his life, the writer-actor-director struggled to finance projects and saw the work he *did* complete wrenched away and re-cut by a motley of producers, philistines, and other enemies of art. By the 1980s, his iconic baritone was reduced to supplying Hasbro's Unicron with gravity.

Callow's biography, however, swabs away this layer of myth, thick as actors' pancake. The first volume, which took us up to the release of *Kane*, complicated the view of Welles as a volcano in a vacuum, who churned up works of genius on his own. In fact, Welles was more like an inspired consolidator of other people's ideas, with a flair for editing, lighting, and spectacle—and a fatal tendency to sudden restlessness. The second volume showed how Welles, far from a victim of the studios, often absented himself from his own productions at critical moments—usually the editing stage. "The student of Welles's life feels like the audience of a melodrama," writes Callow, as Welles begins to drift away from his 1948 adaptation of *Macbeth*. "'Don't go!' one wants to cry. 'Finish the film!' But off our hero canters, oblivious to the destruction of all his dreams."

But Callow's biography of Welles, which will include a fourth volume, does so much more than flush out facts. Callow himself is a celebrated director and character actor—no account of him can seem to resist recalling his memorable turn in *Four Weddings and a Funeral*—who has brought his experiences to a number of celebrated books. Callow, however, doesn't simply recount performances and productions; he critiques them, too, and in a distinctive, witty prose style. Callow sometimes has harsh words for critics (it's an actor thing), but he's quietly become one of our finest interpreters of what can happen on a stage or screen.

"When I was eighteen, I wrote Lawrence Olivier a letter." So begins Callow's 1984 memoir *Being an Actor*—and so began his acting career: writing. ("Language was always the starting point for me," he later notes.) Amazingly, Olivier posted a response, encouraging the teenager to join the National Theatre company. Callow began in the archetypal mailroom, then graduated to the box office. His breakthrough, during a student play of his own devising, is so vividly reported it should be reproduced in course kits:

> In all the anxiety over the show, worrying whether it was clear, whether everybody knew where to come on or go off, I had no time to think about my performance, no time to wonder about its effect on the group.... I just did it. Suddenly for the first time, I was acting. Not performing, or posturing, or puppeteering. I was being in another way.

At a stroke the mask that I had screwed on to my face fell away. I was free, easy, effortless. For the first time since I'd arrived at the Drama Centre I understood what playing a character was. It was giving in to another way of thinking. Giving in was the essential experience.

Being an Actor is a minor classic, part memoir, part textbook, part manifesto. It advances a "thespocentric" vision of theatre, in which actors literally run the show. *Being an Actor* is also brave; it recounts how Callow came to terms with being homosexual—no mean feat for a memoir in the age of Margaret Thatcher.

But it's Callow's commitment to articulating the craft of acting as a form of creation that runs through the book and the rest of his writing. Here's a passage from his biography of Charles Laughton, one of his major subjects:

> His acting faculty was a thing constructed of a million nerves, a-quiver with impulses. Every impulse, as it passed through him, provoked an adjacent impulse: an entire new set of vibrations was sounded, each with implications. So easy to become lost in a baroque tissue of resonating tendrils. But it is exactly this ability to form a character out of a thousand living cells which together form a breathing, complex organism that fitted him so wonderfully for the screen with its microscopic sensitivity. Watching him can be like watching film of plant life: nature's kingdom in a man.

Callow is an unflagging prose stylist, for whom description is an occasion to exercise wit and manufacture metaphor. Unemployment becomes the "primeval slime from which actors emerge and to which, inevitably, they return"; a poem becomes "a piece of wood that the microscope reveals to be, not a solid mass, but a kingdom seething with life, with swarming multitudes of molecules." Time spent among the warm-blooded—actual writers, actors, and directors—has insulated Callow's prose against the predations of jargon. ("Orsonolators" is his coinage for "the army of theoretical academics who have moved in on [Welles] like locusts....")

He also rejects postmodern cant, such as undergrad-grade assertions that people are unknowable and thorny concepts like "truth" require tongs. The humble goal of theatre critics of yesteryear—"to report and evaluate the gestures invented by actors...to report them, to preserve them, to record their power (or feebleness)"—is pretty clearly his goal, too. In short, Callow belongs to a select tradition that includes figures like Jean-Luc Godard and Welles's protégé Peter Bogdanovich—practicing artists who can't help but comment on their art.

One-Man Band, Callow's latest, follows Welles through the fifties and sixties, as he casts about Europe for money and improvises his way through stage productions like *Moby-Dick* and films like *Othello*, *Mr. Arkadin*, and *Chimes at Midnight*. The book reinforces an alternative narrative, first championed by the French and later popularized by Bogdanovich. Welles, his partisans argue, never stopped making masterpieces, even if some were marred by a lack of resources. If anything, he learned, like a sonneteer, to work within ruthless constraints. When costumes failed to materialize on the set of *Othello*, Welles deployed towels and relocated Roderigo's murder to a Turkish bath. When the set itself failed to materialize, he relocated his adaptation of *The Trial* to an empty train station.

The stories are fascinating, but the best passages in *One-Man Band* are energized by Callow the Critic: they record gestures of power and feebleness. He's particularly incisive about Welles's acting, which Welles, so often absorbed in his productions, usually left to the last minute. "[T]o climb the mountain called *Othello*, neither physical appearance nor charisma nor even inspiration will suffice," observes Callow.

> It requires unrelenting hard work, mentally, physically and vocally. Welles seems never entirely to have mastered the text, so inevitably he was always enslaved to it, never able to ride

it, always hanging on for dear life, or putting on the brakes to slow the play down to the speed of his own thought rather than Othello's. He was also unable to reveal the character's detailed progression through the play or indeed its hidden strata.... In the phrase of actor-laddies of yesteryear, he lacked puff: the stamina, both physical and vocal, demanded by these great roles. He was, in a word, unprepared.

There's much to admire here—repetition ("always enslaved to it, never able to ride it"), metaphor ("hidden strata"), a handle on the historical lingo ("puff"), and confidence funneled down to a phrase ("in a word"). Elsewhere, describing Welles's scene-stealing part in *Compulsion*, Callow pumps plasma into a cliché: "Like the great Victorian stars, he speaks slowly and softly, creating time and space around himself. It is unquestionably ham, but it is very thinly sliced."
Even seemingly throwaway phrases like "The slow, selfish growth of a performance within an actor"—a growth Welles almost never allowed himself the time to cultivate—seem loaded with lived experience. Like those of the best critics, Callow's formulations are both apt and inventive. And there are so many to admire. "Like many a critic before him and since, Tynan failed to understand that his darts, so blithely fired off, actually drew blood." Callow can string a pointed insight, of universal worth, at will.
But because he tends to be exacting, the reader tends to trust his praise. His grave judgments, which wreathe certain works in darkness, ensure his celebrations sparkle. Callow is no fanboy and refuses not to find fault with faulty gems like *Othello* and *The Trial*. (I'm a *Trial* apologist myself but would die for Callow's right to be wrong.) The book builds towards Callow's appreciation of *Chimes at Midnight*, Welles's love letter to Shakespeare's Falstaff, a masterpiece that hasn't always been easy to see. The unfinished *Don Quixote*—"his notebook, his diary, his cinematic letter to himself"—is another Wellesian project one wishes were more accessible, at least when Callow writes about it. Great criticism is fantasy archaeology. You can't help but absorb Callow's excitement as he excavates failed

collaborations, missed opportunities, lost works of art, what could have been—the endless counterfactuals that fork off from Welles's many baffling decisions.

Callow's biography has grown more fascinating and useful with each successive volume. The Welles of the first book—the god-like prodigy who let there be *Kane*—we already know about. But the unapologetically purple concluding sentences of *One-Man Band* look forward to the final, more beclouded years of Welles's life—and threaten to make fanboys and -girls of us all:

> [H]e was thrusting out towards unknown regions, dreaming celluloid visions, unceasingly toiling over the chance to extend the ribbon of dreams, as he had so memorably described film-making. It was an epic journey to match the epic of his first fifty years, and the fact that there was so little to show for it is at once tragic and oddly inspiring: there is a nobility, a selflessness to the quest.

Callow, of course, will have more to show for his efforts. His biography of Welles, once completed, will likely be his masterpiece. (Curious readers should also check out his slim, perfect monograph about Laughton's only film, *The Night of the Hunter*.) But *One-Man Band* isn't simply an effort to bring a god to ground; it's a great work of criticism, too. Callow cuts through the smoke that swirls around Welles—that Welles himself often generated, that seemed to pour forth from his iconic cigar—and screens an image of an artist we've never quite known.

(*Partisan*, 2016)

Whit Stillman's Yuppie Trilogy

MEDIEVAL MORALITY PLAYS had vice. Marxists, the bourgeoisie. My English professors, dead white males. These days, we cross our index fingers in the face of privilege. This trendiest of stock villains tends to lurk in the wings of our cultural conversations, only to caper onto stage under a hail of hisses. He sometimes assumes the form of a man-sized Ivy League crest with legs. It's best not to be seen with him.

No one, however, has done more to humanize poor old, two-dimensional Privilege than the filmmaker Whit Stillman. His nineties triptych—*Metropolitan* (1990), *Barcelona* (1994), and *The Last Days of Disco* (1998), newly reissued in a box set by the Criterion Collection—is populated by people it's tempting to hate: the sons and daughters of old money; young men dilating on the matter of female beauty; disco partisans. They revere Carl Barks (as opposed to Karl Marx), the creator of Scrooge McDuck, and they say things like, "That's a great moment in life when you can start sending all your shirts out for laundering." And yet, for all their flaws—worn as conspicuously as Lacoste gators—Stillman remains fond of his preppies and yuppies.

Unsurprisingly, this seems to trouble his critics. As a writer in *Salon* once explained, "You can't always tell at whom he's poking fun, or why, and it becomes unfortunately easy to typecast him as the WASP answer to Woody Allen and conclude that his movies are insufferably irritating documents of privilege."

Clearly, Stillman's comedies of manners make culture writers uncomfortable. In poking fun at characters on both the right and left, they register with no clear party or position—which might strike some of us, at a time when there's support for masonry on the Mexican border, as unthinkable. But what Stillman ultimately sides with is stylish wit. His apolitical movies dare to prize a well-turned one-liner over social justice; they challenge us to embrace aestheticism and check our politics. ("His sense of rigorous style is a way to right the world," is how *The New Yorker*'s Richard Brody has it.) In our sweltering microclimate of outrage and hot takes, Stillman's work—equal parts guilty pleasure and hydrating tonic—can feel unnervingly, irresponsibly cool.

Stillman's first feature, *Metropolitan*, follows ersatz-socialist Tom Townsend (Edward Clements), who takes up with a flock of wealthy young New Yorkers following a debutante ball. They urge Tom to split a cab—and then duly sweep him off to his re-education. There are more balls to come, but most of the movie takes place during the afterparties, which are set in a Park Avenue apartment. No parent ever pokes a head in; these are reactionaries, not radicals, which means they tend to play bridge, debate the merits of *Mansfield Park*, and worry about their extinction, all in formal evening wear. Nick, played by Chris Eigeman (who would go on to become a Stillman regular), is the group's glue: a critic whose beat is kids these days. "Our generation's probably the worst since the Protestant Reformation," he complains.

Then there's Charlie (Taylor Nichols), the group's in-house anthropologist, who comes up with the acronym "UHB," Urban Haute Bourgeoisie, to tag his endangered tribe. Theirs aren't first-world problems so much as one-percent problems.

These also aren't the lethargic elites in Fellini's *La Dolce Vita*, who laze about like statuary. Failings aside, the UHBs are a fount of outrageous verbal energy. (Stillman's screenplay received an Oscar nomination.) At one point, Audrey (played memorably by Carolyn Farina) politely asks Tom why he bothers attending UHB functions in the first place, given his "vehement opposition to deb parties and to conventional society in general." Nick, as full of Wilde as he is wind, swiftly supplies the answer: "He got an invitation." Tom can only concede. "He's right. I got an invitation and didn't particularly have anything else to do." Another UHB helpfully chimes in and chisels a universal truth: "I think that's the case with almost everybody."

In Stillman's movies, a young adult, entrenched in an ideology or narrow way of being, is often buoyed up and out of his trench by the overflowing charisma of characters who would be charmless villains in other films. Take Taylor Nichol's tightly wound salesman in *Barcelona*, who finds his life disrupted by his freeloading cousin, a Navy lieutenant and staunch defender of American exceptionalism. Then there's Dan, the left-wing editor in *The Last Days of Disco*. When his colleagues, Charlotte (Kate Beckinsale) and Alice (Chloë Sevigny), discuss a tip sheet for manufacturing bestsellers, he scoffs:

Dan: That stuff is such crap.
Alice: This does describe a lot of bestsellers, it's true.
Dan (scowling): It's completely formulaic.
Charlotte: Of course it's formulaic. It's a formula.

Dan—who aspires to organize labor—snorts in the face of the girls' apartment-hunting woes. "Aren't your fathers heavily subsidizing your living expenses with big allowances?" But he soon falls for one of their friends and finds himself a convert to the disco culture he previously decried. (Eventually he confesses to having "reactionary thoughts, too.") Like Tom in *Metropolitan*, Dan is full of recently acquired opinions he would like others, usually women, to acquire, too. (His contemporary analogue would be the aggressive mansplainer.)

"He had a mind so fine that no idea could violate it"—what T.S. Eliot (privileged) said about Henry James (ditto) could apply to Stillman or, at least, his movies, in which ideas, like the hollow balls preferred for squash, are mainly for bandying about. Stillman's celebrated dialogue moves at a quick clip, and he tends to hold his shots; in other words, a Stillman movie works at the level of the set piece, the perfect court in which overeducated characters can spar. They "have clever mouths with which to say foolish things," observes the critic Troy Patterson. "However, they are not fools." They acquit themselves stylishly and complete their sentences.

Stillman, an aesthete, doesn't carbon date his movies too carefully. "Not so long ago," declares a card at the start of *Metropolitan*, in type once reserved for party invitations. "The last decade of the Cold War," declares text at the start of *Barcelona*. Stillman is happily careless with history and promotes content from his own, well, privileged life. (As a young man, he really did fall in with UHBs during a season of debutante balls; he worked for Doubleday, adored disco, and spent time in Spain.) Stillman is ultimately—unfashionably—after universal truths about love and friendship. Although the movies have their grounding in particular milieus, they have their top-hatted heads in Platonic clouds, and the audience's pleasure, top of mind.

"I'm sort of anti-modern," Stillman told *Vanity Fair* recently—and it's true that a director who has blocked both a limbo and a cha-cha-cha is probably out of step with our moment. He has a small repertory of actors he tends to resort to and few films to his IMDB page. *The Last Days of Disco* was followed by fourteen years of silence. When he broke it, with his 2011 picture *Damsels in Distress*—in which young people lament the decline of decadence, and dream of inventing dance crazes—he attracted the kind of vitriol once directed at Dadaists and Beats.

But then we've long since metabolized the official, approved methods of the aspiring rebel—disjunction, dissonance, and the like. Stillman, the new Criterion boxset reminds us, is radical precisely because he remains unfashionable. He takes a sympathetic stance towards unsympathetic subjects, and he liberates audiences from the tyranny of ideas through a commitment to aesthetic pleasure: style, wit, and humour. As Stillman's Alice explains to her love interest, who has just pitched the editor an idea for a book, "Like everything, it all depends on execution."

(*Flavorwire*, 2016)

J.G. Ballard's *Concrete Island*

ENGLISH DIRECTOR BEN WHEATLEY's *High-Rise*, out in the United States on May 13, represents the latest effort to extract a movie from J.G. Ballard's so-called "urban disaster trilogy." *High-Rise*, the last novel in the trilogy, first appeared in 1975, and was preceded by *Concrete Island* (1974) and *Crash* (1973). David Cronenberg, a one-man Impossible Missions Force when it comes to adapting the unadaptable, took a shot at bringing *Crash* to screen in the 1990s. (The novel, about a subculture that gets off on car accidents, is short on dialogue and plot.) *High-Rise*, for its part, concerns a class war that reduces each floor of a luxury apartment to a veldt. (Dog is cooked, incest committed.) These are postwar masterpieces, but postmodern assaults on realism, too; neither *Crash* nor *High-Rise* produces a character with which readers can identify for long.

It's baffling, then, that *Concrete Island* has never made it to screen. Though less self-consciously lurid than its bookends, and nowhere near as violent, the middle entry in Ballard's trilogy is perfectly cinematic: it places an accessible protagonist, due for his comeuppance, in peril—then introduces a series of complications. The novel begins with a car crash that maroons an architect, Robert Maitland, on a parcel of disused land enclosed by several motorways. But in trying to flag down a ride, Maitland sustains an injury, which prevents further attempts at the steep embankment. No cars stop to help, and the architect, to his growing disbelief, finds himself trapped on the island, without food or water. It's one of the most ingenious dystopic fictions ever contrived; the crash deposits Maitland very nearly in sight of the office tower where "his secretary was typing the agenda for the following week's finance committee meeting"—but the crash is cataclysmic, too: Maitland might as well be the last person in London.

You can dispatch *Concrete Island* in an evening—as I did the first time I read it; my 1992 Paladin edition runs a mere 126 pages—and wander off with the impression that the novel is testing a hypothesis. The deceptively artless opening sentences cut straight to the crash:

> Soon after three o'clock on the afternoon of April 22nd 1973, a 35-year-old architect named Robert Maitland was driving down the high-speed exit of the Westway interchange in central London. Six hundred yards from the junction with the newly built spur of the M4 motorway, when the Jaguar had already passed the 70 m.p.h. speed limit, a blow-out collapsed the front nearside tyre [sic]. The exploding air reflected from the concrete parapet seemed to detonate inside Robert Maitland's skull.

Ballard's cool prose gives off the chill of the laboratory; this is research study as much as character study, in which variables are introduced and strings pulled. (As Maitland fights for control of the steering wheel, he "jerk[s] his hands like a puppet's.") Up to this point, Maitland's life has been so cushy it has a thread count. It comes with a wife, a mistress, and a crate of white Burgundy in the trunk. Moreover, his faith in civilization is total. "Turning his back on the island, Maitland stepped on to the foot of the embankment and clambered up the soft slope," writes Ballard as the first chapter comes to a close. "He would climb the embankment, wave down a passing car and be on his way."

A series of setbacks and failed attempts to escape, however, will bring him close to death. And soon enough this Crusoe-reboot will encounter other denizens of the island—Jane, a young prostitute, and Proctor, a former circus acrobat with an intellectual disability, the result of a fall. By the end, Maitland has dominated the island, but also devolved enough to lose interest in quitting it: "Maitland tore away the remains of his ragged shirt, and lay barechested in the warm air, the bright sunlight picking out the sticks of his ribs." Privilege has turned predator.

Ballard's book, however, isn't an affirmation of dog-eat-Darwinism. The presiding image of the island's waist-high grass, which claims the chassis of assorted cars, Maitland's included, is terrifying. At the end of the novel, the architect himself seems mindlessly rooted, if not paralyzed. "In some ways the task he had set himself was meaningless," writes Ballard. "Already he felt no real need to leave the island, and this alone confirmed that he had established dominion over it." As speculative fiction goes, this is sophisticated stuff; rather than imagine some fascist, post-apocalyptic society—see the graphic novel *V for Vendetta*, Alan Moore's riposte to Margaret Thatcher's England—Ballard discovered the plausible dystopia in plain sight: a concrete, postwar London in which the marginalized populate literal margins, those ruled lines where city-planning comes to an abrupt stop.

All of that may sound didactic, even over-determined. *Concrete Island*'s peers, *Crash* and *High-Rise*, though mesmerizing, certainly come equipped with passages purpose-built to be circled by students. ("In many ways, the high-rise was a model of all that technology had done to make possible the expression of a truly 'free' psychopathology.") But the language Ballard invents for *Concrete Island* is more evocative, less schematic. His sentences about the crash are crisp and original—"The sequence of violent events only micro-seconds in duration had opened and closed behind him like a vent of hell"—and his characters are more than simply lab mice, lowered into their scenario by length of tail.

After being attacked by Proctor, the injured architect comes to in Jane's living quarters, an abandoned cinema located on the island. He thinks he's been rescued, but Jane, who means to keep Maitland, is evasive about their location. Our initial sense of the novel as a controlled experiment—take one privileged Londoner and apply pressure—starts to dissipate; Ballard hints at backstories and supplies his characters with supple psychologies. Information comes to us, as it comes to Maitland, gradually, through the keyhole of his viewpoint. As the architect's dread deepens, so, too, does ours.

Ballard has authored more conventional works of speculative fiction. His excellent debut, *The Drowned World* (1962), imagines a future in which the polar ice caps have melted and transformed London into a lagoon, stocked with giant mosquitoes and primeval lizards. But as the novelist William Gibson notes, "Upon arriving in the capital-F Future, we discover it, invariably, to be the lower-case now. The best science fiction has always known that, but it was a sort of cultural secret."

It's encouraging, then, that Wheatley has elected to keep his adaptation of *High-Rise* set squarely in the moment that Ballard imagined: a present understudying for the future, in which poor urban planning makes islands of us all. As the trailer reveals, the titular apartment is a Brutalist concoction of poured concrete, the clothing seems beamed in from a key party, and at least one character's head is in the grip of muttonchops. It's the day-for-night future of Kubrick's *A Clockwork Orange* (1971) and Fassbinder's *World on a Wire* (1973)—science fiction that found the seventies to be sufficiently terrifying.

Similarly, there are no zombies in *Concrete Island*—no irrational, irradiated hordes pitched against a heroic individual. Maitland's wasteland isn't the outcome of nuclear war; it's the blank patch at the edge of our blueprints, the social void in our peripheral vision. If there are monsters in Ballard's book, they're the many motorists who regard Maitland blankly as they pass, urged ever onward, in well-defined lanes, by the traffic behind.

(*Flavorwire*, 2016)

Brian Wilson's *Pet Sounds*

IN 2008, WHEN GUNS N' ROSES finally released its album *Chinese Democracy* after working on it for fifteen years, the writer Chuck Klosterman declared the end of a zeitgeist. "*Chinese Democracy* is (pretty much) the last Old Media album we'll ever contemplate in this context," he wrote in his review for *A.V. Club*. "It's the last album that will be marketed as a collection of autonomous-but-connected songs."

But nearly a decade later, the idea of the album-as-event endures. Consider Ryan Adams enthusiastically covering Taylor Swift's *1989* or Kanye West feverishly revising the track-list for *The Life of Pablo*. Within the last several weeks alone, new full-length records by Beyoncé and Radiohead have dropped, defined their blast craters, and triggered countless think pieces.

It wasn't always thus. Popular music's first big, coherent statement—The Beach Boys' *Pet Sounds*, released fifty years ago on May 16, 1966—wasn't an immediate sensation, at least in the US (a worried Capitol Records even rushed out a package of greatest hits, as if to recall to the public the fun, foamy band behind "Surfin' USA"). Over time, however, *Pet Sounds* came to occupy the upper echelons of best-of lists—or at least, the lists in magazines like *Rolling Stone* and MOJO that tended to prefer rock over other genres (and white, male artists over everyone else). Such "rockism" persisted from the 1960s to the 2000s, and during this time, albums fortified by theme, like *Pet Sounds*, were thought to be more "serious" than one-off singles.

Brian Wilson, who wrote *Pet Sounds*, certainly anticipated the modern pop-centric era, which privileges producer over artist and blurs the line between entertainment and art. (Wilson, his fans will delight in reminding you, carbonated classical music with pop.) But if the big-budget artistic statement is now back—if it's okay to be preposterously ambitious again—the current moment owes something to the pretensions of *Pet Sounds*. Wilson's bildungsroman about the life and death of adolescent love wasn't just a great record; it was also a record of a great artist's mind—popular music's first longform investigation into the psyche of an auteur.

Before *Pet Sounds*, there was Frank Sinatra's *In the Wee Small Hours* (1955)—a kind of concept album informed by the singer's recent break from Ava Gardner. But the songs themselves predated the split; they were standards, written at different times by different people, and curated to match Sinatra's mood.

It would be another decade before Wilson composed a concept album of his own. He had quit the road after a mid-flight anxiety attack in 1964 and had come to depend upon a loose collective of Los Angeles session musicians, first assembled by Wilson's idol, Phil Spector. Wilson had figured out that songs weren't enough; production was critical. Moving forward, he would make the backing tracks, while the rest of the band took care of the touring. (They would put down their vocals later.) At this point, The Beach Boys were more or less The Backstreet Boys. Like his Swedish heir Max Martin, the producer and architect behind Britney, Katy, and so many others, Wilson holed up in the studio while attractive avatars fronted the product.

But Wilson didn't simply want to manufacture hits. The Beatles' 1965 album *Rubber Soul* had encouraged him to disdain filler and seek to create a coherent experience. (He had already run a theme through the second side of The Beach Boys' 1965 album *Today!*, girding five songs with a feeling of unity.) *Pet Sounds* would go further: it would walk listeners through a relationship, starting with the youthful optimism of "Wouldn't It Be Nice" and ending with the disillusionment of "Caroline No." It would also double as confessional poetry, the poetry of an artist outpacing his moment.

Songs like "I Just Wasn't Made for These Times" even boasted Kanye-grade complaints like, "Every time I get the inspiration / To go change things around / No one wants to help me look for places / Where new things might be found."

To his credit, Wilson's ambition was cut with a sense of play that pervaded every aspect of *Pet Sounds*. In a move that would've pleased Andy Warhol, Wilson recruited an advertising copywriter to come up with the album's lyrics. In a move that would've pleased a Dadaist, he rattled listeners' sense of sonic possibility. On "God Only Knows," he contrived the clip-clop of horses' hooves using a bottle. Elsewhere, he integrated banjo, bass harmonica, electric bass, kettledrums, and more.

But the result was regarded by many—including some of The Beach Boys who sang on it—as too ambitious for its own good. The great heyday of rock criticism, the 1970s, was still to come, and there was certainly no internet to provide exegeses (read: hot takes). Nevertheless, Wilson patented a type that lives on to this day—the reclusive genius whose instrument is the entire studio. *Pet Sounds* foreshadowed the big-budget psychodramas of the future—albums by Michael Jackson, Prince, Radiohead, and other skittish artists successful enough to find a fully-stocked studio at their ego's disposal.

Anytime a band or musician disappears into a studio to contrive an album-length mystery, the ghost of Wilson is hovering near. Anticipating the working methods of today, he took to recording his work in fragments, which were collaged together later. He came so close to completing another concept album—this one an odyssey through America called *Smile*—that Capitol even commissioned cover art. But he lost his resolve. His bandmates, who preferred applying their vocals to songs about the intersection between surfer and girl, were resistant to Wilson's seemingly arch aspirations. Then there was the ever-present problem of Beatles. It didn't matter that *Pet Sounds* had inspired Paul McCartney to compose a concept album of his own; *Sgt. Pepper's Lonely Hearts Club Band*, which the Beatles launched in 1967, effectively ended the arms race between the two bands. Overwhelmed by the success of *Sgt. Pepper*, the Beach Boy ran ashore.

Today, of course, music fans venerate boldly ambitious statements like *808s & Heartbreak* and *Lemonade*—and romanticize the precocious authors behind them. But in the late sixties, there was no readymade narrative against which to plot Wilson—in part because he was pop's Ur-auteur, first in a line to be populated by Lauryn Hill, Axl Rose, Lee Mavers, and other recluses. He withdrew to a mansion in Bel Air, gained weight, and took up the accoutrements of the legend with lived experience (robe, beard, equity in healthfood store). But the myth is stigmatizing. Wilson was never especially pretentious or tortured. He remained enthralled to the goal of the perfect pop song, with the Spector-produced "Be My Baby" as his sacred text. Wilson even attempted several comebacks, and some of them, like 1977's *Love You*, yielded rewards.

Nevertheless, *Pet Sounds* remains the masterpiece. There's the gorgeous music, which has inspired countless musicians. (REM's 1998 love letter to the Wilson aesthetic, "At My Most Beautiful," quotes sleigh bells, cellos, and rumbling tympani.) But there's also Wilson's approach. Swap out the Hollywood studio peopled with unionized musicians for a laptop loaded with sound files, and the author of *Pet Sounds* looks a lot like the godfather of the current age—the first to assemble hits from fragments, the first to turn an album into an occasion. His approach was especially impressive when you consider that what he was splicing together was tape. (Wilson was artisanal, his heirs, digital.)

With *Pet Sounds*, Wilson brought an ambition to pop that it hadn't previously known and helped make heroes out of producers. "I just wasn't made for these times," he sings towards the end of *Pet Sounds*, a square Beach Boy in a round world. It turns out the lyric was one part boast, one part prognostication.

(*The Atlantic*, 2016)

CHARLES BRUCE'S POEMS

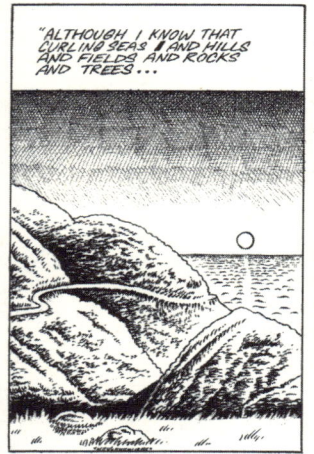

Christian Wiman's *Poetry* and Poetry

"I DON'T REALLY BELIEVE IN Collected Poems," the American poet and critic Christian Wiman has said. "They're almost always bad." Wiman has long believed that real poetry is rare. As editor of the prestigious magazine *Poetry*, a position he held for ten years, he faced a slush pile so big it had slopes, a base camp. But he still struggled to source print-worthy poems.

"If poetry is so rare in the world, if so much of it is dross, just think how much rarer it must surely be in your (our!) own work," he writes in a provocative editorial called "In Praise of Rareness." Wiman's argument—that a person who truly respects poetry will find most of it lacking—is the sort of good sense that nevertheless triggers some poetry readers, who tend to be aspiring poets themselves. People don't prefer to acknowledge that the art they dabble in is probably beyond them. (Full disclosure: Wiman took some of my poems for his magazine. But he rejected many, many more.)

Unsurprisingly, Wiman's high-profile editorship came to overshadow his own poems. So, too, did an essay he wrote about his incurable form of blood cancer and his rediscovery of faith. (The piece went viral in 2007, and led to other essays about God, opening up a new readership for Wiman.) But Wiman's poems, which have been gathered in his new book *Hammer Is the Prayer: Selected Poems*, deserve our attention, too. By striving to be clear and memorable, they dare to address the needs of that mythical unicorn, the general reader. They prove, as Wiman's editorship did, that poetry doesn't have to be a coterie concern.

Typically, American poets reside in academia. They tend to regress to the mean of the MFA, and mostly address one another. It can seem like a pyramid scheme, made up of creative-writing professors and students who aspire to be creative-writing professors. The byproducts—the poems—are preserved in journals no one reads, pressed into place like brittle leaves. (Occasionally, some hiring committee takes their tally.) First books are published through contests and subsidized in part by the entry fee coughed up by the poet. Reviews rarely break what amounts to an unspoken peacetime pact: be positive about your colleagues' work. The net result, suggests Dana Gioia in his landmark 1991 essay "Can Poetry Matter?", is a surplus of poetry for which there's little public appetite. "Like subsidized farming that grows food no one wants," says Gioia, "a poetry industry has been created to serve the interests of the producers and not the consumers."

Wiman, however, took the road less credentialed. Born in West Texas, he chose travel over grad school and hours of self-assigned reading—five hours a day, as prescribed by Dr. Johnson—over syllabi. He was the sort of young person who hankers after "EXPERIENCE" (caps his), who arranges to absorb his Milton in Guatemala, in a room made of tin and cardboard. "It's a small miracle that I didn't take to wearing a cape," he says of his purple youth.

But in time, Wiman came to distinguish himself as an accomplished poet and critic. In 2003, he assumed the helm of *Poetry*. The magazine had recently received a historic donation—approximately $200 million from the heiress to the Eli Lilly pharmaceutical fortune. Other poets, with lectern-long CVs, must've resented Wiman his incredible opportunity. But the outsider turned out to be the perfect candidate to remake the magazine and expand its audience.

Because he respected poetry, he assumed that it could stand up to scrutiny, that it could benefit from some bloodletting. He greenlit young reviewers who weren't afraid to let the air out of reputations they found inflated, and he commissioned prose from marquee names like Christopher Hitchens and Clive James, who possessed an appeal beyond the poetry world. The critical prose in the magazine's back pages was filed to a point, trendy jargon track-changed away.

One April—that's National Poetry Month to the uninitiated—Wiman tacked the headline "National Defibrillation Month" to the cover. Under his watch, circulation tripled from 10,000 to 30,000. It was as if Grub Street had grabbed the little mag by the scruff.

Our interest in poetry tends to be palliative; we assume it's too minor and sickly an art form to give pleasure. (Isn't that what *Game of Thrones* or Drake is for?) But Wiman was committed to reaching the dopamine receptors of *Poetry*'s readers. And it's this same commitment to pleasure that powers the poetry in *Hammer Is the Prayer*. Poems like "Hard Night," "Rhymes for a Watertower," "From a Window," "Five Houses Down," "After the Diagnosis," "Sitting Down to Breakfast Alone," "Small Prayer in a Hard Wind," and "Little Killing Ditty" resist obscurity and insist you get them by heart. They exist out of necessity, not to swell a cv.

They also bypass many of the fruitless debates that have paralyzed and polarized the poetry world. Sometimes Wiman composes in rhyme and meter, sometimes free verse. He rejects the idea that a truly modern poetry, one that mirrors our fragmented moment, should come to the reader in shards. Here's "Poštolka (Prague)," from his second book:

> When I was learning words
> and you were in the bath
> there was a flurry of small birds
> and in the aftermath
>
> of all that panicked flight—
> as if the red dusk willed
> a concentration of its light—
> a falcon on the sill.
>
> It scanned the orchard's bowers,
> then pane by pane it eyed
> the stories facing ours
> but never looked inside.

I called you in to see.
And when you steamed the room
and naked next to me
stood dripping, as a bloom

of blood formed in your cheek
and slowly seemed to melt,
I could almost speak
the love I almost felt.

Wish for something, you said.
A shiver pricked your spine.
The falcon turned its head
and locked its eyes on mine.

For a long moment then
I wished and wished and wished
the moment would not end.
And just like that it vanished.

The sense of impermanence, the speaker's inability to communicate an emotion, the inscrutability of the natural world—these themes wouldn't be out of place in the sort of poems that flaunt their modernity, that tend to refuse any kind of formal whalebone. But Wiman's deceptively retrograde rhyme scheme conspires to move the reader to a conclusion that's all the more harrowing for being set in sing-song trimeter.

Many of Wiman's poems are about faith, mortality, and the rural world he sprang from. Like all great poets, he's in control of his materials and, more importantly, the reader's experience. He sources the right words to help her spot hitherto unrealized resemblances between unlike things. (This is more fun for the reader than it sounds.) A "storm cloud [is] glut with color like a plum." A "dark / doorway" is the "wall's yawn." A hole in a cemetery is "like a shadow standing its ground." A town is "now nothing but a name / at which some bored boy has taken aim, / every letter light-pierced and partial."

Then there's his exquisite rendering of a flock of birds quitting its tree *en masse*: "I saw a tree inside a tree / rise kaleidoscopically // as if the leaves had livelier ghosts." No creative writing workshop has yet to figure out how to equip its tuition-dispensers with the goggles required to glimpse such stuff. Wiman's original but precise metaphors are acts of vision and discovery.

Our current epidemic of fashionably opaque poetry can be traced to patient zero T.S. Eliot. It was Old Possum who propagated the notion that "modern poetry is supposed to be difficult." It's a dangerous idea that has traveled like a clutch of spores across the decades, settling on radicals and reactionaries alike—from the so-called language poet, who makes a great show of disrupting grammar, to the canon-defending Harold Bloom, who makes a great show of grumbling. ("Authentic American poetry," declares Bloom, "is necessarily difficult.") We're not supposed to believe that language can let the world through. We're not supposed to believe in the sort of bygone signifiers of authenticity, like "real poetry" and "right words," with which this essay is cavalierly strewn. Nor are we to believe in the neigh of that one-horned general reader out there in the distance.

But Wiman refuses to be difficult and always aims to delight and move us, whoever we are. Only a handful of working American poets—Daniel Brown, A.E. Stallings, David Yezzi, and Kay Ryan come to mind—share his commitment to clarity and his degree of respect for readers. It's a fragile operation, but these outliers have it figured out: get the right words into the right order, and you can occasionally float a poem, like a paper plane, through the Derridean dry ice, over demographic niches, and into hearts. You can, as Frost put it, "lodge a few poems where they will be hard to get rid of." You can make a marginal art form matter.

"[T]here is a kind of faith that a poet had better not lose," says Wiman, who now teaches at Yale Divinity School. "It is a faith in the mind's ability to find meaning in a world that exists independently of itself, and a concomitant faith in language to serve as a means of doing so." Word by word, Wiman makes you a believer.

(*Slate*, 2016)

Kingsley Amis's *The Alteration*

Imagine a United States in which the president has ordered the Environmental Protection Agency to scrub its website of climate-change content, his counselor and former campaign manager has deployed the phrase "alternative facts," a list of crimes committed by undocumented immigrants is drawn up weekly and posted, and an executive order targeting Muslim travellers has been issued. A sci-fi novelist could do worse than recruit any one of these plot points into a gloomy novel of the future—except, of course, they're not plot points.

In light of these recent developments, it doesn't take much effort to glean why George Orwell's *Nineteen Eighty-Four* is suddenly selling at a newsworthy clip. The story posits a terrifying authoritarian society—but it's likely you already know that, even if you haven't read a page of it. It's the one with Big Brother, the Thought Police, doublethink, Newspeak, the Ministry of Truth. It's certainly not the only novel about the dangers of authoritarianism, but it has a monopoly on all the best iconic figures and phrases. Ironically, Orwell's 1949 classic itself has become a kind of tyrant, glowering like Big Brother from the top of Amazon's bestseller list.

However you feel about *Nineteen Eighty-Four* personally, there are plenty of other great speculative novels about authoritarianism, novels that are less iconic, but no less chilling. One in particular turned forty this past fall to virtually no fanfare, while other books enjoyed a surge of interest. This lack of scrutiny was a shame because *The Alteration*, Kingsley Amis's quirky 1976 foray into counterfactual science fiction, is a masterpiece—and timelier than ever. It posits a world in which truth is trussed up, and sexual identities are policed with horrifying consequences. But, unlike other, more aggressively grim dystopias, it's otherwise a relatively pleasant world, whose horrors blink at readers from between the lines.

The first page of *The Alteration* puts down in a seemingly archaic England, specifically at "Cathedral Basilica of St. George of Coverley, the mother church of all England and of the English Empire overseas." A king has died, other kings have assembled, and the protagonist Hubert Anvil, a young, prepubescent chorister, is delivering a transcendent performance. But it's an odd configuration of kings in attendance, and soon other references start to nag. The cathedral contains frescoes by William Blake…and a mosaic by one David Hockney. And then comes the twist, several pages in, as the massive cathedral disgorges its funeral procession: "In the year of Our Lord one thousand nine hundred and seventy-six, Christendom would see nothing more mournful or more stately."

That's right: it's 1976, and an alteration to history has, in fact, *arrested* history. The Protestant Reformation, it turns out, never took place. The Church of England never parted ways with the Pope, Catholicism dominates the Western world, and the Turks have been branded the enemy. (In this alternate reality, Martin Luther, the great papal critic, became Pope.) It's supposed to be the year the Sex Pistols released "Anarchy in the UK," but large portions of the planet are fixed in medieval deep freeze. Interestingly, there's still something like a brash (if much diminished) New World, called "New England," where there's a "First Citizen" instead of a king. It's a surreal setup, but then so was the episode of *The Simpsons* that imagined a reality star rising to the highest office.

The Alteration, then, is a counterfactual novel in the tradition of Philip K. Dick's *The Man in the High Castle*. (Dick's 1962 science-fiction classic, now reimagined as an Amazon TV series, wonders what would have happened had the Nazis won World War II.) In fact, in a sly wink to Amis's real-world readers, Hubert's choir friends come into possession of a copy of *The Man in the High Castle*.

Dick's book, in the world of *The Alteration*, is an example of "cw"—or "Counterfeit World," a literary subgenre of "Time Romance" (basically, science fiction). Such literature is illegal in Hubert's world, and the youngsters duly marvel at their contraband. From it, they imagine an alternative world history that could very well have been theirs, one in which Martin Luther never becomes Pope, something called *The Origin of Species* sees its way into print, and New England eventually evolves into "the greatest Power in the world." Here, then, is "fake history"—but unlike its mischief-making cousin "fake news," fake history has the positive effect of opening minds muffled by oppression to unimagined social and political possibilities.

Amis's seemingly benign title, *The Alteration*, however, has a second, terrible meaning: Hubert himself is to be "altered." At the novel's outset, church authorities resolve to turn the young chorister into a castrato, the better to embalm his otherworldly voice—and to refrigerate the adolescent in clean, bright, asexual youth. Traumatic surgery, here, is sheathed in the sort of opaque euphemism—see "alternative facts"—that politicians sometimes prefer and that Orwell himself worried about in his classic essay, "Politics and the English Language."

Hubert will attempt to flee his "alteration," but plot is the least of the book's pleasures. Most of the delight (and terror) comes from Amis's wickedly clever world building. For example, as Hubert's friends geek out over *The Man in the High Castle* (the way real-world fanboys might an installment of *Star Wars*) one of them pauses to balk at the idea of a brash English colony across the pond becoming a world power. "That mean little den of thieves and savages…?" he says with disbelief. It's a moment of black comedy, but in 2017 it's also a painful reminder that the pre-eminence of the United States, far from a given, might one day seem like nothing more than preposterous sci-fi: the object of a fanboy's scorn.

In another twist, Amis imagines a society that has largely suppressed science. Electricity has been discovered, but is disdained, the way many now disdain vaccines. Curiously, there are car- and train-like conveyances that propel people about Hubert's otherwise lethargic world—but only because enterprising electricity-denialists have found complicated workarounds. It's hard not to picture climate-change skeptics when reading passages like this:

> [I]gnition was achieved merely by compressing petroleum vapour to a certain density, without the introduction of a spark. That suffix was vital, for the only practicable known means of producing a spark was an electrical one, and matters electrical were held in general disesteem. They were commonly regarded among the people as strange, fearful, even profane; the gentry smiled at the terms of this view while not missing its essential truth: electricity was appallingly dangerous, both as it existed and as it might be developed.

Crucially, unlike *Nineteen Eighty-Four*, there are no scene-stealing villains in *The Alteration*—no Thought Police, no Ministries of Truth—to administer tyranny. Nor do telescreens loom overhead. There's just a mundane, centuries-old consensus that corsets sexuality and chloroforms reason.

In his introduction to the NYRB Classics edition of *The Alteration*, William Gibson calls the book a "study in tyranny, as effective, and terrifying, albeit in its much quieter way, as Orwell's *Nineteen Eighty-Four*." Quiet is the key, well-judged word here. Read between the lines of *The Alteration* and you find Western culture behind bars. Read too quickly and you'll miss the submerged fact that geniuses like Willem de Kooning came to devote their canvasses to religious content, and that many literary classics never came to be. (Instead, Hubert's bookshelf includes an alt-canon of bizarro doppelgangers like *Lord of the Chalices* and *The Wind in the Cloister*.) Even Shakespeare, identified only as the author of "If you prick us, do we not bleed," was excommunicated and expelled from England. No other book dispenses such disastrous fates—noiselessly, behind the scenes—to the liberal heroes and artifacts it's easy to take for granted. Free will has been garroted by rosary beads.

It's easy to glide over many of these details. *The Alteration* requires readers to have a handle on history and be alert to allusions that Amis doesn't especially underline. As a result, the book might not seem like obvious gear for the resistance (whereas Occupy Wall Street readily took up the mask preferred by the protagonist of Alan Moore's graphic novel *V for Vendetta*). Nevertheless, Amis's experiment is an essential entry in a canon that includes *V for Vendetta* as well as other well-known fare like *The Man in the High Castle* and *The Handmaid's Tale*. Dick himself suggests *The Alteration* might be the best "alternate-worlds" novel, period. Amis's subtle, stylish sentences yield no slogans, no iconic images. But those anxious about encroaching tyranny will discover in its pages a grave new world.

(*The Atlantic*, 2017)

Vladimir Nabokov's
Heroic Couplets

I HADN'T WRITTEN POETRY in four years when, all of a sudden, I found myself writing a lot of it, hundreds of lines of the stuff. This was surprising. For one, I thought I'd given up poetry (even if, as Dorothy Parker once put it, "nobody seemed to notice my magnificent gesture"). Also, when I used to write a poem, it was always short. Spilling onto the second page of the Word document was decadence. It was as close as I got to Epic Poetry.

Perhaps I still thought of myself mainly as a critic. Editors sometimes took my pitches, and Twitter sometimes took note. Prose gets more love than poetry. Or hate. But hate's a reaction, at least; someone was reading those essays and reviews. The poems—playing the long game, playing for longevity—had been pitched to the immortal dead.

Plus, it had gotten easy banging out the 1,200-word "take," a word more spat than said. Writers should be wary when writing starts to feel easy. "No tears in the writer, no tears in the reader," said Robert Frost. It's a worn saying, but a solid one, too, like some ancient monument many hands have passed over.

By the spring of 2017, it had begun to occur to me that it might be time to try something harder, something more ambitious, than short lyric poems (which I wasn't writing anyway) or ephemeral prose.

Pale Fire provided a model: a long poem, in heroic couplets, that delivered a compelling story. Nabokov's 999-line masterpiece had plenty of poetry: a pair of scissors is a "dazzling synthesis of sun and star," a winter is "scrape-scooped away"—but it was also unfashionably linear, conspicuously coherent, and clear as a tumbler.

The long poems presented to me in university—*The Waste Land*, *The Cantos*, *The Maximus Poems*—were defiantly unreadable: fragmentary, allusive, evasive. They had their moments; indeed, the dispensation of moments, pottery shards of perception, was often the point. But the shards rarely fit together, and the poems seemed to exist to be explicated, not enjoyed.

The splendidly functional couplets of *Pale Fire*, on the other hand, calmly, firmly carried me along:

> I love you when you're standing on the lawn
> Peering at something in a tree: "It's gone
> It was so small. It might come back" (all this
> Voiced in a whisper softer than a kiss).
> I love you when you call me to admire
> A jet's pink trail above the sunset fire.
> I love you when you're humming as you pack
> A suitcase or the farcical car sack
> With round-trip zipper. And I love you most
> When with a pensive nod you greet her ghost
> And hold her first toy on your palm, or look
> At a postcard from her, found in a book.

Nabokov has pulled off a lot in these twelve lines. He's completed his couplets, which furnish their music but aren't so noisy they can't fade into the background. He's also contrived some first-rate poetic images—"round-trip zipper," "sunset fire"—while engineering a believable, likeable character, a feat any novelist ought to envy. And he's consolidated the reader's interest in the character by hinting at some domestic tragedy.

But the poem remains (to flog another Frostism) a future largely not taken. Few poets have followed the example of *Pale Fire*, with its effortless couplets and engaging narrative—perhaps because it's not quite a real or official poem. Nabokov's couplets, after all, are a means to an end: a means to endnotes, authored by a fictional scholar. And it's the endnotes that make up the bulk of *Pale Fire*'s page count; the ballooning endnotes, the true point of the book, conceal a novel.

Put another way, the poem isn't a pure product of the poetry world. It's a work of art, to be sure, and better than much of what the poetry world produces. But *Pale Fire* is also an outlier, just quirky enough for its example to be safely ignored.

But I couldn't ignore it. And by the fall of 2017, I'd composed the first chunk of what would become *Forgotten Work*. Nabokov's poem was about a poet. Mine, too, was about a maker of music—an indie band. When the story opens, the band is rehearsing in a garage and brainstorming a name for itself. Thus, I had the makings of my very own bildungsroman. The chunk was even (check!) in heroic couplets.

But recklessly, on a whim, I decided to start the next section thirty years in the future. My verse novel wouldn't be about the band, after all; it would be about the band's cult following. What's more, I decided each chapter would reboot the story and focus on a new character, perhaps even further into the future. In other words, with each new chapter, I'd have to establish a new setting, a new set of motivations, a new conflict, a new technological context—all the while ensuring that (a) each line was bopping along in iambic pentameter, and (b) the word at the end of each line had its mate.

It seemed important to make things hard for myself. Not hard in, say, the Oulipian sense; I've never been drawn to the elaborate restraints that some poets make a fetish of (e.g. "Write a poem in which every other word starts with the letter 'z'!"). But I had a sense that if I could clear the hurdles I'd arranged, the book would take care of itself.

The rhyme scheme, it turns out, was a constant collaborator. Completing a rhyme tended to nudge me, and the book, in unanticipated directions. Often, the nudge was negligible, and the book, like an aircraft carrier, barely shifted. But much like a character in some sci-fi story—who goes back in time, displaces a pebble, and returns to the present to find everyone now sports plumage—a rhyming poet's seemingly minor, local choices can ripple out and wrinkle the rest of the work.

Early on, I describe the taste of Hubert, a snobby English student circa 2037:

> Hubert loved looking back. He'd waved off eye
> Replacements; Hubert had a glasses guy
> Who sourced assorted old-school gear for old
> Souls and their skulls. His frames were bold,
> As quaint as whalebone corsets, hunting foxes,
> iPhones, and those primitive Xboxes
> That weren't implanted but, instead, sat on
> Your furniture. He loved the off-brand dawn
> His window ran, recorded when the sun
> Could still be seen. He loved such stuff as *Fun House*, *Horses*, *Astral Weeks*, *The La's*, *Pet Sounds*,
> Thomas Disch's essays, Ezra Pound's
> Translations...

Which came first, the "foxes" or the "Xboxes?" I don't remember. But I do remember having no clear sense of what it meant that the sun could no longer be seen; I just liked the sound of that "off-brand dawn," and anyway, I needed at least the "dawn" because the Xboxes of the future no longer sit "on" furniture. (You can start to see how the rhyme scheme wasn't just a collaborator; at times, it was a dictator.)

Now, the impact of the "foxes/Xboxes" rhyme was microscopic and more or less contained to the passage above. But it turns out that that missing sun, a throwaway prop, would throw its shadow over the rest of the book. After all, and as I discovered a chapter later, humans of the future have been careless. They've teleported so much trash into the exosphere, the trash has cohered into a cloud and come to obscure the sun.

For several years, writing my verse novel, there was always something to wake up to: a plotline to advance, a character to add flesh to, another couplet to complete. Like an AI come into consciousness, *Forgotten Work* came to write itself. What a relief this was. I noted, above, that I'd wanted to try something harder, something more ambitious than the short lyric poem. But I'd be terrified to attempt a short lyric poem now. Where would I even start?

The verse novel liberates poets from waiting around for lightning bolts—there's too much work to do! It also opens us up to poetic opportunities we might not otherwise realize we have. At one point in *Forgotten Work*, I explain a robot dog:

>   White but flecked
> With grainy dots, the Shiba was a plastic
> Model that could stretch and turn elastic,
> Or press through a fence, its body bulging
> Forth as Play-Doh worms, the fence divulging
> Dog.

I love short lyric poems; I fall before Daniel Brown, Kay Ryan, Robyn Sarah, and Samuel Menashe. But I don't know how I'd ever have gotten to an image like that "body bulging / Forth as Play-Doh worms, the fence divulging / Dog," if I'd been writing the regular kind of poem, and not mulling over the makes of robot dog available in the 2050s.

"I became a journalist partly so that I wouldn't ever have to rely on the press for my information," said the late Christopher Hitchens. I sometimes harbour a similar thought when it comes to poetry. The stuff I want to read simply isn't the stuff most poets are offering up (not enough robot dog, for one) so I have to mint it myself. This is why I write less and less about poetry these days—you're welcome!—and also why I can't stop reading works like *Pale Fire* or, say, *Don Juan*.

Written in the nineteenth century, Byron's proto-verse novel strikes me now as more modern than *The Waste Land* (than most poetry, really) even if it's less useful to the professor who has fifty minutes to fill and needs something sticky to explicate. It's faster, funnier, more energetic, more violent. More readable.

I get that I sound like a hopeless crank. Still, I can't help but think that the future of poetry, or *one* future for poetry, can be found in the past, in works like *Pale Fire*, *Don Juan*, and *The Golden Gate*, among others (though not many others!). As another hopeless crank, a character from *Forgotten Work*, reflects in iambs:

> The futures we prefer have long since passed.
> Tomorrow is interred inside the past.

(*Lit Hub*, 2020)

Dave Sim's *Cerebus*

In December 1977, the first issue of *Cerebus*, a comic about an aardvark barbarian, appeared in black and white. Written and illustrated by Dave Sim, a cartoonist who lives in Kitchener, Ontario, *Cerebus* would persist for nearly three decades, expiring in the twenty-first century. At its peak, back when comics had pesky material needs such as ink and distribution, Sim's book enjoyed a print run of 36,000—a feat for a self-published series.

Sim had been inspired by the commercial success of *Howard the Duck*. But while *Howard the Duck* took place in our modern world, Sim selected a medieval backdrop for his own anthropomorphic character. Sim had no deep feeling for the sword-and-sorcery genre; it was merely easier to draw than sci-fi. But *Cerebus* quickly wriggled free of the barbarian shtick, which chafed like chain mail.

The aardvark ran for elected office and became prime minister of Iest, the fictional city state where much of the series is set. Then, he became pope and ascended to the moon. Later, having fallen from power, Cerebus found himself taken in by his ex-girlfriend and her new husband. Next, he spent an entire run of issues holed up at a café, in mourning. Part of the comic's appeal was its ambition; with each new storyline, Sim brought some suitably weighty subject—politics, religion, gender, grief—into view of his distinctive panels, each one framed by his hallmark design: a slightly thorny black line. As he went, he bundled issues, by storyline, into thick softcover editions. (A set of what fans came to call "phonebooks" has followed me through several moves and blows out a shelf in my basement.)

There isn't an adjective that can't be directed at *Cerebus*, which turns forty this month. The series is funny, boring, thrilling, tedious, moving, offensive, satirical, reactionary, innovative, sexist, romantic, and ultimately, as our culture writers like to say, problematic. If the comic came out today, takes like "Aardvarks: I Can't Even" would file themselves.

But despite its problems, Sim's life's work, doled out in monthly doses for twenty-six years, adds up to Canada's most aesthetically accomplished and ambitious graphic novel (followed by Chester Brown's *Louis Riel* and Seth's *Clyde Fans*). Shot through with hairline flaws and cavities, *Cerebus* is nevertheless one of those neglected monuments of Canadian culture—like Peter Van Toorn's book of poems *Mountain Tea* or Mary Margaret O'Hara's album *Miss America*—that your professor never assigns.

It wasn't just Sim's subject matter that was ambitious. Early on, he declared that *Cerebus* would run for exactly 300 issues. That meant twenty-six years of monthly issues, published outside the near-monopoly enjoyed by Marvel and DC, the superhero conglomerates. Sim's underdog product would cease production, around page 6,000, with the planned death of its title character. That meant—if all went according to plan—the final issue would come out in the far-flung future of March 2004.

Sim's bloody-minded pursuit of this milestone made him an oddity among comic artists. So, too, did his advocacy for their creative rights. When Canadian Todd McFarlane helped lead an exodus of artists from Marvel to form an imprint of their own in the nineties, Sim's aardvark showed up in an issue of McFarlane's new venture, *Spawn*, to cheer on the rebellion. (Sim wrote the issue.) Indeed, *Cerebus*, which often parodied the state of the superhero genre, came to be the conscience of a subculture. Sim even printed detailed advice to aspiring cartoonists, from how to pick the right printer to the basics of how to use a nib. (As a teenager, who xeroxed his own comics with friends, I learned how to ink from reading *Cerebus*.) Sim also opened his pages to excerpts from other fledgling indie comics. On the shoulders of his sword-wielding aardvark, countless careers took their first tottering steps.

Sim's heroism, however, was sometimes easier to appreciate than his product. Those trying to sell you on *Cerebus* will insist that the early issues—which constitute a crudely drawn *Conan* parody—must be endured since they introduce many of the series's major characters. Sim himself seems to have taken grim pleasure in pointing out how much effort his life's work requires of readers. ("It's virtually impossible to sell," he's said, "because it's virtually impossible to describe.")

In fact, *Cerebus* was usually about whatever happened to be preoccupying its creator. For instance, when Sim got religious, so, too, did his comic. When Sim wanted to talk to his creation, the aardvark found himself plucked from a bloody fight and plunked down into a postmodern metafiction. When Sim took an obsessive interest in American literature, his book's back pages ballooned with endnotes, and Cerebus turned fanboy, fawning over one Ham Ernestway, a depressive novelist. Sim's book was meticulous about its world building, but blithe, too; the drywall between his aardvark's reality and ours was always porous. At any moment, a real-world figure—a fellow cartoonist, Oscar Wilde, Woody Allen—might suddenly, calmly, populate his panels.

Unlike the typical superhero comic of the time—which ensured that each new instalment was self-contained or, at least, lubricated with a recap—*Cerebus* didn't condescend to the uninitiated. An issue of *Cerebus*, encountered in isolation at a comic shop, was like a section of film snipped free from some larger spool. Here, then, was another part of the appeal: with no Wikipedia at hand, you had to do the adult work of getting up to speed.

But even if you didn't know what was going on, the production values were apt to win you over. "Genuine poetry," argued T.S. Eliot, "can communicate before it is understood." Similarly, the formal polish of a page, even a panel, of *Cerebus* could reassure curious readers that they'd stumbled onto the real thing. Critical to the look of *Cerebus* were the embellishments of Sim's crack collaborator, Gerhard. Early on, Sim recruited the artist to supply his comic with hi-def backgrounds: exquisite crosshatching that cohered as cumuli or gave palace marble its gleam. Gerhard's buildings, another cartoonist's afterthought, were so thorough they seemed to unfold, origami-like, from real-world blueprints. *Cerebus* was a monthly masterclass in what obsessive artists, under a relentless deadline, could accomplish with pen and ink.

Sim made it to March 2004, and the aardvark to his projected demise. But no great fanfare welcomed either event; by then, Sim's comic had shed many of its readers. Indeed, those trying to sell you on *Cerebus* are also likely to warn you off the last third of the series. Like the doomed survivors of a shipwreck who still have access to a working radio, their message would sound something like, "Don't go where we ran aground."

Sim's comic was always controversial. As it progressed, the books became increasingly anti-feminist. Issue 186—as notorious a number to Sim's fans as 237 is to Stephen King's—horrified the comic world. By this point in the series, Cerebus was attempting to usurp Cirin, leader of the matriarchal Cirinists, a totalitarian regime of robed women who had overrun Iest. (Cirinism is the sort of cartoon nightmare that keeps men's rights activists up at night.) Issue 186, however, went further, comparing men to light and women to light-gobbling void. *The Comics Journal*—something like the comic medium's version of *Poetry*—printed responses from the writer Alan Moore, the cartoonist Seth, even Sim's ex-wife. (The headline on the cover: "Dave Sim: Misogynist Guru of Self-Publishers.")

As the series wound down, Sim became increasingly religious and right-wing. (His belief system is bespoke, cadged together from different religions.) The "Latter Days" storyline, in which Cerebus becomes the object of a religious cult, was as deftly illustrated as ever; a casual browse will take your breath away. But it also clubbed readers with pages and pages of textual analysis of the Torah, in dense tablets of tiny type—the preferred mode of the off-the-grid crank. Even Gerhard, still labouring over Sim's backgrounds, was no longer a fan. "It was a strange sort of phenomenon," he told an interviewer, "to be working on a book that I can barely even read any more."

Like Gerhard, many readers who stuck with *Cerebus*, who experienced it in glacial real time, one month at a time, felt betrayed by the turn the series seemed to take. The critic Tegan O'Neil was blunt:

> *Cerebus* towards the end wasn't so much a poor reading experience as the final violent convulsions of a bad marriage... And when it was over I missed it, even though my reaction was as irrational as that of a battered spouse longing for their abuser.

But looking back on the contours and vistas of the completed series as a whole—while ignoring its creator, that volcano off to the side fuming about "leftists" and generations "raised to be women"—provides some perspective. Indeed, *Cerebus* begins to resemble James Joyce's *Ulysses*, another flawed book that dares to encompass all of life.

At the start, *Cerebus*, like *Ulysses*, is charming, readable, and allusive. Then the work grows more ambitious in its world building and more formally experimental, parodying different genres and storytelling styles. Just when you've gotten the hang of it, it double downs on its own difficulty. The longueurs between successful set pieces lengthen, and the later chapters chip away at your patience. But the book still pellets out enough small pleasures and insights about the human condition to keep you turning pages. Plus, there's plenty to occupy those pursuing tenure—booby traps to trip over, allusions to log. In short, it's a brilliant work. But dim in spots. And dumb when it comes to women.

Actually, some of the cartoonist's depictions of women were more nuanced than you might expect. And two late storylines, "Going Home" and "Form and Void," offered rewarding meditations on relationships as well as on writers like F. Scott Fitzgerald and Ernest Hemingway. It's a reminder that the worth of a cultural object can't simply be derived from its politics, however ugly. As O'Neil concludes, despite her disappointment, "[*Cerebus*] will survive because it is simply indispensable." As Alan Moore puts it,

"*Cerebus*, as if I need to say so, is still to comic books what Hydrogen is to the Periodic Table."

If anything, the soul of *Cerebus* is in the details: in the hundreds of local pleasures—plot twists, slapstick gags, and wordless, gallery-grade panels—that, in the aggregate, occupy the bulk of a reader's experience of the work. There are minor delights which include Cerebus learning how to sweep a floor, and sublime ones, such as the two-page panel of the aardvark peering down at Iest (drawn and quartered into farm fields and street grids) as the tower he's sitting on spins toward outer space. I mean the pleasures that exist despite the author's explicit program or most self-defeating, overdetermined intentions and intolerances. As with *Ulysses*, *The Cantos*, *The Merchant of Venice*, and countless other complicated texts, it's complicated. But that's what makes forty-year-old *Cerebus*, though far from woke, a work of art.

(*The Walrus*, 2017)

Kay Ryan's Essays

THE OTHER DAY ON TWITTER, an accomplished poet posted a draft of a poem and invited feedback. "Twitter, help me workshop this!" he cried, the word "Twitter" suggesting he was open to opinions beyond his 10,000 followers.

The tweet brought to mind—as the verb "workshop" itself always does—an essay I first read some fifteen years ago, by the American poet Kay Ryan. Ryan was an outsider in the poetry world. She lived in Northern California, didn't teach creative writing, didn't network. Her poems, too, were outsiders: essay-like, flensed of first-person pronouns, and littered with landmines, buried rhymes that could send you skyward. She was growing in popularity but nobody's idea of a poetry professional—which was probably why *Poetry* magazine, in an act of inspired mischief, dispatched her to a creative writing conference. The resulting essay, "I Go to AWP," is a classic of gonzo travel writing. Ryan attends panels, hankers after free keychains, eats with other poets, and generally recoils in horror.

Part of the pleasure of the piece, especially if you're familiar with the poetry world, is experiencing an insular microclimate through alien eyes. What are "arcs," Ryan wonders, and why should books of poems have them? Moreover, why do poets toss around the word "mentor" with such abandon? And what compels them to bounce, *en masse*, on fancy words like "transgressive" until "the springs pop out"? At every turn, the interloper dilates exquisitely. Here she is on that verb "workshop":

> In the old days before creative writing programs, a workshop was a place, often a basement, where you *sawed* or *hammered*,

drilled or *planed* something. You could not simply *workshop* something. Now you can. You can take something you wrote by yourself to a group and get it workshopped. Sometimes it probably is a lot like getting it hammered. Other writers read your work, give their reactions, and make suggestions for change. A writer might bring a piece back for more workshopping later, even. I have to assume that the writer respects these other writers' opinions, and that just scares the daylights out of me. It doesn't matter if their opinions really are respectable; I just think the writer has given up way too much inside. Let's not share. Really. Go off in your own direction way too far, get lost, test the metal of your work in your own acids. These are experiments you can perform down in that old kind of workshop, where Dad used to hide out from too many other people's claims on him.

Screeds against creative writing programs are easy enough to write, but Ryan is too clever not to step around the pitfalls of the genre: the reactionary politics, the curmudgeonly (if inconveniently accurate) hunch that poetry can't be taught. "It doesn't matter if their opinions really are respectable," she concedes—point to the programs. But then she raises the hammer and nails the problem with the workshop: aspiring poets surrender their stubborn streaks at the door. She proceeds to reclaim—and refurbish—the metaphor, nudging out the crowd in favour of the cranky loner. "Let's not share. Really." It's all so very deft. You barely notice she's laying waste to a vast infrastructure.

Ryan started publishing poetry in the 1980s and was writing in her mature style by the 1990s. But she didn't publish many of her best essays until the aughts. A good number of them appeared in *Poetry*, under Christian Wiman's editorship. They were charming and philosophical. They gave the impression of a master who had waited years to speak her mind; and of a mind that had required those years to mull its concerns: poetry, memory, time, Moore, Frost, Dickinson. The mind seemed calmly, irrefutably, itself. Unlike so many of her contemporaries, who had "given up way too much inside"—to workshops, to the online fracas, to the fiction of fellowship—here was a writer who had stayed steeped in her own acids.

At first, it was the poems that got most of the attention. They appeared to be members of some previously unidentified species of verse that surely must've been with us all along, lurking under some frond. If you thumbed through any of her books, and squinted, they described the same shape over and over: a lean column, typically one per page. "Progress—the idea of progress—doesn't mean anything to me," she said in her *Paris Review* interview. "I don't have to think my books are getting better. I just want to keep going back to the same well to have another little drink."

Ryan started attracting the big awards, and even served as US Poet Laureate, a rare blip in a life of preferring not to. She was suddenly everywhere. My poems started sounding like hers. So, too, did the poems of others.

But it was the essays—in *Poetry* and elsewhere—that stayed with me, quietly, like burrs. (I carried a photocopy of one, a piece about the dangers of notebooks, which first appeared in *Parnassus*, through several moves.) I came to feel that a book of Ryan's essays, if there were ever enough of them, would make a monument: a monument to the independent-minded critic, a figure fast disappearing off the face of the culture. And so, I waited.

Synthesizing Gravity: Selected Prose (Grove 2020), a collection of Ryan's reviews and essays, came out last spring, in the midst of the pandemic. *The New York Times* and a few other places made note of the item, but it quickly fell off radars already preoccupied with COVID. I didn't even know about it until many months later.

But the book might've passed the culture by anyway, pandemic (and Trump and TikTok and Tiger Kings) notwithstanding. Ryan's criticism doesn't engage much with the zeitgeist. Pop culture doesn't particularly figure into her writing, and her references can be bracing curios. (William Bronk's poetry, she writes, is "like the small brown bottle my grandmother carried in her purse and sniffed for the pick-me-up jolt.") She can proceed like a philosopher, with Platonic forms at hand. ("This is actually an abstract walk," she writes in one essay, "one I'm making up, a generalized walk based on what I like. I have usually done this on a bicycle, but I was asked to write about a walk, so I'll walk.") She has the gall to rope us into the first-person plural, the gall to believe in the transcendent. ("There is a permanent time that poetry lets us into. There are doors in all the centuries, feeding into this permanent time.") Her essays are counterintuitive, but never contrarian. ("We must run roughshod over what threaten to become memories.")

Ryan isn't interested in what a Robert Frost poem reveals about his politics, or the economic conditions that shaped Marianne Moore. She has never handled a hot take.

Her reviews and essays are ostensibly about poets and poetry, but they inevitably range further, into stretches of intellectual territory many contemporary critics steer clear of, where grand old ideas loom like the sandstone buttes in Monument Valley. "Something nonsensical in the heart of poetry is the very reason why one can't call poetry 'useful,'" she explains at one point, and then adds, a little later, "This is why Auden and others can say with such confidence that poetry makes nothing happen. That's the relief of it. And the reason why nothing can substitute for it."

We don't expect critics to assert such truths anymore, let alone with such confidence. We expect them to "problematize," to qualify. Ryan's own confidence, then, is thrillingly anachronistic: obstinate, sure, but warming, too, as if a cast-iron stove were squatting in the middle of that valley.

Elsewhere, turning over T.S. Eliot's definition of poetry as "a superior amusement," Ryan observes, "I am reminded by him that though we cannot be exactly precise or complete, that is no reason not to make gigantic statements, for there is great enjoyment in gigantic statements." To borrow a line from Ryan: "I can hardly begin to suggest the courage this...gives to me." After all, so much of our criticism—and its grumpy, online parody "culture writing"—takes a grim pleasure in chipping away at "gigantic statements." But Ryan is perfectly happy standing amid some Stonehenge of "gigantic statements."

Her genius, really, is for metaphor. It's metaphor that makes "gigantic statements" possible—that winterizes her generalizations against our objections. Imagining her readership, she writes:

> When I am writing, I feel that I have insinuated myself at the long, long desk of the gods of literature—more like a trestle table, actually—so long that the gods (who are also eating, disputing, and whatnot, as well as writing) fade away in the distance according to the laws of Renaissance perspective. I am at the table of the gods and I want them to like me. There, I've said it. I want the great masters to enjoy what I write. The noble dead are my readers, and if what I write might jostle them a little, if there were a tiny bit of scooting and shifting along the benches, this would be my thrill. And I would add that the noble dead cannot be pleased with imitations of themselves; they are already quite full of themselves.

You could write a monograph about this passage—its rhetorical subtleties, its sly humour, its beauty. Ryan is animating something like T.S. Eliot's tradition—a grand order of works of art, which adjusts itself slightly as upstart works of art elbow in. But she avoids the loaded word "tradition"; hers is a "trestle table." What's more, she puts up an astonishing tableau: those "gods of literature" dwindling toward some vanishing point "according to the laws of Renaissance perspective." Then comes the disarmingly likeable confession: "I am at the table of the gods and I want them to like me. There, I've said it. I want the great masters to enjoy what I write." It's a hit of pure honesty; after all, isn't the enlightened, contemporary writer supposed to spurn canons and welcome the fellowship of the workshop, of literary community?

And yet Ryan wants her place among the greats—and wants to "jostle" them, no less. The charming cheek of it! In lieu of Eliot's clinical description of how the "existing monuments form an ideal order among themselves, which is modified by the introduction of the new (the really new) work of art among them," we get something much livelier: literary giants "scooting and shifting along the benches" in response to a Ryan poem. Oh, and these aren't simply the "dead white males" of right-thinking discourse, a brick of a phrase that would've sunk the passage. "[T]hey are already quite full of themselves," she jokes, letting the air out of her "noble dead"—and letting air into Eliot's "ideal order," stuffy as a catacomb. Somehow, in a matter of sentences, she's revived the idea of tradition. She's made it okay to aspire to eternity.

"[M]etaphor is where the creative imagination reveals its furthest capacities," writes that old editor of Ryan's, Christian Wiman, in the book's introduction. And metaphor, I'd add, is what can elevate criticism into the realm of art. (There, I've said it—one of those "gigantic statements.") Ryan's essays are works of art, or, at least, contain them: stray images and sentences so strange and immediately memorable they seem like aphorisms in waiting:

> Work which pleases itself first just snips so many binding strings in the minds of others.
>
> We must be less in love with foreground if we want to see far.
>
> ...imagine a glass filled with a supersaturated solution; if you give it a tap, it could turn to crystals. Rereading is like these mysteries.
>
> If a poem sticks you to it, it has failed.

I hasten to add these aren't rare jewels that have been wrested from otherwise prosaic settings; I could've opened the book to any page and found something worth pocketing. Nor do they suggest layers of polish. "A few of these essays have never been seen before," writes Wiman, "and arrived at my door in pencil, each without a word crossed out and bearing such boreal clarity and crisp precisions that I found myself pausing to write things down."

"Boreal clarity" is a jewel of its own; Ryan's prose compels its critics to rally their resources—some of its critics, anyway. When I was in grad school, I wrote a chapter of a dissertation about Ryan. Armed with Bourdieu et al., I scrubbed at her poems and prose. But theory, when applied to a writer who's already defiantly clear, becomes steel wool: it scuffs, it doesn't clarify. Ryan's example challenges us to put aside our critical frameworks and pay attention.

In her essay, "Notes on the Danger of Notebooks," she tells the story of a lecture given by Gertrude Stein. The audience, made up of studious note-takers, is struggling to understand Stein. But a photographer, off to the side, is getting it. He has an "edge," says Ryan; because he's taking pictures, and is half-preoccupied with his camera, he doesn't have the mental space to be actively *trying* to understand the supposedly forbidding modernist. Stein's words break across him, and he is able to merely listen and receive them: a radical posture.

Ryan is always clear, never coyly oblique. Indeed, there's a relief in reading her ruthlessly specific judgments. By that, I don't necessarily mean "fierce opinions of other people's work," though she has those. For instance, she can approach an Emily Dickinson poem with the confidence of a picky reader, not a supplicant, and is perfectly comfortable pointing out that some stanzas aren't that special:

> Dickinson terrain is hard on the brain suspension. In any poem of more than one stanza, one stanza is likely to bottom out.
>
> #1099 has several things not going for it. First, I always worry when it looks like she's going to inhabit an insect. These experiments can go bad in the fey direction. (Recall the "little tippler / leaning against the—sun—") And here she is in stanza one already sensing herself in the early stages of becoming a butterfly.

This is audacious, brazen stuff. We tend to approach figures like Dickinson as towering giants laurelled with cumuli, their texts like tablets handed down from Parnassus. We take their aesthetic decisions for granted, as settled matters, and concentrate mostly on meaning: what is the poem driving at? Or we cut such giants down to size by plumbing trendy depths: what Leon Wieseltier calls the "habit of correcting high thought with the social and economic lowdown." You have to know your mind, and have quite a bit of nerve on hand, to view a Dickinson poem anew; to see it as a compendium of fresh decisions made by a brilliant but fallible artist—and to pass judgments on those decisions.

By "ruthlessly specific judgments," then, I really mean "courageous choices." While most critics celebrate the harvest (read Twitter sometime or virtually any literary journal), Ryan *chooses*: this over that. And the force with which she expresses those preferences can sneak up—and tip you—like a sudden gust. Here she is on the impact of discovering Stevie Smith, and why no other poet, up to that point, could've replaced Smith:

> It seems so unfair, how the heart is. Why couldn't I feel the same about Auden? Surely Auden is profound and so wise and weary and puckish too, obviously a vastly more elastic soul and mind and talent. Or Larkin. Larkin was alive then, when Stevie Smith was, in the seventies. Maybe I didn't know about Larkin then.

As she piles on the superlatives—"profound," "wise," "weary"—she quietly buries Auden, that "obviously" a shield, driven into the soil, mid-sentence, to turn back our objections. She's too smart to attempt a proper frontal attack against Auden or Larkin; it's not them, it's her. "Maybe I didn't know about Larkin then," she writes, the sentence the shrug of an innocent. It doesn't matter if Auden and Larkin are the greater poets. Ryan has made peace with her heart—has even used the word "heart!" You're left with the feeling of wanting to feel for a poet the way Ryan feels for Smith. Your assent is total—even if you disagree.

Ryan goes on to marvel at Smith's poem, "Duty was his Lodestar," which begins by mangling the title: "Duty was my Lobster, my Lobster was she...." Ryan is floored by this mischief, and spends over a page sprawled on the floor, accounting for herself. Here, I will break in on Ryan, a third of the way through:

> It gives me so much hope, to see language get pantsed.
>
> It's one thing to have duty as a lodestar: a high-toned piety one might repeat: perfect for lip service.
>
> It's another thing to have duty as a lobster. It doesn't work at all. It just won't abstract right. The lobster has torn free of duty by the first line. What we get is a clattery lobster dance with breaking-up and making-up.
>
> In fact, we might say—it has just occurred to me—that the joy of this poem is that *it* has torn free of duty. The duty to be more than a prank, duty to rhyme decently, to keep to a rhythm, to find fresh words even.
>
> It's the special fun of laughing someplace you're not supposed to laugh, like church. Because it must be said that the fun results from scrambling the piety; the fun is had at the expense of sobriety. And it wouldn't be much fun to think about the lobster if one were *not* thinking about its not being a lodestar.
>
> Maybe this poem really only works for people who are tyrannized by duty.

I quote from this essay at such length to give a sense of Ryan thinking in real time, but also to convey how her prose can work: proceeding from a minor, playful point—"It gives me so much hope, to see language get pantsed"—to an unlikely, even dark epiphany—"Maybe this poem really only works for people who are tyrannized by duty." Between those polarities, the prose is sneaky, sidling crablike up to its point—though, of course, the sidling, the stylish writing, is the point.

You don't have to be enchanted by the Smith poem to be enchanted by Ryan's enthusiasm for it. Enthusiasm is its own reward. I didn't get this at first. *Poetry* published a letter of mine once, complaining about a short Ryan essay on Bronk. I saw nothing memorable in Bronk's work. But Ryan had already anticipated this. "I don't remember a single individual Bronk poem," she writes in the original piece, "and I don't know if they're actually memorable; anyhow, they don't matter to me in that way." This sort of sophisticated prose soon rubbed off on me. I even came to see myself in Ryan's confessions:

> I have a weak character. I am very susceptible to other people's enthusiasms, at times actually courting them. I like to sit among people who feel strongly about a basketball team, say, and get excited with them. I love to love ouzo with ouzo lovers.

It was endearing to know that Ryan, too, was drawn to enthusiasm—or shall we say the enthusiasm of authority. "We have to listen to so many dumb people; it's such a pleasure to watch somebody's brain working that fast," she says of Linda Gregerson, one of the speakers, at that fateful writing conference, who appealed to the interloper. Ryan thinks a lot about thinking. The effort of the singular mind—as it pulls together scraps and fashions poems—is a recurring trope in *Synthesizing Gravity*: a grave reminder that making art is lonely, difficult watch repair: news no workshop wants to hear.

Still, we cannot entirely dispense with society, with the catalyzing properties of sympathetic editors and readers. Even mavericks like Ryan need their champions. The first decade of the twenty-first century was an especially fecund time for poetry criticism, because of magazines like Wiman's *Poetry*, but others, too. Organs of honest, spirited criticism walked the earth then: *Parnassus*, *Contemporary*

Poetry Review, Books in Canada—all part of the fossil record now. "Everything Kay wrote for *Poetry* was commissioned," Wiman told me. "I was always after her to write prose—and only sometimes succeeded." We might not have had a book like *Synthesizing Gravity*.

We almost certainly won't have another for some time. What scandalized Ryan fifteen years ago—the phenomenon of poets overexposing themselves to the opinions of others—is no longer quarantined in the writing workshop; it pervades social media, to which poets and critics have flocked *en masse*. Groupthink prevails, and writers self-censor—before they can even be policed by others. Young sensibilities praise on Twitter what they disparage in email. (Trust me.) There are a few outliers. The Scottish poetry magazine *The Dark Horse* remains a bastion of scrappy indifference to the convulsions of literary community. William Logan continues to display an undying death wish in his fierce reviews. Mostly, though, the zeitgeist has spooked us: it has scared off many of the uncompromising commentators who would've peopled another age. But there I go again, making gigantic statements.

There's plenty of clamour, of course: plenty of voices professing a passion for poetry. Flip the switch on Twitter and you will find them all over the place (I am there, too!) sharing their likes or, occasionally, organizing into storm clouds against some perceived transgression. There's no shortage of "content," that most contemporary of words. No shortage of people churning out what is ostensibly criticism—for websites, journals, blogs, Substacks. Surely a lot of this work is interesting. Surely we should call the authors "critics." But Ryan seems to me among the last of a kind, and *Synthesizing Gravity*, a monument to a crumbling moment and, shored against it, a singular mind.

(*Lit Hub*, 2021)

Howard Hawks's *Bringing Up Baby*

This month, the upmarket Criterion Collection, which reissues "important classic and contemporary films," dusts off Howard Hawks's 1938 screwball comedy *Bringing Up Baby*. But "dusts off" isn't quite right. Dust could never settle on *Bringing Up Baby*. Hawks's breakneck picture—a vehicle for Cary Grant and, especially, Katharine Hepburn—never stops moving, and its characters never stop talking. It's as packed with kinetic energy as a super ball.

The Criterion Collection tends to specialize in artisanal superfoods: Soviet science-fiction, tortoise-brisk character studies, well-smoked French fare. But if fizzy *Bringing Up Baby*, now available in lavish Blu-ray, isn't a work of towering art, then neither is *Guernica* nor *Gravity's Rainbow*.

The plot is deceptively artless. Grant plays compliant paleontologist David, on the cusp of acquiring (a) an intercostal clavicle, the bone he needs to complete his brontosaurus skeleton, and (b) an equally lifeless wife. (The day before the wedding, the wife-to-be makes no bones about it: David's work is paramount and the marriage "must entail no domestic entanglements of any kind.") Hepburn plays Susan, the relentless, charming aggressor. Susan and David meet-cute on a golf course. David has been trying to woo a wealthy backer; Susan will soon be wooing David. She plays his ball—by mistake?—and they're off.

More plot summary would be pointless. There's a leopard on the loose (the "Baby" of the title), a big-game hunter, a psychiatrist with a facial twitch, pratfalls into water, a rock that's thrown at a balcony, a sleepy man who suddenly appears at said balcony, stolen cars, a chicken-wagon crash, a second leopard, olives underfoot, misunderstandings, mayhem. Susan's dress rips and uncurtains her backside (chastely underweared, but still), while David finds himself in a negligee—and loses himself in the process.

Towards the end, the local jailhouse rounds up all the characters, and a hapless constable tries to parse the chaos. Hepburn has worn down Grant and gotten her man. Grant has gotten his bone. You can guess what happens to the teetering brontosaurus skeleton introduced at the very start of the film. (Says Russian brontosaurus expert Anton Chekov: "If you say in the first chapter that there is a rifle hanging on the wall, in the second or third chapter it absolutely must go off.")

But for all its zaniness, *Bringing Up Baby* is as crisp and contemporary as any movie of the past century. The characters speak quickly—so quickly they often overlap. It's a Babel of voices, in which meaning and identity are, as your English prof once said, fluid. David's transformation from stuffy, museum-grade object to the heroic object of Susan's desire is a study in slippery, post-something selfhood. The famous negligee scene alone could launch a thousand dissertations. (Susan's aunt: "Well, who are you?!?" David: "I don't know. I'm not quite myself today.")

But Susan herself is the centerpiece: a marvel of sexy, self-sufficient, bloody-minded agency, a strain of cinematic woman Hawks specialized in. (See also Angie Dickinson's card-player-with-a-heart-of-gold in *Rio Bravo*, who levels said heart at John Wayne's sheriff, and gets her man quite tidily.) Hepburn's take on the Hawksian woman knows what David needs before he does. She engineers a series of small disasters to keep David close and is blissfully chipper in the face of doom.

When a dog, George, absconds with David's brontosaurus bone, David and Susan set out on the grounds of her aunt's farm in Westlake, Connecticut. "Susan, where is he apt to go?" asks David, desperately, turning in circles. "George is apt to go anywhere," she responds cheerfully. Daring, kooky, and irresistible, she talks a screenplay a minute. But Hepburn's face—whenever we catch it gazing at poor, beleaguered Grant—says it all. She's surely the funniest comedic heroine of all time.

The whole thing is beautifully and simply shot by Hawks. (As Orson Welles once said, comparing Hawks to the director John Ford, "Hawks is great prose; Ford is poetry.") The camera is unfussy and lingers on Hepburn and Grant for long takes, with minimal cutting. The chemistry of these two screwball-crossed stars was clearly real.

"Be rested and on your toes," says filmmaker Peter Bogdanovich on the disc's audio commentary track. It's sound advice for first-time viewers. *Bringing Up Baby* is faster than *The Fast and the Furious* and, in its hyperlinguistic way, more demanding than Tarkovsky, Wenders, Godard—name your cinematic superfood. Wit has never worked more quickly, more intensely. Like Hepburn's deathless, indefatigable Susan, *Bringing Up Baby* wears you out and wins you over.

(*Lit Hub*, 2021)

Jake Tapper's Joke

THE ANCIENT ART OF NAME-CALLING has its visionary poets and lowbrow opportunists. In the visionary camp, there's the late poet-critic Clive James, who once called Arnold Schwarzenegger a "brown condom full of walnuts." And there's the late magazine *Spy*, which, decades ago, correctly identified Donald Trump as a "short-fingered vulgarian." On the lowbrow front, there's, well, Trump, who never demonstrated much imagination, but who knew how to hammer a nail—"Crooked Hillary"—over and over.

The latest innovator in this ever-evolving space is Jake Tapper, who anchors CNN's *The Lead with Jake Tapper*. Some time ago, Tapper took aim at supporters of my country's much-tousled Prime Minister, Justin Trudeau. Tapper had been covering Canada's vaccine distribution, calling it, on air, a "real failure by the Trudeau government…" Later, on Twitter, he wrote: "Careful for acknowledging facts or Tru-Anon will attack you."

Tru-Anon! Tapper's clever adaptation of "QAnon"—the name for the cult of dimwits who believe that Democrats, elites, and other satyrs are administering a global pedophile ring—burbled up through the right-hand column of the Twitter homepage, a grimy aqueduct that explains what's trending at any given moment. Conservatives, naturally, were delighting in Tapper's coinage, but you didn't have to be right wing, or even agree with Tapper about Trudeau's adherents, to admire the poetic chops.

Name-calling doesn't have to be accurate to be effective. Consider the case of Amanda Knox, the American exchange student in Italy, who was arrested in 2007 for the murder of her roommate in a supposed orgy-gone-bad. Tabloids quickly seized on an old nickname of Knox's—"Foxy Knoxy," acquired while playing soccer as a kid—and weaponized it against the beleaguered young woman. (Knox spent four years in prison and was eventually acquitted.) A damaging slur is often lurking on the dark side of a nickname.

That said, the accurate insult is a just insult. It's a scalpel: sharp, light, and compact. It cuts to the rotten core. How perfectly the phrase "Tricky Dick" got at the shriven heart of the eternally crooked Richard Nixon. (His enemies had already tried "Dick Tracy.") But did you know that one Helen Gahagan Douglas, a Democrat, wielded the name "Tricky Dick" during a 1950 political campaign and that the name was not born of Watergate? Me neither!

But then, true poetry often transcends its author, travels beyond its original context, and disperses through the culture. The journalist Paul Greenberg came up with "Slick Willy" in 1980, after Bill Clinton, then Governor of Arkansas, spoke at the Democratic National Convention. Greenberg had balked at how Clinton presented himself as part of a lineage of progressive governors, when, to Greenberg's mind, Clinton had broken the lineage. "Slick Willy" was birthed in the *Pine Bluff Commercial*, but soon sprouted centipede legs and scuttled after Clinton, with frequent stops in the prose of conservatives. Whether we like it or not, a killer insult becomes part of the store of folk sayings. It becomes everyone's.

The least accomplished but most primordial insults are the ones our peers discover in elementary school, riffing on the sounds our hapless names make. In an old *Seinfeld*, Jerry's girlfriend Dolores recalls the "merciless" teasing she endured for having a name that, as she says, "rhymes with a part of the female anatomy." Jerry, at this point, doesn't actually know her name and feels embarrassed to ask. Thus, he's forced to ponder the possibility of "Mulva." Insert laugh track.

Rhyme is one of the first poetic devices a grade-school amateur will reach for. No one got terribly far with my surname—"Guriel" is dactylic and confusing—even if variations on "Girl," "Gorilla," and "Grill Cheese" were manfully attempted. Some rhymes are artless mashups that nevertheless take ("Governator"), while others are so seamless and obvious they must've been conceived on the slopes of Parnassus ("No-Drama Obama").

Then there are rhymes both base and brilliant, uniting Fallen Earth and Heavenly Firmament. In the dark, unlettered ages before the invention of RhymeZone, it took a genius like Lord Byron to figure out what to do about "Wordsworth." Byron's fertile, inspired solution: "Turdsworth."

The true stylist avoids the obvious and puts some effort in. Christopher Hitchens's infamous description of Nobel laureate and Saint Mother Teresa—"thieving, fanatical Albanian dwarf"—is so baroque it practically has its own dome and painted ceiling. It can't help but be remembered.

Indeed, the poet Robert Frost once observed, "The utmost of ambition is to lodge a few poems where they will be hard to get rid of…." That's surely the goal of name-calling, which aspires to produce poetry for the ages. "A village explainer," Gertrude Stein said of Ezra Pound, "excellent if you were a village, but if you were not, not." There's subtle music in Stein's slight: the exquisite alliteration of "explainer" and "excellent," and the damning repetition of "not," that second "not" a nail. Of course, one doesn't need to possess a talent like Stein's to make a slight stick. Once we've heard a "Tricky Dick" we're stuck with it.

And the arms race of Twitter only escalates the art. Zingers are released like trial balloons. Barbs are tested, whetstoned. The relentless one-upmanship, made possible by the platforms of our Silicon Valley betters, ensures that a heat-seeking phrase—"Tru-Anon"—is always only a tweet away. One of the great horrors of the twenty-first century—and there have been so many already—is that everyone is a potential headline writer. You may wish to consult RhymeZone when naming your offspring. You may wish to turn off the mentions.

(*Lit Hub*, 2021)

Byron's Poetical Commandments

The very bingeable Lord Byron is having a moment. In 2019, the first two cantos of his great verse epic *Don Juan* enjoyed their 200th anniversary. This coming Sunday, August 8, 2021, cantos III, IV, and V will turn 200, as well.

Don Juan is a comic masterpiece. It eavesdrops on the exploits of the title character (stress on the surname's first syllable: Don JU-an), a young man who gets himself into scrapes—adultery, shipwrecks, and the like. It remains a model for any poet who wants to go long and recount a story in rhyme and meter.

It's also a work of snarky literary criticism by other means, with occasional shiv-sharp jabs at contemporaries like William Wordsworth and Samuel Taylor Coleridge. Early in the poem, Byron even offers some "poetical commandments," a few stanzas designed to edify (and definitely not troll) his nineteenth-century readers, including lines like:

> Thou shalt believe in Milton, Dryden, Pope;
> Thou shalt not set up Wordsworth, Coleridge, Southey;
> Because the first is crazed beyond all hope,
> The second drunk, the third so quaint and mouthey....

To mark the 200th anniversary, I present an updated set of "poetical commandments" in *Don Juan*'s style: iambic lines arranged in octaves that go ABABABCC. These commandments offer sturdy advice that contemporary Byrons-to-be might wish to consider as they pursue literary immortality and ponder the important stuff:

aesthetic choices, which workshops to apply for, and whether to follow up by email about the status of a poetry submission.

"Thou Shalt Not Take or Teach an MFA"
or, Poetical Commandments for the Twenty-first Century

Thou shalt not write a line that's not five feet.
Thou shalt put down that book by Leonard Cohen.
Thou shalt not share book contracts via tweet.
Thou shalt not follow up about thy poem
Nor link its brethren in a book-length suite.
Avoid the open mic, the Word that's Spoken.
Thou shalt not take or teach an MFA.
(See Homer; Dickinson; and Ryan, Kay.)

By all means, focus on the epigram—
On verse that's entertaining. Crystalline.
(By all means, Google "J.V. Cunningham"
And poet's-poet types like "Daryl Hine.")
Thou shalt not craft one's poems for the Gram
Nor reach out to an editor online.
No emailed Word docs, please. Submittable.
Thou shalt write poems that are readable.

Avoid the triple-headed, water-pitchered panel.
Avoid AWP, tote bags, Anne Carson.
Thou shalt not shun nor mob nor pulp nor cancel.
Thou shalt not burn offending books. (That's arson.)
Thou shalt not tag a well-known poet's handle
Nor drop the word "conceptual." (That's jargon.)
Turn off alerts: thy smartphone's singing sirens.
Thou shalt read only timeless hot takes—Byron's.

(*Lit Hub*, 2021)

Truman Capote's Blurb for *A Separate Peace*

Few Canadian writers have been more deliriously blurbed than Anne Carson. "[T]he most exciting poet writing in English today," declared Michael Ondaatje. "...I would read anything she wrote," proclaimed Susan Sontag. These and other big names gracing her early books—Alice Munro, Guy Davenport—projected a gravity field. They had the power to pull you in, even if the book itself turned out to be a gas giant: impressively opaque, but ultimately vaporous.

You can imagine my surprise, then, when I discovered a doctored blurb about Carson, attributed to yours truly, on the Random House website. I had recently panned Carson's book *Red Doc>* in *Poetry* magazine, and some collagist had reordered sentences from my review to suggest a positive appraisal. But why the desperate measures? Carson certainly isn't wanting in the sort of glowing press that produces ember-like pull-quotes. (The doctored blurb has since been pulled from the page promoting *Red Doc>*, but it endures on Amazon.)

We like to pretend that blurbs are a trivial, necessary evil, like the corporate logos that plaster the sides of race cars. But blurbs matter. I have bought books because of an artful, well-placed endorsement. I bet you have, too. Middleman, matchmaker, lubricant—some blurb once stood between you and a book you now love.

First, taxonomy: there are two distinct classes of blurb. Some are solicited in advance of a book's publication; others are pull-quotes, extracted from reviews. The solicited blurb, arranged by publisher or author, is obviously the inferior specimen. A person can be asked to endorse a book and truly—sincerely—mean it. But his lab-grown praise is, at bottom, a favour in aid of marketing. The review blurb, on the other hand, is by its very nature superior. No one compelled the reviewer to plug the book, and he could just as easily have panned it. The review is the natural breeding ground of trustworthy blurbs.

Even among the lower order of solicited blurbs, however, there's a hierarchy. The best of these come from recognizable names that require no further qualifier, like Stephen King. It's always slightly pitiful when a blurb has to assure us that the blurbist is the author of something:

"Scary as hell." –Franklin J. Donnelly, author of *Bite Marks and Blood Lines: The Ultimate Vampire Encyclopedia*

Obviously, such blurbists are nobodies who diminish the very books they've been asked to help shift. They are fourth choices, fifth choices. If your name needs a qualifier, you're not ready to write blurbs for people.

Proportion is also an indicator of quality. It's not promising when a book's first few pages are nothing but blurbs—pull-quotes from an endless roll call of major newspapers and magazines, each one ecstatic. (See, for example, *The Brief Wondrous Life of Oscar Wao* in paperback.) Few books deserve that much praise (few books deserve praise, period) and it's a minority of critics who can identify them anyway. The avalanche of good press is often triggered by groupthink: the unconscious, uncoordinated conspiracy that develops when the editors who assign reviews have bought into some book's advance marketing or are responding to the pressures of the zeitgeist.

One or two decisive blurbs is a much better look. You can trust the book that carefully curates its praise. My copy of *Lolita* features a single statement from *Vanity Fair*: "The only convincing love story of our century." Blurbs should drop the mic.

Good books attract good blurbists. Bad books are often betrayed by their blurbists' technique. "Technique is the test of sincerity," said the poet Ezra Pound. "If a thing isn't worth getting the technique to say, it is of inferior value." Let's take a closer look at a blurb by the esteemed culture review USA Today:

> Few books require a 'highly flammable' warning, but *The Brief Wondrous Life of Oscar Wao*, Junot Díaz's long-awaited first novel, will burn its way into your heart and sizzle your senses. Díaz's novel is drenched in the heated rhythms of the real world as much as it is laced with magical realism and classic fantasy stories.

I'm a sucker for alliteration, but "sizzle your senses" is what I'd use to explain the concept to middle schoolers. Also, all books, not "few," are "highly flammable"—that's science. And how can a book be both "drenched" and "laced"? The prose of Díaz's insincere blurbist doesn't pass Pound's test.

For contrast, here's what sober Alison Bechdel says on the back of Katie Roiphe's essay collection *In Praise of Messy Lives*:

> Katie Roiphe does not so much explode pieties as slice them open and prod their strands apart with equal parts rigor and transfixed, childlike curiosity.

No senses were sizzled in the making of that blurb. There's music, but it's subtle. There's imagery, too, but no clichés. No hearts. Bechdel is getting at Roiphe's calm, surgical precision in a similarly calm and surgical way. Clearly, Roiphe's stylish writing is worth the pains Bechdel's prose takes.

But nevermind Pound's test. Which book sounds more promising—the one that slices and prods with "transfixed, childlike curiosity?" Or the one that sizzles and leaves you with heartburn?

The philosopher Michel Foucault once wondered if a laundry list, discovered among an author's papers, should count as part of his oeuvre. It's the sort of mind-expanding query that works best when the mind is located in the undergraduate skull. It draws attention to how we blithely privilege some artifacts over others when deciding what comes under the category of art. But it's still a stunt; Foucault wasn't encouraging a devotion to laundry lists.

Blurbs, on the other hand, are a species of micro-criticism worthy of our scrutiny. And because criticism can aspire to the condition of art, so, too, can the humble blurb. I love the obsessives who have tracked and preserved the various endorsements authored by the reclusive novelist Thomas Pynchon. These fanatics know that even Pynchon's scraps are events. They know that blurbs, when composed by great writers, carry trace elements of genius.

The jacket of Christopher Hitchens's memoir has a generous line by Gore Vidal: "I have been asked whether I wish to nominate a successor, an inheritor, a dauphin or delfino. I have decided to name Christopher Hitchens." But the blurb is crossed out, and next to it, in red handwriting: "no, CH." Hitchens fell out with Vidal after 9/11. His annotation of Vidal's high praise is snarky. Sneaky. He gets to benefit from the honorific even as he appears to reject it. This is the coffin-cool anti-blurb in all its chilliness.

Then there's Adam Kirsch, who called Slavoj Žižek, "the most dangerous philosopher in the West" in an essay for *The New Republic*. (Kirsch was repelled by Žižek's apparent embrace of violence.) Žižek, naturally, turned around and redeployed the phrase as praise on his next book.

Blurbs can be weaponized. They can be turned back on the blurbist like the dagger he holds in his hand, the one he thought he was wielding.

It's human nature to stand in front of a bathroom mirror and accept an award you haven't actually won; to imagine blurbs praising books you haven't actually written. At one point in *Ulysses*, the mind of aspiring poet Stephen Dedalus races:

> Books you were going to write with letters for titles. Have you read his F? O yes, but I prefer Q. Yes, but W is wonderful. O yes, W.

It's always easier to author responses to books than the actual books. But most real-world endorsements might as well be describing fantastical works. Like relentless missionaries, blurbs are always bringing the good news. The blurbist may harbour genuine doubts about a particular novel or collection of essays, but these are always left behind in the original review—or submerged. Everything is a masterpiece, a must-read, a page-turner, a dazzler, a Roman Candle.

We would be blinded to have so many brilliant books. A human-scale effort that responds to the needs of smart readers is always preferable, and always harder to find. "A quietly vital and cleanly written novel that moves, page by page, towards a most interesting target." That's Truman Capote's blurb for *A Separate Peace*. And in an age of souped-up superlatives, isn't the phrase "most interesting" instantly trustworthy? Wouldn't you prefer to read something "quietly vital and cleanly written?"

It's remarkably easy to appear to possess an aggressively quirky voice (see Carson or Díaz). It's devilishly hard to write cleanly and interest readers. The best blurb, which is to say the best criticism, checks its superlatives and reveals the critic to be a human reader, greedy for intelligent distraction. For delight. He demands shrewd engineering, not literary excellence. Of course, it's the conspicuous appearance of the latter that sells books and wins awards. But it's the former that everyone secretly wants.

(*The Walrus*, 2016)

CHRISTOPHER LEHMANN-HAUPT'S BLURB FOR *GRAVITY'S RAINBOW*

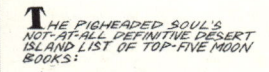

William Gibson's Realism

JOHNNY IS A WALKING HARD drive: a courier-cum-USB-stick. Anxious clients pay to stash data in his head. He has no access to the data; the right password, spoken aloud, triggers "idiot/savant" mode—and gets him talking.

One day, Johnny discovers there's a contract on his life. (Apparently, his head contains "hundreds of megabytes" pilfered from the Yakuza.) He falls in with a street tough named Molly Millions. Molly has mirrored lenses for eyes and keeps retractable scalpels beneath burgundy fingernails. A Yakuza assassin on their heels, Molly and Johnny eventually retreat to "Lo Tek" country, up in the rafters of one of the sprawling geodesic domes that span cities and their mushrooming subcultures.

It's been four decades since William Gibson's short story "Johnny Mnemonic" appeared in the May 1981 issue of *Omni* magazine. He'd already published a couple of pieces, but "Johnny" was a landmark feat of fiction: in a matter of eight magazine pages, Gibson roughed out the contours of an entire world.

The world Gibson was building was a wormhole away from most science fiction—from space-opera optimism and the sort of intergalactic intrigue that's settled by laser sword. Gibson's heroes were hustlers, their turf the congested city. They used substances, skirted the law, and self-edited via surgery (see Molly's nails). He provided more detail, the following year, in the story "Burning Chrome," which coined the term "cyberspace": a boundless 3-D grid, "an abstract representation of the relationships between data systems"—a kind of web. And then, in 1984, he went even deeper with *Neuromancer*. His zeitgeist-rattling debut novel was about a hacker for hire who navigated cyberspace using a modem and an Ono-Sendai Cyberspace 7 deck, a Gibson confection that rests on his hacker's lap (and sounds a lot like a modern-day laptop).

In time, the "cyberspace" coinage went viral the vintage way: it travelled from printed page to rapt fanboy. *Neuromancer* scooped up the available awards, generated two sequels, and popularized a sci-fi subgenre, "cyberpunk," a nuisance term (see also "grunge" or "millennial") that leapt from think piece to think piece like an augmented tick.

But *Neuromancer* was more than just an act of prescience that predicted something like the web. As Gibson himself has pointed out, the book was really about its moment. With conspicuous references to plastic surgery, the idle rich, and multinational corporations, the world of *Neuromancer* and its brethren, the so-called Sprawl novels, was a proxy for the decadent 1980s. In other words, Gibson was a serious writer prodding at the excesses of his present—and in brilliant prose to boot, prose that dared to reckon with the very grain of the environments it imagined. Gibson had spliced the DNA of realism into science fiction.

The Vancouver-based author went on to produce over a dozen books, help launch another subgenre (steampunk), inspire U2, and even trigger a fashion trend (the "normcore" aesthetic of the 2010s can convincingly be traced to the habits of a Gibson character who's "allergic" to brands). But "Johnny Mnemonic" was the first broadcast of Gibson's brilliance. Four decades on, telegraphing the style and concerns of the books to come, "Johnny Mnemonic" remains a bracing reminder that Gibson, more than a pop prophet, is one of our best writers.

For all its obsession with the future, science fiction ages quickly. Still, some of the prognostications of "Johnny Mnemonic" have held up. "We're an information economy," narrates Johnny at one point:

> They teach you that in school. What they don't tell you is that it's impossible to move, to live, to operate at any level

without leaving traces, bits, seemingly meaningless fragments of personal information. Fragments that can be retrieved, amplified.

Gibson didn't quite predict cookies and social media, but "Johnny Mnemonic" nails our hermit-proofed paradigm. Even the story's premise—that the most precious commodity is data—rhymes neatly with twenty-first-century anxieties about privacy and cryptocurrency.

And yet, the most radical thing about Gibson's story is its realism. At the very beginning, Johnny delivers some tough-guy talk:

> I put the shotgun in an Adidas bag and padded it out with four pairs of tennis socks, not my style at all, but that was what I was aiming for: If they think you're crude, go technical; if they think you're technical, go crude.

That Adidas bag was as stunning, in its day, as a phaser; sci-fi rarely deigned to mention such base details as brands. A year after the publication of "Johnny Mnemonic," the movie *Blade Runner* posited a similarly radical (and radically banal) point in one of its most iconic scenes: the hover cars of the far-flung future, when they finally get aloft, will fling themselves past sky-high ads for Coca-Cola.

"Johnny Mnemonic" also reflects Gibson's fascination with the cadged-together, a fixation, really, that runs through his work—from the artistic AI that remixes rubbish into dioramas in *Count Zero* to the squatter-occupied bridge in *Virtual Light*: a "patchwork carnival of scavenged surfaces." Here's a description of the ramshackle turf on which Lo Tek street fights unfold:

> The Killing Floor was eight meters on a side. A giant had threaded steel cable back and forth through a junkyard and drawn it all taut. It creaked when it moved, and it moved constantly, swaying and bucking as the gathering Lo Teks arranged themselves on the shelf of plywood surrounding

it. The wood was silver with age, polished with long use and deeply etched with initials, threats, declarations of passion.

When I tweeted once about the debris that fills his fiction, Gibson responded: "The mostly American sci-fi I started with as a reader seldom got it that futures are built of pasts." Gibson's vision of tomorrow always keeps some clutter in view—"the chassis of a junked console" in *Neuromancer*, "the tattered yellow wall of *National Geographics*" in *Virtual Light*. (Actually, by my count, there are at least three such walls of shelved *National Geographics* in Gibson's body of work; the denizens of his futures can't seem to divest themselves of print media.) Debris provides density, a backdrop against which hi-def futures can properly pop.

Even that opening monologue of Johnny's—"If they think you're crude, go technical; if they think you're technical, go crude"—reminds us that progress is a feint. To prep a shotgun, Johnny notes that he'd "had to turn both these twelve-gauge shells from brass stock, on a lathe, and then load them myself; I'd had to dig up an old microfiche with instructions for hand-loading cartridges."

Gibson's characters are often connoisseurs, preloaded with nostalgia streaks. There's the brand expert in *Pattern Recognition* who covets her "fanatical museum-grade replica of a US MA-1 flying jacket," the work of "Japanese obsessives." There's the restless publicist in *The Peripheral* who longs for an artisanal past. Gibson himself once made a living as a "picker," sourcing antiques for collectors. There may be no purer distillation of temporal tension in all of Gibson's fiction than the tableau of Johnny and Molly "crouched in the narrow gap between a surgical boutique and an antique shop" as rain from a "ruptured geodesic" falls behind them.

The future shock of "Johnny Mnemonic"—including sharp details like "tooth-bud transplants from Dobermans"—is so distracting it's easy to miss how graciously economical Gibson is; unremarked-upon references to "Mercedes electrics" and a "tendon stapler" pass by quickly, trusting their reader to fill in the rest.

There are certainly apprentice moments in "Johnny Mnemonic": overwrought lines, the noir poetry of a novice. (See, for instance, "The Drome stank of biz, a metallic tang of nervous tension.") But, for the most part, the story is delicately observed and pledges a fealty to physics and the implications of plot. When Molly, talking to Johnny, climbs up "through a hole in a sheet of corrugated plastic," the sheet muffles her voice. And, when the Yakuza assassin removes his thumb tip and unspools a length of "monomolecular filament"—a wire the width of a molecule—the prose is precise and devastating:

> Just a suggestion of a bow, and his left thumb falls off. It's a conjuring trick. The thumb hangs suspended. Mirrors? Wires? And Ralfi stops, his back to us, dark crescents of sweat under the armpits of his pale summer suit. He knows. He must have known. And then the joke-shop thumbtip, heavy as lead, arcs out in a lightning yo-yo trick, and the invisible thread connecting it to the killer's hand passes laterally through Ralfi's skull, just above his eyebrows, whips up, and descends, slicing the pear-shaped torso diagonally from shoulder to rib cage. Cuts so fine that no blood flows until synapses misfire and the first tremors surrender the body to gravity.
>
> Ralfi tumbled apart in a pink cloud of fluids, the three mismatched sections rolling forward onto the tiled pavement. In total silence.

The "conjuring trick," the floating thumb, the body parts "rolling forward," the "total silence"—had Gibson somehow once witnessed the results of an execution by invisible wire?

Panicking, Johnny discharges his shotgun. By this point, the reader may reasonably have forgotten that the shotgun is still sheathed in its Adidas bag. But Gibson hasn't—and he takes pains to document the by-product: "I was covered in scorched white fluff. The tennis socks. The gym bag was a ragged plastic cuff around my wrist." Fiction, let alone science fiction, is rarely as tactile as Gibson's.

Later, after the Yakuza assassin slices off his own hand by mistake and falls through the Killing Floor, the principals rummage around for the hand. Says Johnny: "All we found was a graceful curve in one piece of rusted steel, where the molecule went through. Its edge was bright as new chrome." That bright wound—reminding us that the new is ever present beneath the old, a gleam waiting to be revealed in rust—is as correct a detail as sci-fi has ever produced.

Perhaps Gibson's genius, then, is taking the actions and reactions of his characters seriously. Over thirty years after the Yakuza assassin's wire trick, in the 2014 novel *The Peripheral*, a magistrate of twenty-second-century London, Ainsley Lowbeer, produces a different sort of weapon, a shape-shifting baton that can summon a drone strike. A threat is near, and the weapon, a "tipstaff," begins to

> morph again, becoming a baroque, long-barreled gilt pistol, with fluted ivory grips, which Lowbeer lifted, aimed, and fired. There was an explosion, painfully loud, but from somewhere across the lower level, the pistol having made no sound at all. Then a ringing silence, in which could be heard an apparent rain of small objects, striking walls and flagstones. Someone began to scream.
>
> "Bloody hell," said Lowbeer, her tone one of concerned surprise, the pistol having become the tipstaff again.

The succession of double-take-inducing details is exquisitely managed. Gibson doesn't explain how the tipstaff works or why it assumes the look of a "baroque" pistol; alert readers will get that tipstaffs are the products of nanotech and nostalgia, of advanced societies that have aestheticized how they do harm. (It's as if someone called in an airstrike on a rotary phone.) A lesser writer, of course, would've insisted that the pistol do the firing, but Lowbeer's ornamental weapon disgorges nothing, not a peep. The explosion is *elsewhere*, and Gibson is mindful that explosions have epilogues, the follow-up sound of raining objects "striking walls and flagstones.

Someone began to scream." Two chapters later, as wreckage is combed, we learn that the screaming belongs to a woman, physically uninjured. "'See to her,' he'd heard Lowbeer say, to someone unseen, 'immediately.'" Lowbeer is concerned about trauma. It turns out that the magistrate never intended her drones to inflict so much damage; the approaching threat contained an explosive.

Maybe this doesn't thrill you, but Gibson's ability to release his characters into a scene and work out the logical (though not immediately obvious) impacts of their pinballing sets him far above most writers. It's a rare quality, this knack for accounting. And it can't be easily installed, slotted into a creative-writing student's mind, say.

Like virtually everything that followed "Johnny Mnemonic," *The Peripheral* also extended Gibson's punditry, his habit of filleting the present with the edge of the future. Climate change and pandemics have wracked Lowbeer's world, and Russian oligarchs loom. Even Lowbeer's drones—the book calls them "flashbots"—quote our era's impersonalized take on warfare. Gibson continues to iterate new futures to reskin our ever-shifting present.

Johnny and Molly decide to linger among the Lo Teks; characters in Gibson's fictions often find their way into loose, makeshift communities. It's a happy ending, though *Neuromancer* writes over it when Molly recounts Johnny's inevitable darker fate. And a still-darker fate waited further on: a movie with Keanu Reeves and Dolph Lundgren, he of He-Man fame, reached the big screen (remember when screens were big?) in 1995 and duly flopped.

But the original 1981 story, which can be found at the very start of *Burning Chrome*, a collection of Gibson's short fiction, has a deeper legacy. It created a world, sure, but a writer, too. And, after all these years, it remains unforgettable, which merely means its sentences stay with you, as if they've been permanently uploaded.

(*The Walrus*, 2021)

J.G. Ballard's
The Drowned World

CHRISTOPHER HITCHENS condemned multitudes: Henry Kissinger, the Clintons, aggressive sommeliers, God. Even science fiction—the late critic loathed the stuff. But one day, friend and novelist Martin Amis delivered unto Hitchens a care package containing three works in the genre by the English writer J. G. Ballard. "Any one of these," Hitchens later wrote, "would have done the trick." A sci-fi skeptic had been converted.

One of Amis's picks, *The Drowned World*, turned sixty this year. It helped launch not only Ballard's career back in 1962 (the older Amis, Kingsley, loved it, too) but also a modern subgenre of sci-fi about climate disasters (later called "cli-fi") that's now almost as prevalent as carbon. Recent entries include Kim Stanley Robinson's 2020 novel, *The Ministry for the Future*, Jon Raymond's *Denial*, out this month, and the forthcoming story anthology *Terraform*.

But *The Drowned World*, one of several early Ballard novels about climate, is not concerned with raising its readers' consciousness or sounding the alarm about humanity's carelessness. In the novel, it's solar storms, not fossil fuels, that have warmed the Earth's atmosphere, dissolved glaciers, and displaced vast quantities of silt. Europe and North America have become sweltering, half-submerged jungles, and what's left of our species—about five million people—has retreated to the polar caps. The sub-tropical Arctic Circle now clocks in at a balmy 85 degrees Fahrenheit.

At the start of the book, a team of scientists has been mapping London, which is steeped in stagnant water. There's room to stretch languidly out; Robert Kerans, the book's protagonist, occupies a suite in the abandoned, half-submerged Ritz, "the rich blue moulds sprouting from the carpets in the dark corridors adding to its nineteenth century dignity." Solar radiation has had a curious impact: Kerans's suite overlooks a lagoon rife with giant mosquitoes, bats, iguanas, and "freak botanical forms," all resembling their prehistoric antecedents.

But when the scientists and their military escort are instructed to head north to avoid rising temperatures and storms, Kerans and a few colleagues find themselves oddly resistant to leaving—and decide to linger. They've acclimated to the drowned world; the solar radiation, it seems, has kicked up a layer of primordial silt in their minds.

There's a heavy-handed scene in Bruce Sterling's otherwise fascinating 1994 cli-fi novel, *Heavy Weather*, in which someone wonders aloud, "When do you think the human race conclusively lost control over its own destiny?"—prompting other right-thinking characters to reel off various real-world culprits, including wars and failures of political will.

But there's no such moralizing in Ballard; his approach is as cool as a pair of calipers. Asked by an interviewer if there was a "moral purpose" to his work, Ballard replied, "I am not sure about that. I see myself more as a kind of investigator, a scout who is sent on ahead to see if the water is drinkable or not."

In one of *The Drowned World*'s many stunning set pieces, a looter named Strangman is draining one of London's lagoons in search of sunken treasure. Kerans's colleague Beatrice is horrified at the result:

> She gazed out at the emerging city, an expression of revulsion on her tense face, physically repelled by the sharp acrid smells of the exposed water-weeds and algae, the damp barnacled forms of rusting litter. Veils of scum draped from the criss-crossing telegraph wires and tilting neon signs, and a thin coating of silt cloaked the faces of the buildings, turning the once limpid beauty of the underwater city into a drained and festering sewer.

One reads *The Drowned World* with dread and then, increasingly, fascination: it's hard not to find Ballard's contemporary ruins and irradiated jungles seductive. Ballard has suggested that the sight of annual floods in Shanghai might have inspired the novel's landscape. During World War II, he spent part of his childhood in a Shanghai internment camp, which became the setting of his best-known book, the 1984 novel *Empire of the Sun*. "I remember looking from our camp, Lunghua, eight miles out, towards the French concession which occupied the south half of the city," he once recalled. "I would see the apartment houses rising from these great sheets of water." Primal memories appear to have propelled the author as well as his characters.

Ballard, who died in 2009, is less a prophet than, as Hitchens came to consider him, "our great specialist in catastrophe." Like Kerans, "a second Adam" in the book's closing beats, *The Drowned World* stands uneasily near the start of a lineage. It won't compel you to curb your carbon emissions, but it will keep you reading. Come on in, says the catastrophist. The water's fine.

(*Air Mail*, 2022)

Monte Hellman's
Two-Lane Blacktop

*E*ASY RIDER, BADLANDS, THELMA & LOUISE—the list of American road movies is long and winding. But the very best of the lot also happens to be the least iconic. It didn't explain the mood of a generation and demurred on delivering a manifesto. But if no eras were defined in the making of *Two-Lane Blacktop*, which turned fifty in July, that's because Monte Hellman's existential 1971 film about drag racing transcended its era, even if it stalled at the box office.

The picture featured at least one and a half stars: a bona fide Beach Boy, Dennis Wilson, and an up-and-coming singer-songwriter, James Taylor. The premise, too, seemed built for speed. Taylor and Wilson roam the countryside in a stripped-down '55 Chevy, challenging easy marks to street races. Taylor is the nameless "Driver" behind the wheel, Wilson, the wingman "Mechanic," who tends to the engine. They land themselves in a cross-country race with Warren Oates's character, owner of a gleaming new Pontiac GTO. (The end credits call him "GTO"; in *Two-Lane Blacktop*, you are what you drive.) A young free spirit—"the Girl," played by Laurie Bird—tags along. (She sneaks into the '55 Chevy's backseat early on: a wrench dropped into the works.) The race is for "pinks," which means that the winner gets the loser's car.

The buzz was as loud as a rebuilt engine. *Esquire* printed the entire screenplay, by novelist Rudy Wurlitzer and actor Will Corry, ahead of the picture's release. The cover of the April 1971 issue displayed a hitchhiking Bird and declared *Two-Lane Blacktop* the "movie of the year."

But the movie bewildered audiences. The cross-country race—spoiler?—sputters out when Bird straddles some random guy's motorcycle at a bar and pulls away. The characters barely speak to one another, and there's no score, just the occasional song trickling from a radio. Hellman's static camera doesn't even stick with the cars during many of the races, instead calmly watching them roar past or dwindle in the distance. It's as if Samuel Beckett had directed *The Fast and the Furious*. *Two-Lane Blacktop* bombed, and by January 1972, *Esquire* had given itself the "Nobody's Perfect Award" for hyping the film—an accolade that was part of the magazine's annual "Dubious Achievements" list.

The crash could have been foreseen. In fact, Beckett was an artistic hero of Hellman's. A decade before, Hellman had directed the first Los Angeles stage production of Beckett's *Waiting for Godot*. Later, he went to work for B-movie king Roger Corman. When Corman green-lighted two cheapo Westerns, Hellman delivered two art-house objects, *The Shooting* (1966) and *Ride in the Whirlwind* (1968), both of which starred a then-unknown Jack Nicholson. The French loved them.

Hellman, it became clear to those watching closely, was a serious artist who only appeared to traffic in genre trash. He made the most of his opportunities, and as the years passed, fans and critics came to a consensus: in *Two-Lane Blacktop*, he'd made a masterpiece. (Says the filmmaker Richard Linklater: "it's like a drive-in movie directed by a French New Wave director.")

Sure, the characters barely speak, but the story's all there in Bird's face, as she sits in the back seat and stares longingly at Taylor while massaging Wilson's neck. In another scene, Hellman shoots Bird and Taylor from the back seat as Taylor tries to teach her how to shift gears, his hand on hers. (Bird's shoulders hunch and heave in silent laughter.) Oates, the veteran character actor, is chattier than the rest. But his face, swept variously by warmth, sadness, and confusion, betrays his desperation to connect with others on the road.

The vistas are wide-screen, and Hellman frequently shoots real people in real environments. He infiltrates the drag-racing subculture and moves among its obsessives with documentary precision. Even the leads were non-actors. (Neither Taylor, Wilson, nor Bird had ever been in a movie before.)

The movie ends, appropriately enough, in the middle of a race, when the film stock appears to melt. That moment may have burned up *Two-Lane Blacktop*'s commercial prospects, doing yet more doughnuts on the audience's patience. But it left its mark on cinema. Today, we'd call it "meta" and applaud the way the film confounds the conventional American road movie.

But moviegoers primed for another guitar-spangled *Easy Rider* balked. Perhaps Hellman's themes were too universal. Taylor's Driver doesn't know how to tell Bird's Girl what's in his heart. Oates doesn't know how to get taken seriously as a sophisticate. (He keeps a wet bar in the trunk and an onboard record collection for any occasion.) Then there's the gorgeous clothing, which carbon dates no one: Oates's cashmere sweaters (a revolving cast of them), Taylor's light-blue work shirt, Bird's pink-dress-worn-over-jeans.

Most of the principals soon passed away: Bird by suicide in 1979, and Oates and Wilson a few years later, by heart attack and drowning, respectively. Hellman died in April of this year, just shy of the anniversary. But *Two-Lane Blacktop*, which was added to the Criterion Collection in 2007, has traveled across fifty years, a cult following of obsessive fans in tow.

(*Air Mail*, 2021)

A.E. Stallings's Poems

THE AUDIENCE FOR CONTEMPORARY poetry, like the audience for child pageants, is made up mostly of aspirants and their loved ones. Sure, Instagram sensation Rupi Kaur sells books, but she's the Instapoet who proves the rule. The poetry world is insular; a large, independent readership for the real stuff remains a fantasy.

But A. E. Stallings, an American poet, translator, and critic who lives in Athens, Greece, writes as if the whole world is reading. It certainly should be; Stallings's new book, *This Afterlife: Selected Poems*, is a major event. A mid-career retrospective, *This Afterlife* gathers work—witty, moving, and engaging poems on parenting, everyday life, and mythology—from her first four books. Stallings's beat is the universal, and her poetry assumes the existence of yeti: smart non-specialists who read poems for pleasure.

Here's the final stretch of "Silence":

> It's the room
> In which melody moves, the medium
> Through which thought travels, it is golden, best,
> Welcome relief to talk-worn tedium.
> Before the word itself, it was the womb.
> It has a measure. Music calls it rest.

The lines are packed with payoffs: alliteration ("talk-worn tedium"), rehabilitated cliché ("it is golden"), metaphorical aplomb ("it was the womb"), and that final, arresting observation about music.

The poem itself is musical—a sonnet. Stallings, a virtuoso when it comes to writing in traditional forms, is not afraid to rhyme. "There are no tired rhymes," she wrote over a decade ago in *Poetry* magazine, where I first discovered her. "There are no forbidden rhymes. Rhymes are not predictable unless lines are. Death and breath, womb and tomb, love and of, moon, June, spoon, all still have great poems ahead of them." For a time, under Christian Wiman's shrewd editorship, *Poetry* threatened to command a large general readership. The presence in his pages of writers such as Stallings—alongside the likes of Christopher Hitchens, Neko Case, Richard Rorty, and Alfred Molina—was a big part of the reason why.

This Afterlife is not quite a greatest hits. The competent poems from her debut, *Archaic Smile* (1999), comprise the weakest leg of the book and should've been culled. No matter: by her third collection, 2012's *Olives*, Stallings was discovering eternal truths such as this one, from "Another Bedtime Story":

> One day you realize it. It doesn't need to be said—
> Just as you turn the page—*the end*—and close the cover—
> All, all of the stories are about going to bed.

Stallings's poems about her kids are among her best. She concludes a piece to her daughter, Atalanta, with a string of sonic effects that carries the unresisting reader to an ingeniously abrupt ending:

> O apple of my eye, the world will drop
> Many gilded baubles at your feet
> To break your stride: don't look down, don't stoop
>
> To scoop them up, don't stop.

That "stop" is startling, resolving the rhyme with "drop," confidently left dangling a few lines earlier.

Stallings is the sort of poet who can seemingly do anything. She's a dab hand at personification. (See, for instance, "Accident Waiting to Happen," where she writes, "I'm bright and unstable / As a just-mopped floor, / I'm a curtain near a candle, / Finger in the door.") She can knock out an entire poem using nothing but the letters in the word "olives." ("Is love / so evil? / Is Eve? Lo, / love vies / evolves.") And she can animate the inanimate—from jigsaw puzzles to glitter—with panache. Here are four lines from "Scissors":

> Knives at cross-purposes, bereaving
> Cleavers to each other cleaving:
>
> Open, shut; give and take,
> All dichotomy in their wake.

We don't usually think of poetry as a form of entertainment—a degraded word—but mischievous formulations such as "bereaving / Cleavers to each other cleaving" leave you feeling giddy.

The poetry world tends to reward opacity and mediocrity. Poems that give pleasure are suspect. But Stallings is the sort of poet who actually deserves her plaudits: an outlier with a commitment to the reader's delight. She has come close to a Pulitzer and a National Book Critics Circle Award, but prizes are ultimately a feint; they belong to the realm of reputation, politics, career. Poems are either memorable or not, and *This Afterlife* is loaded with the real stuff, the right stuff, the kind of lines you remember—lines with an afterlife.

(*Air Mail*, 2022)

Tom Scioli's Graphic Biography of Stan Lee

IN THE OPENING PAGES of Tom Scioli's new graphic biography, *I Am Stan*, an elderly Stan Lee is signing autographs at an event. But the aging co-creator of Spider-Man, the X-Men, and other world-conquering IP is unsure. "Stan Lee," says the minder behind him. "S. T. A. N. L. E. E." It's a dark moment for Lee, a writer who helped bring so many brightly costumed heroes to print and a salesman who's rarely silent over the course of the book.

Scioli, a Pittsburgh-based cartoonist and the author of *Jack Kirby: The Epic Life of the King of Comics*, another graphic biography, tends to reboot his style to suit his subject. In his Kirby book, Scioli left his pencils uninked (a nod to Kirby, who was usually inked by others) and deployed a six-panel grid (a layout Kirby often used). In *I Am Stan*, Scioli stacks up page-wide horizontal panels, which give his word balloons plenty of room to expand. Lee, who helped usher in the modern era of Marvel Comics, is always talking—telling stories, soothing disgruntled artists, pitching schemes, and manufacturing myths.

When, after years of mixed success in the comics industry, Lee and Kirby hit their stride, Scioli's panoramas fill with Kirby's cigar smoke and, crucially, tail-less word balloons. "Monster hero," "beauty and the beast," "nuclear terror," "mutation"—these and other unattributed phrases float around Lee and Kirby as they dream up the Incredible Hulk.

"I had to come up with a way of having these guys have these kind of conversations," Scioli said in a recent interview with Ed

Piskor, another Pittsburgh-based maverick who has taken his own revisionist approach to Marvel myths. Scioli's wariness of putting words in mouths is well founded, for at the heart of the story of Marvel Comics lurks a radioactive question: just who exactly created the spandexed heroes and heavies who dominate our summer blockbusters?

The answer remains murky, thanks in part to the so-called Marvel Method, the collaborative process Lee came to insist his writers and artists follow. In lieu of writing a script, the Marvel writer brainstorms a story with his penciller. Next, the penciller goes off and draws the comic, inventing details, even characters (while not getting any additional fee or credit for writing—a sticking point that will bring Lee into conflict with the great comic artist Wally Wood).

Finally, the writer, inspired by the pictures, adds words. "You end up with an action-driven story with snappy dialogue that complements what's going on visually," Lee tells Roy Thomas, a writer he poaches from DC, Marvel's main competitor. "You can't argue with the results," Thomas replies.

The pages of *I Am Stan* in which Lee, Kirby, and a handful of others mint many of Marvel's classic characters make up one of the most compelling depictions of messy, inspired collaboration I've ever read. At one point, Lee and Kirby talk out a story for the Fantastic Four. Free-floating word balloons—"sky on fire," "world-eater," "Galactus"—hover above Lee's and Kirby's silhouettes. In the next panel, Kirby delivers the pages. "Here's the Galactus story, Stanley. It's a doozy." Lee inspects the art. "Who's the nut on the surfboard, Jack?" "Well, the way I see it," says Kirby, "a guy as powerful as Galactus needs a herald. I call him 'the surfer.'" Thus did Kirby, alone at his drawing board, conjure the Silver Surfer from the void, challenging Lee, as writer, to rise to the occasion. ("How do I come up with words to match this?" Lee wonders.)

Elsewhere, Kirby presents Lee with his latest idea, Spider-Man, which Lee then passes to the artist Steve Ditko to play with—and which Lee will later campaign for, in the face of the publisher's hostility. ("I don't like it, Stanley. Spiders don't sell.") We're also the spider on the wall as Ditko proposes a rectangle, featuring Spider-Man's head, on the upper-left corner of the book's cover. ("It will make it easier for the kids to find the comic," says Ditko.) Lee will add the company name to that rectangle and put it on all Marvel covers—an iconic brand beacon. Scioli's unstated thesis is clear: these billion-dollar properties were far from inevitable. They were batted around, rejected, resuscitated, and refined by multiple men, with Lee as an essential manager-cum-hype man.

At times, swelling word balloons press in on Lee from both sides, as if to suggest a fast talker buckling under the weight of his own words. Too much text is often a sign of failure in comics, a visual medium. But Scioli's bursting (and charmingly hand-lettered) balloons remind us at every turn that Lee's superpower was talk—a power he sometimes used for evil. When Kirby's family sues for royalties, Lee gives a deposition in which he downplays his erstwhile collaborator's role in the Galactus story.

But we see a frail, fallible human, too. A troubled Lee exits Kirby's funeral early—and misses the moment when Kirby's wife says, "Where's Stan? Bring him up here. I want to give him a hug and let everybody know there are no hard feelings. Jack would want that."

The last stretch of *I Am Stan* makes for tough reading. Here, the comics legend becomes a caricature of decline—clashing with his daughter, involving himself with dubious business partners, kibitzing with Larry King, and launching an ill-advised Web venture called Stan Lee Media.

Scioli never takes sides, though, and each of his pages works like a self-contained strip that reveals yet another dimension of his controversial subject. Ultimately, *I Am Stan* is a graphic masterpiece about a man who, like the best Marvel characters, was one part hero, one part monster.

(*Air Mail*, 2023)

Jason Guriel's Guilty Pleasure

I WAS AS SURPRISED AS anyone when I became obsessed with comics again last year, at the advanced age of forty-five. As a kid, I loved reading *G.I. Joe* and *The Amazing Spider-Man*. I loved the way they materialized like magic on the newsstand every month, and I loved the fantastical contents: microclimates conjured with pencils, brushes, and Dr. Martin's dyes. Later, as teenagers in the nineties, my friends and I self-published our own comics, xeroxing pages drawn on Bristol board and hawking them downtown.

In time, my passion slipped from panels to poems. The feat of minting similes as magical as Jane Kenyon's description of wind-stirred leaves—"they show their light undersides, / turning all at once / like a school of fish"—captivated me. No rulers or lettering guides required.

But after finishing work on a nearly 400-page novel in rhyming couplets, I felt restless. One of my old friends, his house now free of kids, had started drawing comics again. He got me thinking about the artists I used to love; a Google search got me to Ed Piskor and Jim Rugg's YouTube channel.

Mostly off camera, the two Pittsburgh cartoonists scrutinized the comics I'd grown up reading—and pointed me toward what I'd missed. Their enthusiasm was instructive. They'd marvel at the extracurricular work Chris Ware put into his sketchbook *after* a full day of drawing. They'd gape at Alex Toth's willingness to white-out a street scene he'd drawn in a window for the sake of economy and clarity.

Soon, I found myself at art stores, stocking up on Japanese Micron pens and, eventually, Copic multiliners, Piskor's preferred marker for inking. My back began to ache, so my wife ordered an angled drawing board for Father's Day.

The act of drawing panels again brought everything back. Comics were a core part of my childhood. My parents didn't have a lot of money, but they could always spring for an *Archie*. Really, it was the row of *Archie* digests lining the shelf by my bed that taught me to read. They helped run out the clock on those interminable Sundays before we'd amassed a decent VHS library. Decades-old scotch tape still holds together my copy of the first issue of *G.I. Joe*.

Before Netflix, before the internet, before they cast Robert Downey Jr. as Iron Man, comics provided a cheap and plentiful form of narrative entertainment. If you craved Spider-Man content in the 1980s, you had to make do with the monthly comic book, created by human hands under airtight deadlines. In that slow, reptilian age before reply all, original art was physically couriered from penciller to letterer to inker to colourist. Eventually, advances in digital wizardry made today's deafeningly dull Marvel movie feasible. But the analogue medium of comics used to have the monopoly on superhero IP.

You could buy comics everywhere, it seemed—at the grocery store checkout or off the spinner rack in a bookstore's basement. I sourced issues of *Daredevil* (from the much-loved Ann Nocenti and John Romita Jr. run) at a hobby shop in Cloverdale Mall. I acquired a splendid X-Men Annual (#12) at my local variety store, the book pencilled by Arthur Adams, a notoriously painstaking artist. Marvel comics are my memory-triggering madeleine.

The comic book long ago fled the newsstand. The saddle-stapled product of my youth—the flimsy periodical now called a "floppy"—is pricier these days and mostly relegated to the specialty comic shop. Meanwhile, my seven-year-old borrows graphic novels from his school library, and *The New York Times Book Review* covers new releases by Seth, Chester Brown, and Daniel Clowes. The guilty pleasure has acquired respectability.

Still, on a recent flight, I couldn't bring myself to break out the graphic novel I'd packed in my carry-on. Look, I'm forty-six. A Gen

Xer. I'll never entirely erase in my mind the non-repro blue line between low and high art. I still recall when comics were childish, outlaw, and slightly problematic.

I might even prefer them that way. Give me the scatological transgressions of Brown's *Yummy Fur*, the scabrous snark of Clowes's *Eightball*, the kinetic Kirbyisms of Tom Scioli's *American Barbarian*, the spandex-adjacent violence of Michel Fiffe's *Copra*. Give me drawings inked by hand, off-white newsprint, and no computer fonts. Give me cyan, magenta, yellow, and black. Give me back my four-colour youth.

(*The Walrus*, 2024)

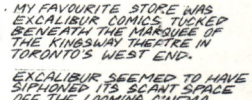

Holiday Shopping IRL

ONLINE SHOPPING HAS been on the rise for the last two decades, spiking abruptly (and unsurprisingly) during the pandemic. My household certainly did its part; for the past few years, we filled our digital shopping cart, struggled to recall the credit card number, and summoned groceries, kids' clothing, books, and CDs (yes, I still buy them) to the porch.

I was grateful for the delivery trucks, suddenly everywhere and idling. But by 2021, I'd had enough of scrolling. I was missing an essential human activity, a vital practice necessary to the nourishment and advancement of the soul. I was missing it so much, in fact, I wrote a small book about it: a longform ode to the art of in-person browsing. To browse is to wriggle free of algorithms, strike out for brick-and-mortar stores, and wrangle actual stuff—books, DVDs, and records—in proximity to other corporeal forms. To browse is to open oneself up to boredom, aimlessness, and, crucially, serendipity. It's to wander the world with one's smartphone firmly pocketed.

Browsing in person is especially helpful during the holidays. You might have a specific list in mind, but browsing expands that mind, exposing it to unforeseen possibilities—arranged on shelves by human hands. Sure, shops can be hectic during the holidays. But there's plenty of festive stimuli to savour: the non-denominational Starbucks cup, the visions of sugar plum fairies, the Vince Guaraldi.

Online holiday shopping, on the other hand, dispenses with the hustle and bustle of real-world browsing—but all the pleasure, too. It boils the full-bodied practice of perusing material reality in person down to thumb and screen. It relegates the shopper to their browser—and reduces browsing to scrolling. It's a poisoned chalice, packaged in bubble wrap.

When I was in my early twenties, holiday shopping was a breeze. I had a small family with virtually no extended relatives. I dealt with Christmas mostly by way of gift card, no browsing required. The cards were acquired on foot, usually at a mall. My sister liked a Canadian clothing chain called Jacob (now mostly defunct), and my mom was partial to The Bay (an iconic department store) and Tim Hortons (an iconic purveyor of bad coffee). My father collected stamps, so the Canada Post counter, at the back of Shoppers Drug Mart, sufficed.

Now, twenty years later, the pool of giftees has swelled. My father is gone, but my sister has a husband and three children. My wife and I have two young kids, who require toys from Santa's workshop, not gift cards. What's more, the wife has family, and the family is serious about gift-giving. My in-laws even exchange stockings, a ritual I've come to adopt. The stockings are great fun but require brain power. And browsing. Lots of browsing.

Before the pandemic, my wife and I did a lot of in-person holiday browsing. We had our shopping lists, sure, but we benefited from the chance finds made possible when navigating a brick-and-mortar store. (Plus, assembling the manifold elements of a stocking—especially a kid's—was easy to do when confronted with shelves and bins.) For my part, I knew I could simply show up at a Kate Spade, pan my gaze across the shop, and zero in on a couple quick wins—a wallet, say, or necklace.

But during the pandemic, our analogue browsing tailed off. Toronto's second lockdown began on November 23, 2020, a month ahead of Christmas. By that point, online shopping seemed like a no-brainer, even if some stores were still open to foot traffic.

The digital shopping cart, to be sure, is tantalizingly convenient. You submit what you're after to the search bar, scroll through a linear list of options, and click. Sure, you're strong-armed directly to some product page and thus aren't very likely to stumble on something unexpected. (The algorithm is the enemy of chance finds.) But online shopping is easy and safe—at least for the people placing the order. A shiver passes through some distant fulfilment centre, and a box embarks for your address, the human labour faceless. It's long been the optimal transaction for grinches who object to crowds and Christmas music—and it was handy for those with compromised health or a cautious disposition. Why *not* shop online?

The eye-straining screens, for one. If you work all day in front of a laptop, you might not want to spend your evening there, too. Online holiday shopping sends you back to your screen—or the screen of your significant other, that loved one who wants to walk you through gift options and solicit your opinion. (Watching someone else scroll a laptop is surely one of the penances described in *terza rima* by Dante.)

Worse, those gift options are hypothetical, even when they purport to be in stock. Not infrequently has my household arrived at a consumer decision and triumphantly clicked "checkout" only to find that the desired tchotchke, available only moments ago, is out of stock, the tech-bro deities having hurled a thunderbolt at our hubris.

This doesn't happen when eyeballing the available stock in a store. Cashmere and non-fiction and Nintendo Switches don't dissolve to smoke when you reach for them. The bounty is whatever you can see and heft—or whatever the sales associate, returning from some backroom, has managed to rustle up. Oh, and discovering that a store doesn't have something you're looking for is nowhere near as frustrating as the email with the subject header: "There have been a few changes to your order," which I received on the very day I was editing this piece.

Put another way, in-person browsing is instantly illuminating. Last November, ahead of the second pandemic Christmas, my wife and I took a turn around a half-empty Toys "R" Us and filled a shopping cart—the old-school kind—with gifts for the kids. Although we'd been shopping online as well, the full and physical cart was clarifying. No futzing with dozens of open browsers, no balancing scales in our mind, no surprises; we could see what was in front of us and judge what we had for each child. The real-world shelves presented options we could reach for and examine. A novelty in our digital world: to have a grasp on the actual size and quality of things.

What's more, there are no mysterious delays when you wheel your cart to the register. The sales associate hands over your bagged items; you bring said items home. But not a year has gone by when some opaque shipping snafu didn't leave me or a loved one shy a crucial gift come Christmas morning.

In-person browsing also helps prevent your dwelling from devolving into a warehouse of filthy, corrugated boxes from Halloween through Christmas Eve. Maybe this isn't a problem for you; maybe you're organized. But as packages arrive at my address, the harried adults hustle them to the basement—away from the pupils and paws of small children—where they pile up like the crates in Xanadu at the end of *Citizen Kane*. Someone might slit open a box to confirm what's inside. But they inevitably procrastinate on the processing of cardboard and plastic and bubble wrap because there are dishes to wash and lunches to assemble and, of course, more boxes to summon.

All that packaging and reliance on fast shipping is a gut-punch to the climate. According to Martina Igini, those delivery vans idling in your neighborhood are often half empty so that companies can make their narrow shipping windows. "[W]hen consumers opt for a fast delivery," she writes, "the emissions far exceed those generated from in-person shopping." (I'll leave it to you, Dear Scroller, to Google "fulfilment centre working conditions.")

Browsing isn't just better for carbon levels; it's better for the soul. Online shopping promises abundance, but too many choices can paralyze. (To click or not to click?) It certainly *seems* like you have agency when scrolling; after all, you can hop from hyperlink to hyperlink or fan out your browsers like trading cards. But you're also potentially at the mercy of consumer-gouging algorithms and the whims of websites that suddenly, like Bartleby, prefer not to load.

Most crucially: en route to the things you *think* you want, you will sometimes stumble on the unanticipated things you actually *need*. You will also encounter other souls, whose job it is to help you. Sometimes you even run into people you know. Serendipity presides over browsing like a goddess her realm; your scrolling, on the other hand, is the purview of some asshole in Silicon Valley.

My family will certainly do its share of online shopping this year. But now that the three-year-old is properly vaccinated, there's no real excuse not to return to brick-and-mortar stores and browse again. There will be light-entwined and wonder-inducing fir trees, intricate window dioramas, cosplay Kris Kringles (and their elven support staff), carollers we'll try not to make eye contact with, the call of coffee kiosks, and, on the PA, some of the finest studio recordings by Elvis, Mariah, and Darlene.

Am I being sentimental? Maybe. But the youngest members of the household—who aren't yet cynical about the seasonal worker behind the Santa Claus beard—will be thrilled. What a gift.

(*The Atlantic*, 2022)

Brief Recommendations

The Portable Dorothy Parker

You likely already own this book because of the handsome cover by Seth—or your nostalgia for flappers. *The Portable Dorothy Parker* is made up mostly of Parker's fiction and poetry, but the last seventy pages are given over to reviews of books and plays, filed for *Vanity Fair, The New Yorker,* and *Esquire.* Considering the reckless things that have been written about reviews—remember when Jan Zwicky noted that critics, faced with bad books, should "keep [their] mouths shut"? when she equated negative reviews to "sadistic behaviour"?—reading Parker is a relief. A member of the Algonquin Round Table, around which New York's wits famously assembled, Parker knew what we, in the Epoch of Likes and Follows, would like to forget: most of the art that wants our time is only going to waste it. Ruthless, maybe, but her devotion was to readers, not writers. "I tried, for my first duty is toward you…" she reports of one of her efforts to reckon with a book. "Unhappily, it was like counting those sheep over that fence; before I had listed the first hundred I was safely asleep." Parker wakes you up.

(*The National Post*, 2013)

Barbarian Days: A Surfing Life

I will read anything if the sentences are good enough; style beats subject matter—or, more accurately, buoys it. (Style, of course, doesn't mean "beautiful writing" or Michael Ondaatje.) Many have already praised the memoir *Barbarian Days: A Surfing Life*, which came to paperback in April. It's a brilliant book about dimly-lit depths: that subculture of people—mostly men—who keep an eye on surf forecasts (these are a thing) and who can wax opaquely on such arcana as board design or a particular coast's pathology. Previously, this world lacked its ambassador; he is now, and for all time, William Finnegan, a staff writer at *The New Yorker*, once known mainly for war writing. Finnegan faced an enormous technical challenge: over hundreds of pages, try to pin down and describe the behaviour of water—and the men who make it their obsession—without boring the uninitiated. But like Montaigne in a wet suit, he pulls it off, again and again. *Barbarian Days* channels one man's lived experience of waves into a work of art.

(*The Walrus*, 2016)

The Castle of Indolence: On Poetry, Poets, and Poetasters

QUOTING A BLURB by Harold Bloom ought to strip a critic of credentials. But Bloom's plug of the late Thomas Disch is exactly right and a model of meaningful understatement: "One of our mere handful of accurate critics of contemporary poetry." Disch was an independent mind and a confusing figure. He wrote poetry and reviews, but also science fiction novels. He appeared in progressive magazines (*The Nation*) and conservative ones (*The New Criterion*). Where he was clear was in his care for readers, which made him an enemy of postmodern posturing and what he called, with politically incorrect gusto, "the academic ghetto that can do double duty as a quarantine ward." Disch's book, which came out in the nineties and collects his reviews of poetry, is not much talked about these days. But above a landscape that's positively sick with MFA programs and self-promotion, *The Castle of Indolence* calmly pokes its single, slender spire. The spire is a syringe.

(*The National Post*, 2013)

Blow Out

IN THE LONG OPENING shot of *Blow Out*—available next week in 4K from the Criterion Collection—we share a set of eyes with a serial killer who's cornered a coed in a shower stall. The coed whimpers, and we cut to a screening room where a slasher-movie sound tech, played by John Travolta, is laughing; he's going to need to record a better scream. So begins Brian De Palma's 1981 thriller, a meta masterpiece and one of Quentin Tarantino's favourite pictures. The premise remixes Michelangelo Antonioni's *Blow-Up*, about a photographer who thinks he's captured a murder on film. Sourcing sound effects near some woods, Travolta's character accidentally records a blowout, a shot-out tire that sends a car off the road and kills one of its occupants, a presidential hopeful. Soon after, the sound tech falls for a makeup artist (Nancy Allen), who's mixed up in the conspiracy. (Dennis Franz and John Lithgow also deliver terrific turns as a sleazy photographer and a psychopathic heavy.) De Palma himself is at his most resourceful, splitting his screen and recruiting the inventor of the Steadicam to film that opening set piece of slasher pulp. An unbroken, revolving take of the sound tech discovering that all his reels have been erased gives the movie its dizzying, paranoid centre. Forty years later, *Blow Out*'s ending still creeps up and garrotes you.

(*Air Mail*, 2022)

Too-Rye-Ay (As It Should Have Sounded)

"YOU HAVEN'T HEARD THE LAST of them," Homer Simpson once said of Dexys Midnight Runners, the one-hit wonder behind "Come On Eileen." But the joke was on American audiences; in the UK, Dexys was an institution, with a trio of excellent albums to its name. The second of those, 1982's *Too-Rye-Ay*, the one bearing "Come On Eileen," has now turned forty—and grown a shaggy subtitle for its re-release. That subtitle bespeaks a fussy vision; lead singer

Kevin Rowland was part auteur, part autocrat, endlessly revising his band's sound, attire, and personnel. To wit: after the first Dexys LP, 1980's rousing *Searching for the Young Soul Rebels*, Rowland compelled his horn section to take up the viola and cello—to mixed results. Course-correcting, he pilfered the idea of using violins—and the slow-fast dynamic for "Come On Eileen"—from a demo by former bandmate Kevin Archer. Rowland also snagged the demo's violinist, Helen Bevington, whom he renamed "Helen O'Hara" for maximum Celtic vibes, and with whom he conducted a doomed romance. (Genius steals.) The resulting music—delivered by an affably ragged iteration of Dexys, their dungarees immortalized on MTV—was disarming and irresistible, a counter-intuitive hybrid of Celtic and soul impulses. Wherever there were ears, "Come On Eileen" was a hit. The album's mix, though, never sounded quite right to Rowland. A late, neglected triumph (1985's *Don't Stand Me Down*), addiction, and the dole office lay ahead for Rowland—but rehab and redemption, too. Archer now receives royalties for his influence on "Come On Eileen," and Rowland, in recent years, has recorded some of his best music while stewarding the Dexys legacy. The new edition—*Too-Rye-Ay (As It Should Have Sounded)*, on vinyl and CD—corrects the original mix, replaces the cover art, adds bonus tracks, and ultimately offers a fresh take on a scruffy classic.

(*Air Mail*, 2022)

Godzilla Monsterpiece Theatre

KING KONG, MOTHRA, the Japan Self-Defence Force, the Avengers—the tireless IP known as "Godzilla" has faced many foes across various media since its debut in Ishirō Honda's eponymous 1954 film. But Tom Scioli's new three-issue comic series for IDW, *Godzilla Monsterpiece Theatre*, presents the monster-cum-metaphor-for-nuclear-dread with an unlikely obstacle: Gilded Age wealth. The premise is priceless: what if Godzilla turned up in the Roaring Twenties, destroyed the opulent mansion of F. Scott Fitzgerald's Jay Gatsby, and left Daisy, object of Gatsby's love, lost at sea? ("Do you hear that crowd roar?!" says a flapper, mid-Charleston, as Godzilla looms above Gatsby's estate.) *The Great Gatsby*, staple of high-school curricula, helpfully passed into the public domain in 2021. Thus, Gatsby himself is free to rally Thomas Edison, Sherlock Holmes (public domain, class of 2023), and other thought leaders to take on the scaly threat—all in brightly coloured, widescreen panels, which make plenty of room for killer parties and kaiju. Scioli, the iconoclastic cartoonist behind graphic biographies of Jack Kirby and Stan Lee, has a tendency to revive legacy brands that, like sea monsters, occasionally go dormant, including GI Joe, Transformers, Go-Bots, and other fanboy franchises. At one point in *Godzilla Monsterpiece Theatre*, Scioli deploys the famous final sentence of Fitzgerald's novel—"So we beat on, boats against the current, borne back ceaselessly into the past"—as Fitzgerald's characters, drenched by a Godzilla-induced wave, try to make an escape by boat. Elsewhere, standing in a giant footprint stamped into a cornfield, Sherlock Holmes declares, in word bubble, "The game is afoot." *Godzilla Monsterpiece Theatre* is an irreverent mashup: equal parts classic monster and modernist classic.

(*Air Mail*, 2024)

This Makes That

For years, the Chicago-based cartoonist Ivan Brunetti taught art in college; new work was rare. Thankfully, the artist behind the celebrated comic *Schizo* and sundry *New Yorker* covers continues to produce books for kids. His latest entry, *This Makes That*, follows a classroom as it devises lemon-powered LEDs, "unpoppable" soap bubbles, and more. The drawings are immensely likable—and immediately recognizable. "I have gone through life squinting at a very flat world," Brunetti, who is beset by "severe myopia," has written. But the cartoonist, a devotee of Charles Schultz, makes flatness a virtue. Brunetti's geometric characters, drawn with templates, French curves, and other old-school drafting tools, are defiantly two-dimensional. They occupy a world in which cars yawn to accommodate large circular heads and tables rest on the page like unconstructed boxes. Discerning parents will want *This Makes That* for their four-to-six-year-olds. Connoisseurs of a master cartoonist will want it for their eyeballs.

(*Air Mail*, 2025)

The Dilettante: Reviews, Essays, and Rants

OKAY, THIS BOOK DOESN'T actually exist—but if it did, it would compile Stephen Metcalf's "Dilettante" column, which he filed for *Slate* over the last decade, and which you can find online. (The diehard fan of book reviews and essays often has to clip and assemble.) It would also include some of Metcalf's other magazine writing as well as select transcripts of the various podcasts he's recorded. A student of the late philosopher Richard Rorty and a former speechwriter for Hillary Clinton, Metcalf is that rare thing: a progressive who's unafraid of making evaluative judgments; a curmudgeonly connoisseur who can talk late-capitalism. (Foucault? Yea. Deleuze and Guattari? Nay.) He can cover a lot of ground—he's been tough on Springsteen, *The Searchers*, libertarianism—but like many top magazine writers, he dissolves in the acid bath of his best lines. (About the movie *Blade Runner*: "...it murmurs beautifully in the background." About the novel *Beloved*: "It draws up so elegantly on the blackboard.") The best general American critic without a book to his byline.

(*The National Post*, 2013)

Loathe

Carl Wilson's Case for Celine Dion

In my youth, in Toronto, it was the mark of cool to declare an interest in something called "Britpop," which meant bands like Blur, Pulp, and Oasis. There was the club that played their music and the shop where an aspiring anglophile could acquire his Fred Perry, his Vespa. Paul Weller impersonators walked the Earth or, at least, a stretch of College Street.

I adored Britpop but didn't know about the club or shop. I lived in the suburbs and caught Blur by chance on TV, a Mesolithic form of YouTube, which was programmed by our elders and dominated by Nirvana's successors: the music my primitive high school preferred. I didn't know that Blur formed part of a kit that could furnish me with an identity and set me apart—but then neither did my peers, to whom a Fred Perry shirt would've signified "golf." Blur was a band, not a badge. Had I wanted an outsider identity, I suppose I could've deepened my connection to the local goths. But the face paint seemed like work.

It's now the mark of cool to declare that a preference for a genre like Brit-pop is, in part, the province of sociology, and signals something about my milieu, my desired tribal identity. It's also *de rigueur* to be a little bit, well, blurry in matters of taste. We're to take, with our Britpop, something borrowed, something corny—something hip hop, something country—and be embarrassed about none of it. Blushing at guilty pleasures is as retrograde as the Garden of Eden.

Blame recent shifts in technology and the way we categorize art. We've been liberated from having to have taste by recommendation engines and iPod shuffles, which allow unlikely juxtapositions and don't judge. We've also been liberated by "poptimism," whose major text, Carl Wilson's *Let's Talk About Love*, has just been reissued. It's a conversion narrative; Wilson starts out a snob, a music critic at a Montreal weekly, who finds himself seeing red when Elliott Smith is overshadowed by Celine Dion at the 1998 Oscars. Wilson sets out to understand his hatred of Dion and, more generally, how taste is formed. (It's socially determined—sort of.) He learns about Quebec, travels to Vegas to see Dion perform, and corresponds with some of her fans. By the end, a snob has changed his tune: all you need is love.

Wilson's slim monograph first appeared in 2007; the new edition arrives a mere seven years later, with a mild thump: appreciative essays by the likes of James Franco, Nick Hornby, the guy who played bass in Nirvana, and others have brought the book to a respectable width. In fact, they account for nearly half the page count.

But is *Let's Talk About Love*, which borrows its title from Dion's 1997 album, already a classic deserving of the deluxe treatment? "By the early twentieth century," writes Wilson, "almost no one believes in them"—that is, categories like "highbrow" and "lowbrow." And yet the frisson his project was calculated to create depended on his audience's understanding of—even investment in—such categories. Like other contrarians—see Jonah Weiner, who defended Limp Bizkit, "the most hated band ever," in 2009—Wilson needs a subject that is sufficiently south of the brow.

He sets up the book as a thought experiment. "If I end up warming to her music, that will be one lesson; if I don't, we might draw others." But it's hard to buy the real-time rhetoric, to accept that the critic, on page 21, is setting out on a journey of self-discovery as opposed to writing backwards, from the conclusion. "Maybe if hating Celine Dion is wrong, I don't want to be right," he says early on: fighting words. But such flare-ups are conspicuously short-lived. Wilson can deliver an inspired takedown of Las Vegas (the city leaves him "feeling insignificant and micro-penised"), but his contempt for the Canadian singer is unconvincing—when he remembers to express it at all. His description of how Dion's records wallop him like a "wet, live kitten" comes so late in the book it's as if Wilson is rebooting our belief in his project's premise.

Part of the problem: the project feels overdetermined. The anaphoric chapter titles—"Let's Talk About Hate," "Let's Talk About Taste," "Let's Talk with Some Fans"—betray the book pitch. Indeed, the book often seems built from checked boxes. You get the obligatory trip to Vegas, the time spent with the fans, the taste of Quebecois politics, the touch of Kant.

Even more predictable is a tendency to suddenly reverse course on an argument. Wilson is always doubling back, as if anticipating your objection; he's always armed with yet another study, another counterargument. You shouldn't enjoy that shot at Oprah Winfrey for long; several pages later, Wilson will call attention to his snobbery, implicating your own. Nor should you entertain the thought that there's something snobby in his anti-snobbery; Wilson will soon enough interview a fan who has "a streak of snobbery in her anti-snobbery." Nor should you be entirely shaken by his account of how sociology explains your taste; after burning up ten pages on it, he confesses he only half-believes the stuff. The dead-ends and reversals wouldn't be so annoying if one didn't suspect he already had the destination in mind.

In short, Wilson's book could never have ended with the critic doubling down on his snobbery; the needs of his project demanded otherwise. A mere page after declaring, "Maybe if hating Celine Dion is wrong, I don't want to be right," he's already wondering if he won't find something "human" in Dion's work after all. While a messily self-reflexive writer like David Foster Wallace truly wrestles with himself—with predilections, prejudices—Wilson bets on his fuzzy side and throws the fight.

What *Let's Talk About Love* was really battling all along was negative criticism. It's the book the "poptimist" moment wanted, but it's also the byproduct of a larger trend, whose roots reach back to 1993, when Wallace, writing about US fiction, declared irony dead. "Today's risks are different," he argued. "The new rebels might be artists willing to risk ... accusations of sentimentality, melodrama. Of overcredulity. Of softness." In the wake of this kind of thinking—which created the context for such phenomena as *The Believer* magazine—irony becomes sarcasm, and negative criticism, just plain mean.

Despite the fact that Wilson is capable of sharp words, which are usually directed at other critics—"That jerk in the *Independent*"—he wants you to sheathe yours, and talk up your experience of the stuff you love: "to show what it is like for me to like it, and invite you to compare." (In other words, Wilson's weapon is a wagged finger.) He can't fully embrace the music, but Dion, he discovers, is a person with a context. Her fans are people, too. People who need people—or, anyway, power ballads.

Let's Talk About Love is a crafty book, even if you can't help but harbour the gut feeling that certain cultural products are better than others, and that criticism ought to find an entertaining way to give voice to guts. His account of the work of the sociologist Pierre Bourdieu is super readable, the stuff about Vegas pretty funny. In one particularly compelling stretch, he complicates the tendency of critics to prefer a modern, darker art to one that has an excess of emotion and sentiment.

Still, it's hard not to feel troubled by the sort of thinking that powers a book-length argument for being nice to artists instead of honest with ourselves—but there I go again, talking feelings: a win for Wilson's side, or proof that, for all its intellectual gamesmanship, his book can't redeem the perpetrator of "My Heart Will Go On"? Whatever the answer, when it comes to criticism, positivity has left a dubious legacy. It's now mostly a feint, and reactions to negative reviews are often and ironically more nasty than the offending reviews. Cries for sympathetic dialogue are less democratic than Wilson seems to think; they muffle dissent by other means.

Indeed, some of the essays in the new edition Auto-Tune indignant censoriousness to the key of politically correct compassion. One contributor checks Wilson's use of "goopiest" to describe a Phil Collins tune: "Gentle, Carl." Another contributor, having been informed that Judy Garland is "corny" by a friend, thinks to himself, "F— you, my friend!" and then, "Are you even my friend?" One wonders what Wilson's contributors would make of such bullies as Oscar Wilde or Dorothy Parker.

But if Wilson's book is already a classic, if poptimism is as passé as punk sincerity, if policed compassion is a thing of the past or, at least, the aughts, perhaps there's cause to take heart. Go ahead and feel guilty about that guilty pleasure. My snob will go on.

(*The National Post*, 2014)

Michael Robbins's Shtick

IN THE EARLY EIGHTIES, when it came time for the Replacements to title their third album, they went with a wink: *Let It Be*, the name of the Beatles classic. "[N]othing is sacred," said Paul Westerberg, the Replacements' chief songwriter. "[T]he Beatles were just a fine rock & roll band." Released in 1984, the Replacements' *Let It Be* had little to do with Lennon and McCartney. It concerned androgyny, music videos, and the limits of Reagan-era social media (i.e., answering machines). It blew some raspberries, too: a song about a "boner," an ironic Kiss cover. The postmodern pranksters toyed with titling the follow up, *Let It Bleed*. (They went with *Tim* instead.)

Michael Robbins's second collection of poems takes its title from Simone de Beauvoir's feminist classic, *The Second Sex*. Is Robbins being, as they say on NBC's *Community*, "meta"? Is this progressive poetry? ("I stick my gender in a blender..." goes one line.) Or is the appropriation merely a provocation? Will the prankster call his third book, *The Booty Myth*? In general, Robbins tends to repurpose the words of others: lines, lyrics, titles, and clichés.

He also tends to repeat what works. He hasn't much altered his approach since 2009, when he published four stanzas in *The New Yorker* titled "Alien vs. Predator." The stanzas dispatched a shiver across the internet. They inspired a range of responses, from amateur animation to a *Village Voice* profile. They got Robbins a book (of the same title) with Penguin, which chewed through five printings and was reviewed in *The New York Times*. Hollywood took just enough of an interest to determine the book couldn't be adapted.

What was it about Robbins's stanzas? Here's the first one, from "Alien vs. Predator":

> Praise *this* world, Rilke says, the jerk.
> We'd stay up all night. Every angel's
> berserk. Hell, if you slit monkeys
> for a living, you'd pray to me, too.
> I'm not so forgiving. I'm rubber, you're glue.

The allusiveness and irreverence, the clichés and clipped sentences, the semi-regular beat and rhymes—the essential elements of Robbins's poetry, in place from the start, amounted to something like a voice. It was the cartoony culmination of its influences—the restlessness of John Ashbery and the shock doggerel of Frederick Seidel. Moreover, the voice's references to pop culture struck some non-poetry readers as novel.

It didn't matter that Thom Gunn had composed verse about Elvis Presley a half century ago or that Philip Larkin had name-checked The Beatles; Robbins presented a curiosity to content creators: a Kansas-born, up-from-his-bootstraps bard, who referenced Best Buy within breaths of Rilke. In the author photo for his first book, he boasts a Slayer t-shirt and holds a plastic cup of something. Headphones circle his neck like an airplane pillow. If author photos had audio, his would be ticking with treble. It gave the impression of a twenty-first-century everyman who has briefly surfaced from his feed—what we used to call "white noise"—to register his bemusement and confusion. Think Prufrock, augmented by smartphone and blended ice drink.

In *The Second Sex*, Robbins assigns this persona to current events, gender relations, and the topic of Michael Robbins—and he feeds the persona lines as memorable as any in recent American poetry. In one poem, he deploys a metaphor that's hard to forget:

> The camel can't come to the phone.
> This is for the drone-in-chief.
> Mumbai used to be Bombay.
> The bomb bay opens with a queef.

In an elegy for Michael Jackson, he gets the reader's mind racing, then trips it up, using nothing more than smartly placed line-breaks:

> He lay with many a kid. I don't know
> and you shouldn't act
> like you know what he did.

Robbins's voice is hotheaded and hapless, a little bit country and a little left of centre. "I don't believe you: God is great," he says in one poem, putting atheists like the late Christopher Hitchens in the crosshairs. "I feel like a natural woman / is just too real for me," he says in another, splicing Carole King with the modern-day male whose experience of women is mostly by way of browser.

It's a mesmerizing persona when encountered as a one-off in a magazine. It's perfect for circling parts of, for putting into the hands of the uninitiated, for the block quote. But across the length of a book, the second in two years? The subverted clichés—"I plant my fat on the land," "I can't tell my bright from my left"—start to sound rote. Predictably provocative, the poems themselves start to seem less like discrete units (each with an internal integrity all its own) than a means to a shtick.

"You were always wide open to changing the stanza order," the poet Anthony Madrid says to Robbins in a recent online conversation. But when a poet writes the sort of poems whose parts can be shuffled easily, it's easy to forget which ones house the lines you actually like, where the lines fit, what the poems are called.

"You are lazy," Madrid also points out, same conversation. And while a few pieces in *The Second Sex*—like "Not Fade Away," a brilliant elegy for fallen pop stars—are fully lit from start to finish, plenty of other stanzas, plucked from different poems, back up Madrid's claim. Take this:

> Got an empty shoe box for Xmas.
> Every Xmas, same shoe box.
> The theater of my dreams
> I called it, for I dreamed of shoes.

Or this:

> Dallas is nice this time of year.
> Been there, done that, Debbie cheers.
> She's living in Silicon Valley now
> with a husband, two kids.

Or this:

> The womb's a fine and private place,
> or am I thinking of a doughnut?
> You ask me, the hippies still have
> a lot to answer for. But no one
> ever asks me. I smell pasta.

Or this:

> You ask what time the elephant
> sat upon the fence.
> Sounds to me like time to get
> a few new elephants.

Actually, I've planted a stanza from one of Robbins's fans among the four above[1]. A sharply defined voice is inevitably double-edged; because it's instantly recognizable, it can be hard to parse from its imitators. (Or, to put it in a couplet of my own version of Robbinspeak: "A poet has hit the end of the line / Has hit me baby one more time.") Of course, it may be unrealistic to expect Robbins to sit tight and polish his work. After all, his restless, up-to-the-microsecond poetry is in part *about* a world that Tweets before it thinks.

The Second Sex is still a rush job, though. If the American poet William Carlos Williams was right, and poems are machines, then Robbins's best are like those drones Amazon proposes will one day deliver our literature and toilet paper: sleek content delivery systems that ruthlessly zero in on, and engage, our attention. But the poet should take note of his predecessor, Seidel, who waited sixteen years to follow up a scandalous debut.

---

1 It's stanza number two.

The more effective move after making a statement like *Alien vs. Predator*—and the more provocative prank—might've been to appropriate the one strategy a successful poet can afford, but which Robbins doesn't seem to have much considered: a little bit of strategic silence.

(*The New Republic*, 2014)

The *Best American* Anthologies' Boosterism

"WILL THE NEAR FUTURE necessitate warning labels in front of all published material?" asks Robert Atwan in the foreword to *The Best American Essays 2014*. Atwan is worried about trigger warnings, indications of an "opinionated, partisan atmosphere" where people fear what they might read. In these climes, the essay, he suggests, might be a "risky and endangered method of communication."

There's a whole family of these *Best American* books, and if they share a trait, it's a predisposition toward anxiety. Each selects the "best" examples of one genre from last year's magazines. The first anthology, *Best American Short Stories*, came out in 1915. But over half of the active titles have launched in the last fifteen years, as the franchise has expanded to accommodate genres like comics, even infographics. (Can we expect a *Best American Tweets*? *Best American GIFs*?) There are also the outcasts and misfits. God may be dead, but something called *Best Spiritual Writing*, once part of the *Best American* series, continues to resurrect itself. *Best American Poetry* is another off-brand item, with a publisher all its own. Canada has an edition, too, which occasionally includes one of my poems.

The anxiety coursing through the opening matter of some of these paperbacks concerns the zeitgeist. David Lehman, series editor for *Best American Poetry*, doesn't quote a single line of verse in his 13-page foreword to the latest edition—the longest of all the forewords in this year's *Best American* series. Instead, he dilates on Twitter, "the tyranny of technology," and the downtrodden humanities. (In fact, in the 2009 edition, Lehman cited something I wrote, as proof of a "hostile universe.")

Glenn Stout, in *Best American Sports Writing*, describes ours as "metric-driven times," in which we tend to "reduce everything to data—sales figures, 'starred' reviews, Facebook shares." Heidi Pitlor, in *Best American Short Stories*, finds the number of writers watching *The Bachelor* "perplexingly enormous" and is resolved to spend less time online this year. (She is going to try to convince local bookstores to start trivia nights.) At least Jennifer Egan, who did the final selection for Pitlor, recognizes how quickly some "new threat" can supersede the last. Still, she can't help but place her "responses to our warp-speed technological change…on a spectrum from anxiety to terror."

It's true these are tough times for the book industry (even if the *Best American* brand continues to metastasize—*Science Fiction and Fantasy* is slated for 2015). It's also true, as Egan suggests, that people, when consulting smartphones on the train, are probably playing games and not, say, working their way through *The Recognitions*. Fear of the zeitgeist may be a natural response when one is mulling the state of the nation's art.

Boosterism is another. According to Tim Folger, who edits *Best American Science and Nature Writing*, "you will find in these pages the most important journalism of our time, the stories that will last." According to Lehman, there's a "harvest of poems" to "glean." "[P]lenty more where that came from," says Egan, having talked up a couple of her own selections.

But when stories, essays, and poems come steeped in overheated gushing, they can start to look like steamed broccoli—the healthy portion of the reader's plate. Such boosterism also encourages aspiring writers—one of the key demographics at which these books subtly tilt—to assume they have something to contribute to the harvest, when in fact they might be better off fussing with that smartphone. Some of the editors even dangle bait: detailed instructions for submitting work by mail. The work, of course, must already be published, and even then, one suspects the instructions don't apply to everyone. An Ian Frazier or Annie Proulx—both of whom appear in *Best American* books this year—surely has no need to address envelopes.

Stout, in his foreword, tells a particularly attractive story about a young person, "as yet undecided on a career." One day, the young person encountered a sportswriter on public transit. How does one become a writer? wondered the young person. "As they parted [the sportswriter] simply handed the young writer-to-be his copy of *The Best American Sports Writing*. 'Just read this,' he said." Lehman, for his part, delights in relaying that the 1990 edition of *Best American Poems* was the first book of poems this year's editor, Terrance Hayes, ever bought, and that Hayes owns the lot of them. He has also consulted his Freud: because all of us have the capacity to dream or make slips of the tongue, Lehman reasons, becoming a poet is merely a matter of learning technique. "It took the advent of creative writing as an academic field to institutionalize what might be a natural tendency in American democracy." Certainly these books offer the civilian a sense of the range of American stories, essays, and poems—and the fantasy that she might be able to publish one.

But a closer look at Lehman's contribution to the series reveals flaws in the fantasy. *The Best American Poetry* compiles roughly seventy-five poems every year and prints under each one its provenance: the magazine where it first appeared. (Other volumes, like *Best American Short Stories*, print fewer selections.) Presumably, then, to have made the cut for Lehman's book, a poem has already had to survive several editors, each with a gate to keep. In some cases, it has had to endure a special horror: the scrutiny of creative writing students, who often serve as first readers for university-based journals. Thousands of negative micro-reviews—meted out as slush piles were dispatched—barnacle the underside of Lehman's buoyant book.

I wouldn't have it any other way. I count on discerning editors to sift and cull. But Lehman's brand of boosterism would like to pretend we can do without this form of honest criticism. When it comes to what makes a poem the "best," Hayes, the poet Lehman tapped to make the final selection, is fashionably unhelpful. "You know when a poem moves you just as you know when good music moves you, regardless of its genre or style," Hayes says. "The problems arise when we are asked to explain *why we like what we like*. It's a problem for everyone, save a few deluded scholars, I guess."

Hayes says he doesn't "mind critics," but he reduces them to a dated caricature, whose bursts of hot air are brought down a degree or two by Hayes's cool. "I'm not ashamed to say I wanted a diverse mix," says Hayes, knowing perfectly well that declaring an interest in diversity, far from shameful, only shames the rest of us, who merely—thoughtlessly—wanted to read the best, most entertaining poems, and not revel in the plurality of American poetry.

More problematically, it's the sheer fact of the harvest—as opposed to individual stalks—that Lehman celebrates:

> In the proliferation of competent poems, poems that meet a certain standard of artistic finish but may lack staying power, I cannot see much harm except to note one inevitable consequence, which is that of inflation. In economics, inflation takes the form of a devaluation of currency. In poetry, inflation lessens the value that the culture attaches to any individual poem.

Lehman is less interested in excellent poems, which can only be consumed one at a time, than an idea, "poetry," which he sets in opposition to the brutal zeitgeist. In 2013, he had it that "poetry is tolerated but pales in power, status, and everything else to punditry of even the blandest and most conventional sort." In 2012: "Poetry has managed to thrive in the face of all the technological changes that seem, on the surface at least, so hostile to the muse." But as Gore Vidal reminded us, "The Novel doesn't exist. There are only novels." Poetry doesn't exist either. *The Best American Boosterism* would have you believe otherwise. But there are only poems, some more deserving of a reader's time than others.

Not all the editors in the *Best American* series balk at honest criticism. Egan sets out her criteria for a good short story, and then pulls specific examples from her own selection. Bill Kartalopoulos, at the start of *Best American Comics*, celebrates the way "networked technology" has democratized discussion, but notes that "critical distinction…can elevate the field." Otto Penzler, in *Best American Mystery Stories*, acknowledges the importance of "subjectivity," but points out that some works are "transcendently exquisite." Not all the editors engage in boosterism on behalf of some put-upon genre.

Lehman, however, is convinced the reader's life "depends on" poetry. He chooses to end his foreword by chastising those magazine editors who "continue to fall" for the death-of-poetry pitch—an "evergreen." Readers of Lehman's own evergreen should be wary of anthology editors who feel compelled to measure their genre against the moment, and don't have the good sense to get out of the way of the work they mean to introduce. They should be wary of editors who, fearing the reader may cast it aside, swaddle their product in layers of optimism. "Nothing stinks like a pile of unpublished poetry," wrote Sylvia Plath. The same might be said of an annual anthology that greets its readers through a gritted smile.

(*The New Republic*, 2014)

Kenneth Goldsmith's Stunts

LAST WEEK AT BROWN UNIVERSITY, the poet Kenneth Goldsmith delivered a new work called "The Body of Michael Brown," based on the unarmed black teenager gunned down by Ferguson police officer Darren Wilson in 2014; the poem Goldsmith read aloud was a "remix" of the autopsy report. (Goldsmith made adjustments, like translating medical jargon and moving a comment about Brown's "unremarkable" genitalia to the poem's climax.) As he read for thirty minutes, the poet stood beneath a blown-up image of Brown in graduation cap and gown. Audience response was mixed—"mostly quiet."

This was nothing new for Goldsmith, a so-called "conceptual poet." He has devoted whole books to found texts: traffic reports, weather reports, transcripts of broadcasts. He once retyped an entire issue of *The New York Times* and titled the result *Day*. He teaches a course called "Uncreative Writing," in which "students are penalized for showing any shred of originality and creativity."

A century ago, Marcel Duchamp made a name for himself by attempting to place a signed urinal in an art exhibition; Goldsmith's project is to install the prepackaged and prosaic into poetry. "I don't write anything new or original," Goldsmith assures us. "I copy pre-existing texts and move information from one place to another. A child could do what I do, but wouldn't dare to for fear of being called stupid."

Unsurprisingly, nearly a century after Duchamp's readymade, Goldsmith has encountered substantially less bafflement and resistance than the Dadaist. It's not just that we long ago internalized Duchamp's provocations; it's also that Goldsmith is, like Warhol, a PR pro, one of those savvy ambassadors who prefer the "mainstream"—a dorm-room noun, which Goldsmith has nevertheless dinged other poets with—to the margin. Goldsmith has appeared on *The Colbert Report*, served as MOMA's Poet Laureate, and read traffic reports to President Obama at a White House poetry reading. And yet the persona he presents is earnest, feckless, hopeless. (Another era would have pegged him a primitivist.) "I am a dumb writer, perhaps one of the dumbest that's ever lived," he writes, straight face ruffled by the slightest of winks. You are meant to be scandalized—but charmed, too.

But although Goldsmith champions the repurposing of texts that browsers make plentiful—like autopsy reports—he is in fact a relentless author of original content: his own image. Goldsmith's lively, mischievous personality can't help but eclipse his ephemeral, incidental works. Ironically, then, he projects a greater sense of self than those staid contemporaries of his who take it for granted that poems are expressive, the issue of people.

As news of the Brown reading spread, however, that personality found itself in trouble. The internet rightly pointed out that a white poet had appropriated and exploited the experience of a black victim of police violence. Cathy Park Hong tweeted that "Kenneth Goldsmith has reached new racist lows yet elite institutions continue to pay him guest speaker fees." Other outraged missives were issued, favourited, and retweeted. One tweet, an apparent death threat, got a Twitter account suspended. One wonders: did the conceptual poet take solace in these acts of repurposing?

Articles lit up *The Huffington Post*, *The Guardian*, *The National Post*, *Flavorwire*. Goldsmith fanned the flame war with a Facebook post defending his performance, which he judged "powerful." It's sometimes said that an event like this breaks the internet, but it really only manipulates it. One was reminded of the scene in *Die Hard*, where the FBI cuts the power to a building that has been occupied by terrorists. The terrorists are actually crack bank robbers led by Alan Rickman, who required the power cut in order to disable a lock and get to a vault. If Goldsmith is Rickman, then the rest of us are the hapless, predictable FBI, responding on cue to the poet's provocation.

But I'll bite. The poet's stunt was (to copy-paste the poet's own earlier self-description) dumb. And yet: is this a case of an otherwise responsible subgenre going too far? Or does the use of Brown's autopsy report expose a preexisting emptiness in conceptual poetry's chest cavity? When Stephen Colbert interviewed Goldsmith about his book *Seven American Deaths and Disasters*, even Colbert removed tongue from cheek long enough to concede feeling uncomfortable. "When I read this, I feel like I'm some sort of time-travelling aesthete who is coming in to sample other people's shock and tragedy," he said. "I'm tasting their disbelief and the way it's changing them forever...and it feels vampiric."

The recontextualized text, of course, has less cynical, more responsible exemplars. One of the very best was produced by W. B. Yeats. In 1936, the Irish poet arranged Victorian critic Walter Pater's prose description of the *Mona Lisa* into lines and put them at the front of the *Oxford Book of Modern Verse*.

"Only by printing it in *vers libre* can one show its revolutionary importance," claimed Yeats, who felt that Pater's prose had influenced a generation of poets. It was as if someone had unearthed a snippet of some seminal interview with Elvis and tapped it to lead off a mixtape that included The Beatles, The Stones, and Dylan. Here is "Mona Lisa," by Pater the Poet:

> She is older than the rocks among which she sits;
> Like the Vampire,
> She has been dead many times,
> And learned the secrets of the grave;
> And has been a diver in deep seas,
> And keeps their fallen day about her;
> And trafficked for strange webs with Eastern merchants;
> And, as Leda,
> Was the mother of Helen of Troy,
> And, as St Anne,
> Was the mother of Mary;

> And all this has been to her but as the sound of lyres and
>   flutes,
> And lives
> Only in the delicacy
> With which it has moulded the changing lineaments,
> And tinged the eyelids and the hands.

Yeats was hardly a champion of free verse. But he found in Pater's prose enough of the stuff of poetry—simile, alliteration, meter, anaphora—to justify the imposition of line breaks. Yeats's was a controversial act of recontextualization; it used free verse, a fashionable mode among forward-tilting modernists, to lash them to a past some were leaning away from. But it was in the service of celebrating Pater, of bringing something beautiful to the reader's attention, of trying to train our attention on the poetic possibilities of the language he had recovered and made strange. "Mona Lisa" places the Irishman in a tradition stretching back to other, more famous chisellers like Michelangelo, who saw blocks of stone pre-loaded with angels.

There are no angels in Goldsmith's brand of conceptual art: no concealed music, no gems half-encrusted by context. There is nothing for the audience to discover, except its own frustration, outrage, or boredom—which earlier avant-gardists could at least pretend were necessary conditions to making the audience more critical. But the beneficiary of Goldsmith's acts of recontextualization is Goldsmith, who doesn't even require readers:

> My books are better thought about than read. They're insanely dull and unreadable; I mean, do you really want to sit down and read a year's worth of weather reports.... I don't. But they're wonderful to talk about and think about, to dip in and out of, to hold, to have on your shelf. In fact, I say that I don't have a readership, I have a thinkership.

You don't need to experience Goldsmith's volume of weather reports nor have seen his reading of the autopsy report (which the courageous iconoclast has asked Brown University not to release); you need only know about them, have heard tell of them. The point of Yeats's found poem is what someone else accomplished. The point of Goldsmith's was entirely selfish, was about what Goldsmith did or is said to have done. This is poetry as clickbait, hearsay, publicity stunt.

Did a recently shot black teenager look like sufficiently newsy fodder to a conceptual poet? Maybe not; maybe Goldsmith's intentions were less cynical. But a subgenre that must cultivate buzz because it has renounced readers—because the author is dead, anyway—will find itself tempted to ever-escalating and offensive acts of provocation. In other words, the kind of conceptual poet Goldsmith has come to embody—Google-hit-grabbing, anti-humanist, insensitive—may have found himself at a dead end.

(*The New Republic*, 2014)

Jonathan Galassi's First Novel

In Roberto Bolaño's novel *The Savage Detectives*, an Impala's worth of poets embarks on a road trip to track down their idol, the hopelessly obscure Cesárea Tinajero. The poets identify with something called "visceral realism," a literary school Tinajero founded long ago. But Tinajero now resides somewhere off the grid of avant-garde history, her reputation kept afloat by word of mouth. Bolaño's heroes haven't even *read* Tinajero when they first set out on their quest; there's nothing to read! They eventually turn up a single item: an unremarkable concrete poem Bolaño's poets fail to find unremarkable.

Unlike Tinajero, Ida Perkins, the fictional poet in Jonathan Galassi's debut novel *Muse*, possesses an oeuvre and a public. Moreover, she's a fantastical index of one man's sense of what matters—a well-placed man who has eyeballed recent literary history up close. Galassi, after all, is a translator, a former *Paris Review* editor, an accomplished poet, and, most conspicuously, the head of Farrar, Straus & Giroux, which stables John Ashbery, Elizabeth Bishop, August Kleinzahler, and many others. *Muse* focuses on Paul Dukach, an editor who works for a storied house not unlike FSG. (Purcell & Stern, we're told, is the smallest of the big New York publishers.)

Paul's obsession is Perkins, the property of a rival house, Impetus (*biggest* of the *small* New York publishers). When the book begins, Paul has never met his idol, but will soon strike out for Venice, where she lives. He will come into possession of an unpublished Perkins manuscript and a revelation about a love affair.

An insider might be tempted to channel one's inner sleuth and draw chalk lines from Galassi's creations to their corresponding, real-world counterparts. For a time, I figured Impetus was an analogue for something like James Laughlin's New Directions, which trucks in experimental writing, has published Anne Carson, and keeps Ezra Pound in print. But New Directions shows up in Galassi's book, too. (Part of the fun of *Muse* is the way it generates friction: forcing real phenomena to rub shoulders with imaginary ones.)

Galassi's novel probably *does* conceal gossipy references to actual people: prickly talents he's handled with garden gloves, bedhead reputations he's styled. And to be sure, the publishing world provides Galassi with satire-rich setting. (The novel's rival publishers—one experimental, the other more commercial—parody the petty rivalries among literary types, who tend to specialize in hair-splitting.) But Galassi's book deserves more than gotcha-grade guesswork.

What *Muse* is really about is fandom, about devoting one's life to the life's work of another: what all great editors come to do. In other words, what Galassi has created in *Muse* is a justification of his own life's work. And what he's created in Perkins is an improbable fantasy: the Ur-acquisition all editors dream of. "Ida was one of those rare poets who bridge the divide between aesthetic schools," the novel assures us. She unifies Beats, formalists, Sylvia Plath, Adrienne Rich, and at least one Kennedy. She sees her lines turned into platinum by Carly Simon and Carole King, dabbles in Maoism, may have attended Woodstock, "was the only person ever to appear simultaneously on the covers of *Rolling Stone*, *Tel Quel*, and *Interview*." Magazines like *Time* and "even the *Reader's Digest*...were desperate to write about her." She ranges so assuredly over twentieth-century culture, it's a wonder Galassi doesn't place her at a block party at the birth of hip hop, or in the background of the Zapruder footage, next to Forrest Gump.

A poet who appears in *Rolling Stone* may be a fantasy, but it's a charming one, and perhaps even a sly act of revenge on a world that has other, crasser plans for cover stories. Galassi worked at Random House in the 1980s, but was fired in 1986, because his books weren't commercial enough. The underdog, however, was soon snapped up by FSG, where, ironically enough, he had a major commercial success with Scott Turow's legal thriller, *Presumed Innocent*. His tenure at FSG has also coincided with the publication of more prestigious works like Bolaño's *The Savage Detectives*, Denis Johnson's *Tree of Smoke*, and Marilynne Robinson's *Gilead*. Among the many reasons to root for *Muse* is the gut feeling that its author would seem to know—would surely *have* to know, given his years in publishing—what makes for a good novel.

But if Ida seems newsreel-thin, so do most of *Muse*'s relentlessly quirky characters. There's the crack team of editors who work at Purcell & Stern, "a raggle-taggle gatherum of talented misfits"—a kind, if unoriginal, character sketch. There's the screwball literary agent, Roz Horowitz, "a canny old bird" who slings shit like, "Watch it, kiddo," and "That and a nickel will buy you exactly nothing." And there's Paul's boss, Homer, the sort of cartoon a creative writing student might draw up if tasked with picturing a publisher, whom Galassi feeds such lines as "This is going to turn the literary world on its tail" and "I'm smacking my lips. Get yourself home today, baby." But it's not just what they say, but how they say it. "'Don't tell me you had to sleep with her,' [Homer] guffawed," when "said" would have done perfectly fine work. Perhaps these figures riff on real people, but they're still so kaleidoscopically colourful they blow the spectrum and hurt the eyes.

It's uncomfortable to remind a brilliant editor to show, not tell, especially when one has entertained dreams of being published by the editor's press. But Galassi fails to trust his reader. "'How did that novel by what's her name, Fran Drescher, do?'" he has Homer say at one point, and then appends, in case you missed his point, "Homer was incorrigibly terrible with names." Or consider this three-sentence exchange, between Paul and Ida, which condescends to the reader no less than three times, cudgeling her with theme:

> "Well, I can see you haven't learned much in your young years!" Ida shot back derisively.
>
> "Forgive me, Ms. Perkins, but I hope you can appreciate how

large you and Mr. Outerbridge loom in the imaginations of some of us," he replied, perhaps a bit assertively.

"You're not one of those despicable literary sleuths who thinks he can deduce every last little sordid biographical detail from a writer's work, are you?" Ida asked, with ill-concealed suspicion.

Much of the first half of *Muse* reads like prologue: backstory to some other, better book in which characters reveal the finer points of their selves through dialogue and action. As it stands, Galassi's novel is so top-heavy with history and exposition, its big revelation means little to the reader, who must take the narrator's word that the characters are worth caring about. Moreover, the reader's sense of a stock world populated by placards is reinforced, page after page, by clichés like "taken a shine," "the way a cat plays with a mouse," "larger than life," "whetted the appetite," "heartless world," "pure gold," "a thorn in the side," "rat's nest," "out of the blue," "wee hours," "dream come true," and "heart in his mouth," among many, many others.

One can't help but wonder how a novel by a man who presides over one of publishing's most prestigious houses seems to have largely escaped blue pencils.

What redeems *Muse*—or what can be salvaged from it—are the poems Galassi gifts to Ida Perkins. Novels about fictional poets, like *The Savage Detectives* and *The Anthologist*, tend to do the poets a favour and leave their poems off-page. But Galassi proves, as Nabokov did in *Pale Fire*, that exemplary poetry can be willed to order. Galassi isn't Nabokov, but the poems he concocts are clean columns of free verse, flecked with internal rhyme and lovely turns:

> How to go on
> with this
> heaviness all
> this despair
> being kind
> reasonable

> practical
> organized fair
> when what I
> want is to shut
> the door open
> your locket and
> finger your hair

Fandom, *Muse* suggests, is its own act of creation. "Thanks to Ida...poetry not infrequently found itself at the heart of American culture and society," we're told, and if that's wishful thinking, it's also wonderful science fiction. But it's not just that *Muse* posits a compelling counterfactual universe in which poetry fans might like to dwell. In fact, an imaginary editor's extreme devotion to his idol has driven the real-world Galassi to an oddball achievement: the composition of a micro-oeuvre of fine poems that don't quite belong to him.

Ida Perkins certainly deserves inclusion in *The Norton Anthology of Imaginary Poetry*—an imaginary book, at present, but one that some great editor or other might be able to bring into being.

(*The New Republic*, 2015)

Jeffrey Eugenides's
The Virgin Suicides

According to the publisher Picador, *The Virgin Suicides*, Jeffrey Eugenides's 1993 debut, is now a "modern classic, a lyrical and timeless tale of sex and suicide." Last month, the novel joined Hermann Hesse's *Steppenwolf* and Marilynne Robinson's *Housekeeping* as part of a series of smart, jacketless miniatures that, should you squint, could double as Victorian vanity editions.

It's easy enough, of course, to balk at book marketing; after all, isn't a novel canonized (or not) at the whim of the ruling party of critics, editors, educators, and other imperialist heavies? Isn't "the classic" what graduate curricula call a "construct"?

Nevertheless, the notion of the classic matters to people who buy books. Moreover, Eugenides's novel has persisted. To those entrusted with filling classroom silence, it's a conversation starter; to young readers, it's a rite of passage—or a pivot into puberty. ("I turned thirteen, and then I read *The Virgin Suicides*," says wunderkind and magazine editor Tavi Gevinson.) Then there are the hipsters of a certain cohort (the present author bows his head here) who saw in Sofia Coppola's stylish 1999 film adaptation a style manual.

But if *The Virgin Suicides* is a classic, it's also a time capsule, an exemplar of the thwarted detective fiction common in the eighties and nineties. The novel proposes an especially opaque mystery—why did five teenagers commit suicide?—and then doubles down on the frosted glass. "In the end we had pieces of the puzzle," explains the narrator, "but no matter how we put them together, gaps remained, oddly shaped emptinesses mapped by what surrounded them, like countries we couldn't name." Teachable to a fault, Eugenides's novel has all over it the fingerprints of an era obsessed with signs, maps, legibility, the embodied text, the gap between signifier and signified, and other useful classroom props.

Eugenides's novel is narrated in first-person plural by a group of men who, as adolescents, lived in purple-prose-inducing proximity to the Lisbon sisters: five teenagers presided over by a puritanical mother and father. Early on, one of the sisters, Cecilia, hurls herself upon a spiked fence. Following her suicide, the remaining sisters are kept under tight wraps—and surveillance constricts further when Lux, the Lisbon outfitted with a rebellious streak, fails to make it home on time after the one and only dance the girls are permitted to attend. The Lisbon house promptly falls into the sort of Gothic decay that allows teachers to talk genre. Meanwhile, the boys across the street struggle to find ways to communicate with the girls. The novel ends with more suicides, which will haunt the narrators, for whom the sisters function as a five-headed Lolita—or a troupe of manic-pixie-dream-girl guides.

There's much to admire about the book, including the collective narrative voice that predates the watercooler "we" in *Then We Came to the End*, Joshua Ferris's 2007 novel about workplace. There are also the hi-res set pieces, more vivid and telling than any teen's Tumblr:

> He came back to us with stories of bedrooms filled with crumpled panties, of stuffed animals hugged to death by the passion of the girls, of a crucifix draped with a brassiere, of gauzy chambers of canopied beds, and of the effluvia of so many young girls becoming women together in the same cramped space. In the bathroom, running the faucet to cloak the sounds of his search, Peter Sissen found Mary Lisbon's secret cache of cosmetics tied up in a sock under the sink: tubes of red lipstick and the second skin of blush and base, and the depilatory wax that informed us she had a moustache we had never seen.

Through the accretion of precise detail in this scene, Eugenides disperses some of the purple fog; the girls, it turns out, are less ethereal than the boys thought. But there's craft here, too, a subtle latticework of alliteration—for example, "crumpled," "crucifix," and "cramped." The novel is at its best in these moments, when it employs precise but artful prose to bring focus to bric-a-brac or to put a point on details. After Cecilia is retrieved from the fence, the exposition is especially exacting: "As they carried her away, the sawed-off stake lifted the sheet like a tent post." Eugenides is careful to cut the dry ice generated by the boys with the occasional beam of crisp light.

The book is at its worst when, instead of putting a point on the details, it resolves to have points to make: the past can't be recovered, for example, or truth is hopelessly subjective. Eugenides styles his present-day narrators as middle-aged, amateur detectives. They interview witnesses, fuss over photographs, and refer us to various exhibits. The men, of course, aren't actually detectives, or even characters, really. At times they seem like little more than stylized obsessives, serving at the pleasure of the novel's epistemological lectern.

They also belong to a lineage of pseudo-sleuths, including the archive-scouring second person in Timothy Findley's *The Wars* (1977), somber Patrick Lewis in Michael Ondaatje's *In the Skin of a Lion* (1987), the doomed obsessives in Paul Auster's New York Trilogy (1985–1986), and the questing poets in Roberto Bolaño's *The Savage Detectives* (1998). *The Virgin Suicides* is in part a product of a pre-Pinterest time when old photos and the contents of archives produced pangs of hopelessness in the hearts of our novelists, and when efforts to drag the past could only flounder.

More generally, the novel unspools plenty of rope with which those characters who dare to seek something like truth can tie their necks. Experts are summoned so that they can be dismissed. One character, a reductive journalist who covers Cecilia's suicide, seems to exist to boil off nuance. Another character, a doctor, guesses that the Lisbon sisters had PTSD, but he also describes them as "lemmings." (Men of science are jerks like that.) The novel reels off a series of suicide stats, which the sort of person who self-selects as a patron of "literary" novels isn't expected to take seriously. It even presents a television show that gives airtime to young people who have attempted suicide. But the narrators are too hep to be convinced: "We listened to them, but it was clear they'd received too much therapy to know the truth."

Near the end, the narrators conclude that "The essence of the suicides consisted not of sadness or mystery but simple selfishness," and that "we will never find the pieces to put them back together." But that's not quite right. What really killed the Lisbon sisters—what tied one to a beam, consigned another to carbon monoxide—was a literary zeitgeist that fetishized epistemological problems. And yet what readers remember about the novel aren't the photos, nor the lost records, nor the gaps dutifully circled. What readers retain are living, illuminated images like that "white stripe Uncle Tucker later saw on Lux's coat [which] came from the goal line she lay down upon. Throughout the act, headlights came across the field, sweeping over them, lighting up the goalpost."

That's blindingly good, and mirrors the moment in *Lolita*, an obvious influence, when the young Humbert Humbert and his proto-beloved "found a desolate stretch of sand, and there, in the violet shadow of some red rocks forming a kind of cave, had a brief session of avid caresses, with somebody's lost pair of sunglasses for only witness."

Whether or not *The Virgin Suicides* is a classic is beside the point. When the novel holsters its heavy hands and simply observes adolescence in all its tactile detail, it produces moments that threaten to stay with readers forever.

(*The Walrus*, 2015)

David Foster Wallace's Criticism

There's a certain irony in making a feature film about David Foster Wallace: funneling the most voluminous of writers, he of the endless endnotes with their own gravitational pull, into the multiplex. The market, of course, is primed for a movie. DFW's fans have already consumed every available product—not just his terrific short stories or his 900-plus-page dystopian novel on TV, tennis, and addiction, *Infinite Jest*, but his critical essays, his Kenyon College commencement address, and his gonzo forays into reporting and travel writing. For the completist, there are also his interviews with *Rolling Stone* journalist David Lipsky from the 1996 book tour for *Infinite Jest*, which have now been adapted as *The End of the Tour*. (Jason Segel bandanas up and plays DFW.) But what emerges from those interviews—fodder for a work of entertainment—is Wallace's deep aversion to, well, entertainment.

"I think that if there is a sort of sadness for people under forty-five, it has something to do with pleasure, and achievement, and entertainment—like a sort of emptiness at the heart of what they thought was going on," says Segel as Wallace, in the trailer. For most of his career, Wallace suggested that art ought to be difficult, that pleasure is suspect, and that entertainment is compromised. Art, Wallace told Lipsky, is a sort of superfood that "requires you to *work*." (Italics his.) Entertainment is candy whose "chief job is to make you so riveted by it that you can't tear your eyes away, so the advertisers can advertise."

It's taken a decade or so for me to wean myself off DFW's criticism and his dorm-room ideas about entertainment; really, it was easy to gloss over the moralizing. For those who read them in real time, Wallace's critical pieces were prescient responses to the enthusiasms and obsessions of the time—David Lynch, Mark Leyner, and Image-Fiction. (They appeared in niche publications such as *The Review of Contemporary Fiction* and *Premiere*.) For most of the rest of us—who read the essays when they appeared later, in collections like *A Supposedly Fun Thing I'll Never Do Again*—they meted out smaller doses of the idiosyncratic voice behind *Infinite Jest*. That voice hadn't exactly been deployed on behalf of a generation, but it seemed to be the private discovery of droves of us, who were overeducated, steeped in pop culture, and unable to quiet our minds. "He'd done a thing that was casual and gigantic," Lipsky wrote, "he'd captured everybody's brain voice."

By the time many of us got around to reading Wallace's early critical essays, they were already period pieces—artifacts of the anti-corporate nineties, when it would've seemed necessary to decry the negative effects of television or bring down Brett Easton Ellis's cohort. Nevertheless, after *Infinite Jest*, we were prepared to consume whatever variety and quantity of DFW we could. The subject matter hardly mattered. We read Wallace for his ever-prisming self-reflections; mashups of the academic and colloquial; footnotes that plunged the reader into fine print; and the sort of sense of humor that breaks into an essay, on its twenty-ninth page, with the heading: "I do have a thesis." We read Wallace because he was a lot of fun—even when he was warning us about the dangers of having too much fun.

"E Unibus Pluram: Television and US Fiction" is the most ambitious of his critical essays—the one that advanced a worldview, jabbed a sharp into a culture enflamed by irony, and powered his most memorable fiction: *Infinite Jest* and short stories like "My Appearance" and "The Depressed Person." Wallace began this tour de force by pointing out that fiction writers, anti-social by nature, constitute an ideal audience for television: they can observe others from the comfort of their own living rooms. (Wallace wrote at a time when people watched TV in living rooms.)

He went on to diagnose how a particular strain of rebellious irony—which postwar American novelists had weaponized and leveled at various forms of authority—had come to be appropriated by media personalities and corporations. Pepsi and Isuzu, for example, had learned how to mock the oily salesmanship to which TV audiences, increasingly savvy and cynical, had grown impervious. Hip knowingness had saturated US culture. Irony, once a potent mode of critique, was impotent: deadpan on arrival.

Wallace then shifted his focus to show how postmodern writers like Leyner had internalized this defunct posture, resulting in "wonderful and oddly hollow" postmodern prose: "there's a bar on the highway which caters almost exclusively to authority figures and the only drink it serves is lite beer and the only food it serves is surf and turf and the place is filled with cops and state troopers and gym teachers...". He ended the essay with a prediction—and potential cure. "The next real literary 'rebels' in this country," he wrote,

> might well emerge as some weird bunch of *anti*-rebels, born oglers who dare somehow to back away from ironic watching, who have the childish gall actually to endorse and instantiate single-entendre principles. Who treat of plain old untrendy human troubles and emotions in US life with reverence and conviction.

It's a rousing passage, and it spawned the likes of Dave Eggers, *The Believer*, and other aggressively wide-eyed, cynicism-free phenomena. But then the essay is such a remarkable performance it's easy to miss Wallace's moralistic tendency to treat television as a social ill.

Wallace's view of entertainment was ungenerous and immature. When Lipsky suggests to Wallace that *Die Hard* is "smarter than most art movies," Wallace, constant killjoy, can't resist reminding the poor fool that it's "also very formulaic, and rather cynically reusing a lot of old formulas." Seduction is a constant source of anxiety, and the overall impression is of a serious kid, the only one who's done the readings, trying to keep the conversation on track.

Entertainment, suggests Wallace in a later piece on Kafka, serves up escapism and reassurance, concepts Wallace seems to think are self-evidently bad. His conception of audiences was also simplistic. "We as an audience," he claims in a profile of David Lynch, "have certain core certainties about sowing and reaping, and these certainties need to be affirmed and massaged." But Wallace himself implies, through his reading of TV history, that one of the chief reasons advertisers adopt techniques like irony is because people change. They adapt to, and grow alienated from, conventions. They certainly don't constitute an inert, sprawling corpus, to which electrodes easily clip.

Wallace's view of art simply couldn't admit entertainment without vaporizing it. To his inner graduate student—a Terminator armed with semiotics—TV commercials resembled easy, radar-red prey, overlaid with crosshairs. They certainly weren't sources of inspiration, as they could be for other, more generous critics. Consider Camille Paglia's rapturous paean to the television of her childhood:

> Burned into my memory, for example, is a late-1950s TV commercial for M&M's chocolate candies. A sultry cartoon peanut, sunbathing on a chaise longue, said in a twanging Southern drawl: "I'm an M&M peanut / Toasted to a golden brown / Dipped in creamy milk chocolate / And covered in a thin candy shell!" Illustrating each line, she prettily dove into a swimming pool of melted chocolate and popped out on the other side to strike a pose and be instantly toweled in her monogrammed candy wrap. I felt then, and still do, that the M&M peanut's jingle was a vivacious poem and that the creative team who produced that ad were folk artists, anonymous as the artisans of medieval cathedrals.

Unlike Paglia, whose imagination transforms admen into artisans, Wallace has little to say in his formal criticism about masterfully constructed pop artifacts that give pleasure to an audience. It's almost impossible to imagine a substantial, celebratory essay by Wallace about Brian Wilson's *Pet Sounds* or Ivan Reitman's *Ghostbusters*, works of genius produced by geniuses of the system. When Wallace does briefly praise a movie like *Terminator* or *Aliens*, it's largely because it refuses commercial compromises.

He certainly couldn't imagine the post-*Sopranos* Golden Age of Television we came to occupy, gilded with *Breaking Bad* and *The Wire*. But then he couldn't always weigh the true worth of what was in front of him either. "Television's greatest minute-by-minute appeal is that it engages without demanding," he writes. But doesn't a smart, old sitcom like *All in the Family*—which had laughs, political talk, and something critical to say about American society in the 1970s—put paid to Wallace's caricature?

Wallace would most acutely dramatize the terrible dangers of entertainment in *Infinite Jest*, which posits a video so captivating it renders its audience immobile. Unable to care for themselves, the transfixed viewers eventually expire. Was Wallace projecting an anxiety about his own vulnerability to entertainment onto the rest of us? He certainly recognized the pleasures of television and, more generally, entertainment. In an early interview, he confesses to consuming a "daily megadose of TV" and worries about his own tendency to want to entertain others. In a foreshadowing of the fatal video in *Infinite Jest*, he declares,

> I think it's impossible to spend that many slack-jawed, spittle-chinned, formative hours in front of commercial art without internalizing the idea that one of the main goals of art is simply to "entertain," give people sheer pleasure. Except to what end, this pleasure-giving? Because, of course, TV's "real" agenda is to be "liked," because if you like what you're seeing, you'll stay tuned.... And sometimes when I look at my own stuff I feel like I absorbed too much of this raison. I'll catch myself thinking up gags or trying formal stunt-pilotry and see that none of this stuff is really in the service of the story itself; it's serving the rather darker

purpose of communicating to the reader "Hey! Look at me! Have a look at what a good writer I am! Like me!"

But Wallace's anti-entertainment ideas have become so influential precisely because he wrote about them in an entertaining way—and *The End of the Tour* will, undoubtedly, be entertaining and spread his views ever more widely.

Not too long ago, while taking part in a panel on criticism, I pointed out that poetry was too often regarded as a source of nutrients rather than pleasure. A young woman in the audience took issue and, with admirable sincerity, alerted me to the dangers of entertainment. She was wielding, naturally, Wallace's essay on television—as clunky a weapon as a cathode ray tube. Why would anyone read the doom-laden Wallace on television now, in the medium's Golden Age? Only later did it occur to me that Wallace sticks with people—especially young people—in part because he's addictive to read. Bad for you in bulk, but so much fun from sentence to sentence.

(*The New Republic*, 2015)

Criticism's Selfie Habit

Browsing the arts and culture pages of various websites recently, I kept running smack into it: the first-person pronoun, as conspicuous as a Corinthian column. It sprang up in essay after essay—and right behind it, a critic in the mood to share. Many of these essays were ostensibly works of criticism about some artist or cultural product. But each one seemed to be armed with a selfie stick, aimed at the essayist. Here are some of their sentences:

> I was thirteen in those pre-Internet days when you needed a cool friend or sibling to introduce you to new music, especially in smaller cities like my hometown of Winnipeg.

> Fukien (or Fujian) is my mother's home province, the place she and her parents immigrated from in the 1950s. So when I hear "Fukien," I'm not thinking about a cuisine. I'm thinking about the place my family came from, and of the long history of migration that they're a part of.

> Maybe I'm a self-flagellating weirdo, but pretense is a personal tendency of which I'm all too acutely aware.

> The first time a girl ever called me pretty, she was absolutely stoned.

For the record, the pieces that play host to these sentences are about: the rock band the Replacements; a recent *New Yorker* poem by Calvin Trillin; Dan Fox's book *Pretentiousness: Why It Matters*; and the late singer-songwriter Elliott Smith. But I could've pointed to plenty of other recent examples of critics pointing at themselves.

Contemporary criticism is positively crowded with first-person pronouns, micro-doses of memoir, brief hits of biography. Critics don't simply wrestle with their assigned cultural object; they wrestle with themselves, as well. Recent examples suggest a spectrum, from reviews that harmlessly kick off with a personal anecdote, to hybrid pieces that blend literary criticism and longform memoir.

Some of these pieces are certainly excellent, and, as an editor, I've certainly commissioned my share of what might be called "confessional criticism." I've even written some, too. But—confession!—I've never felt especially good about it. Relating works of art to one's life, after all, is easy. (No reference library required.) Moreover, the confessional voice is dangerously attractive; as Virginia Woolf put it, "under the decent veil of print one can indulge one's egoism to the full." Such a voice doesn't necessarily guarantee more honest criticism, and, in some ways, its subtle designs on the reader make it even more deserving of our wariness.

How did our critics get so confessional? At mid-century, a group sometimes called the "New Critics" enclosed themselves in an impersonal style, a Darth Vader mask through which they filtered their analyses. Figures such as Northrop Frye believed that works of literature had allusive tendrils in one another, forming a vast, apprehensible system—and so the aspiration was to sound objective, like a botanist scrutinizing roots.

Even those not officially associated with the movement, like Edmund Wilson, found it useful to leverage the clinical language of science, which supplied a sense of authority. "It is my purpose in this book to try to trace the origins of certain tendencies in contemporary literature and to show their development in the work of six contemporary writers," he declares at the start of *Axel's Castle*, his celebrated study of Symbolism. Peak chill would be achieved by the theory types—Jacques Derrida and Judith Butler, for instance—whose voices came packed in dense, icy jargon that required a doctorate to chisel through.

There were always alternatives, of course, running parallel to the more imperious critics. Dorothy Parker deployed a chatty, engaging avatar in her book and theatre pieces. Randall Jarrell's poetry criticism, Pauline Kael's film reviews, and Lester Bangs's music writing all seemed fired by irrefutable furnaces: living, breathing personalities.

Although many of these critics weren't strangers to the first-person pronoun, they often only *appeared* to write in a personal voice; their reviews and critical essays revealed little about themselves. If anything, they tended to favor a hollow "I," a handy prop like the cardboard tube that girds a few yards of giftwrap. It's the sort of pronoun I've employed here, meant to give voice to an argument as opposed to a person. An "I" that's a close, less clinical cousin of "one." A convention, a convenience.

But in recent years, there's been a surge in confessional criticism. This can probably be traced to several things: our declining belief in a tradition or canon (whose dead white masterworks once ensured that critics shared a set of reference points *outside* the self), the exodus of writers towards the internet (which enables the immediate posting of one's personality), our ever-metastasizing regard for pop culture (which demands a critical response of commensurate informality), and, of course, David Foster Wallace.

Wallace wasn't primarily a critic, but the critical essays he published in the 1990s and 2000s presented a model to my generation. He eschewed irony, embraced sincerity, and choppered himself into his analyses of assorted cultural phenomena. "Today is Press Day at the Illinois State Fair in Springfield," begins an early essay, "and I'm supposed to be at the fairgrounds by 9:00 a.m. to get my credentials. I imagine credentials to be a small white card in the band of a fedora."

The voice Wallace patented—endearingly amateur, impressively brainy—couldn't help but appeal to other writers, especially younger ones. Half wide-eyed, half winking, it supplemented deep learning with self-deprecation, a colloquial tone, and personal experience.

When he wrote about the politics of dictionaries, Wallace brought up a difficult encounter with a student. When he analyzed the films of David Lynch, he recalled the night he saw *Blue Velvet* for the first time.

Many of today's most prominent critics seem to spring from Wallace's DNA. They call attention to their foibles, embrace sincerity, and locate cultural objects in relation to their own lives. Consider the opening of Leslie Jamison's essay about James Agee, from her influential collection *The Empathy Exams* (2014):

> Many nights that autumn I went to a bar where the floor was covered with peanut shells, and I drank, and I read James Agee. Liquor carried his trauma all through me, twisted me pliable to the loss, and I wasn't afraid to think like this—pliable to the loss—because I was drunk, and drunk meant sentiment was not only permissible but imperative.

Jamison begins with a personal anecdote, brings in Agee, and then swiftly flushes out the potentially objectionable lines (like "pliable to the loss") before the reader can object to them. She moves on to discuss Agee's book *Let Us Now Praise Famous Men*, but discusses herself, too: the aftermath of a recent assault, a move to New Haven. "So I read Agee thinking about his own guilt when he was supposed to be thinking about three Alabama families, and I thought about myself when I was supposed to be thinking about Agee."

On its own, this can seem like engaging, moving stuff. As part of a trend, it blends into a choir of exceedingly competent critics who can't seem to keep themselves out of their sentences. For example, there's Geoff Dyer, who has written several books in this vein: one about his obsession with the film *Stalker*, another, about his failed attempt to write a book about D. H. Lawrence. (Dyer claims he's allergic to Wallace, but the striking resemblance has been noted.) Then there's John Jeremiah Sullivan, who can't write an essay about the meaning of Axl Rose without showing up as the supporting act. "I'd been shuffling around a surprisingly pretty, sunny, newly renovated downtown Lafayette for a couple of days," he writes, of the city where Rose was born, "scraping at whatever I could find." Like Jamison, Sullivan is careful to remind us that, next to civilians, writers are indecently self-interested.

Then there's Carl Wilson, who examines a loathing for Celine Dion's music in his oft-celebrated book *Let's Talk About Love: A Journey to the End of Taste*. Wilson offers engaging readings on how taste is constructed and why our culture distrusts sentimentality. But he also feels moved to describe the afternoon his "future ex-wife" sang some Buddy Holly to him, thawing the one-time snob's heart. "I don't think I have ever been moved, even in our wedding vows, by a profession of love," declares Wilson. "I've seldom felt so honoured, so human, so sure that merely human was enough." The chapter closes with something like the climax to a power ballad: Wilson screwing up the nerve to finally review Dion's blockbuster album *Let's Talk About Love*. "All right, Celine, I'm ready. Bring it on."

Your tolerance for this sort of thing is, of course, going to be personal—largely a matter of stomach acid (yours) and style (the critic's). But style only goes so far. A critic's desire to ensure that she comes off as messily human may come from an honest place, but it's hard to distinguish seemingly sincere moments of self-critique—"I was supposed to be thinking about Agee"—from rhetorical strategies designed to win readers over. "I'm not the most reliable narrator," writes Katy Waldman in a recent, stylish essay about anorexia narratives that's part memoir, part lit-crit. But the unreliable narrator is a cliché, and such confessions have long since become codified and suspect. Put another way: copping to unreliability is a quick, painless way to earn your reader's trust and, well, *prove* your reliability. Even Wallace himself worried about the efficacy of self-reflexivity.

None of this is to suggest that critics should sink a dentist's sharp into their prose, inject artificial chill into their voice, aspire to the frozen state of Eliot, Adorno, and the like. But they should want to be wary of the zeitgeist. If criticism has reached peak confession, critics would do well to simply scrutinize the cultural product at hand (as well as its influences, social context, and, yes, tradition; we need to read beyond ourselves) and put a temporary moratorium on the memoir—especially if the picture painted is of a quirky, sincere, self-deprecatory soul.

Reviews and essays that call attention to the critic are kind of like those movies that insist the viewer wear 3-D glasses. They promise depth, middle distance, a more fulsome experience, three-dimensionality: some additional layer of life. But the promise is redundant. Good criticism, like good films, will always give the impression of depth, of a presiding, trustworthy personality. Smart sentences, one after the other, are usually heartbeat enough.

(*The Walrus*, 2016)

Bob Dylan's Nobel Prize

It's not just that the lyrics—when isolated from his iconic drone, from the ironic bleats of his harmonica—have none of the density of real poetry. It's that they gave the Nobel to the wrong Dylan. By "wrong Dylan," I mean the literary Dylan, the serious Dylan, the Dylan who, as the press release assures us in perishable prose, "created new poetic expressions within the great American song tradition."

(In the background, as I type this, ABC News is perpetrating more perishable prose, including phrases like "anthems for the civil rights movement" and "defining a generation.")

But the right Dylan—the best Dylan—would never attract a Nobel. This is the Dylan who cut Woodstock a wide swath, who jolted his first fans, the self-righteous folk purists, out of their safe space when he went electric. This is the Dylan of concision and melody, the author of economical punk ("Outlaw Blues"), delirious pop ("I Want You"), stirring blues ("It Takes a Lot to Laugh, It Takes a Train to Cry"), and one perfect Beatles parody ("4th Time Around").

Put another way, I like Dylan for all the wrong reasons, and I like very little of him. I find myself skipping the self-consciously poetic epics like "Mr. Tambourine Man," "Visions of Johanna," and "Sad Eyed Lady of the Lowlands." Beyond the five-minute mark, with yet another verse of surreal, portentous images on the way, Dylan's songs lose their grip on me.

But I imagine that's about when they grab hold of Dylanologists—or Nobel committee members.

(*The Walrus*, 2016)

Literary Community's Pitfalls

THE "PUGILIST POET" August Kleinzahler is one of the prickliest loners in American letters. It's no accident, then, that his new book, *Sallies, Romps, Portraits, and Send-Offs: Selected Prose 2000-2016*, offers up a number of portraits of forgotten poets and critics—all, to a man, idiosyncratic cranks.

There's Thom Gunn, who had a "strong dislike" for "literary gatherings." There's Kenneth Cox, who reveled in the death of his literary enemies, and "sought and achieved almost complete invisibility outside of his writings." Roy Fisher carried on like an island of one: "A lifelong, rather cheerful agoraphobe and hermit, neglect suits him." Lorine Niedecker quarantined herself on an actual island and accessed the world, when she needed to, by post. Christopher Middleton was "incapable of schmoozing, and his career suffered accordingly." Basil Bunting "liked to live by his wits outside the prescriptions of any institution." When this "obstinate, rambunctious, impulsive" poet stooped to teach creative writing, he took precisely zero interest in his students' creations. Classes were held at his bungalow, and he mostly read at the course registrants until, one by one, they dropped out.

In recent decades, however, the idea of the writer as an individualistic outsider has acquired a layer of dust. We used to be okay with literary types asserting independent, fortified egos. Poets and novelists were almost *expected* to be aloof, even anti-social. But today, we're too savvy to indulge such a romantic myth. The aloof rebel is nothing more than an affectation, we tell ourselves, a pair of Ray-Bans you slip on. When Bob Dylan was slow to acknowledge his Nobel Prize for Literature, many were scandalized. "It's impolite and arrogant," huffed a member of the Swedish Academy.

What, then, has displaced the idiosyncratic recluse? Literary community—that is, a supportive web of likeminded practitioners, braided together and ready to enfold you. In recent years, thoughtful poet-critics like Stewart Cole have made an eloquent case for the distinction between community and scene, and the desirability of the former over the latter. Jess Taylor has also reflected at great length on the subject. (Her ultimate conclusion: "We must keep building in order for our community to be sustained, and for it to grow and thrive.") Tatiana Morand has critiqued her own shyness and pledged to make an effort to make CanLit "a more welcoming community." The tagline for the Canadian Women in the Literary Arts organization is "Fostering Community for Canadian Women Working in the Literary Arts." The fine print underlying such fine feelings is clear: community is an unalloyed good.

Writing is such grueling, lonely work, that it's not hard to see the appeal of any thinking that encourages you to engage with other carbon-based lifeforms. Plus, didn't graduate school insist that writers are socially constructed anyway, the products of power and privilege? You might as well accept that you're a node in a network.

But you don't have to buy into the myth of the Byronic bard to worry about the way our novelists and poets—valued for their independence of vision and language—now pine to be part of the crowd. What do we lose when writers are afraid to stand alone?

Let's be clear: writers always occupy some sort of social context. The Dadaists had Cabaret Voltaire; Dorothy Parker, the Algonquin Hotel. Margaret Atwood cut her teeth in Toronto coffeehouses. Christopher Hitchens, Martin Amis, and Clive James honed their wit upon the whetstone of their Friday lunches—"the potential stuff of a new 'Bloomsbury' legend," Hitchens half-joked. Even the hermetic Emily Dickinson, who asserted that "The Soul selects her own Society," had the society of Thomas Wentworth Higginson, a Unitarian minister. Higginson occasionally corresponded with the recluse and helped see Dickinson's first collection to print after her death.

But while no one is truly isolated, writers have become more entangled than ever. Workshops, readings, book launches, conferences, artists' colonies, and other glorified mixers increasingly press literary types upon one another. Creative writing instructors urge their charges to get out there and network. Social media ensures we're always connected. Open letters demand our signatures. The contemporary acknowledgements page is a goblet that runneth over. (The fine poet Michael Prior thanks more than sixty people in his recent debut.) It's now almost unthinkable not to run your manuscript by a long receiving line of applauding peers.

But be careful: those same peers might one day boo and jeer. Literary controversies are now less about aesthetic feuds and more about group outrage. (See Boydengate. See the Steven Galloway intrigue.) "The left is in shambles in North America," writes Carmen Aguirre. "It has become the new puritanical church, shaming, bullying, condemning, and expelling anyone in its ranks who is seen as taking a misstep." Similarly, if you break with orthodoxy in the literary world, you will find yourself branded a heretic. When I suggested in *The Walrus* that critics should reference themselves a little less in their reviews and essays—brilliant advice I'm clearly forgoing—I might as well have draped myself in "Make America Great Again" bunting or throttled a sloth on YouTube. Writers I was once friendly with disappeared. Writers I'd never met fumed on social media. The whiff of scorched bridge practically wafted through the WIFI.

The most consistent complaint directed at my essay? That it was, in effect, anti-community. One writer accused me of trying to push away the "routinely marginalized, whose points of view are less frequently given voice." Another said that my thesis "overlooks that subjective approaches to criticism allow for a broader inclusion of vantage points."

Canadian poets are especially energetic tribalists. They tend to swerve and feint *en masse* like a school of tuna. Perhaps they recognize artist-as-individual as a bad career move. Exiling oneself to the metaphorical basement, as novelists often do, won't yield a tangible payoff like a bestseller. Instead, the material rewards for poets often come in the form of, well, more community! Teaching gigs, invitations to read, and the interest of grant and prize juries. The $150,000 Griffin Poetry Prize, in particular, has often seemed like one of the most blatant of literary cliques, with many apparent tendrils lashing together judges and winners.

At a more basic level, however, literary community can have a deadly impact. The most obvious fatality: your critical faculty. It becomes harder to file an honest review of a book if you're always rubbing shoulders. Not long after I first started writing criticism, I ventured out to a reading on the invitation of an editor—and almost immediately encountered a poet whose debut I'd recently been assigned to review. His poetry was dull, but he seemed decent enough. It took me months to file my piece, and even then I pulled my final punch—and I'm one of the few jerks in Canada willing to bloody a book of poetry. How are younger, less jerky writers ever going to develop the independent spirit required to lob a rotten tomato if they've committed themselves to nurturing the community garden?

That's the ultimate casualty here—an independent spirit. And while most Canadian poetry critics rarely sound a negative note, most Canadian poets sound indistinguishable. If you could shake the bylines free from a volume of *The Best Canadian Poetry*, you'd have a devil of a time restoring them to their rightful poems.

"'What is the role of the writer to her society?' was a question Wallace Stevens took up and his answer was: none," says Souvankham Thammavongsa, a poet whose strange poetic miniatures underscore her belief that she represents a constituency of one. A writer's real responsibility, she suggests, is "to build a voice and to keep building that voice." This stands in stark contrast to the civic-minded suggestion that writers apply their bricks and mortar to some cloud-city of togetherness. The latter sounds lovely, the former, merely honest.

The poet Kay Ryan, one of a few one-offs still around, has written eloquently about the need for writers—especially younger ones—to develop a carapace against what she calls "camaraderie."

For Ryan, this means avoiding the delivery systems by which literary community, like a virus, transmits itself: workshops and conferences. It means shrugging off the endless obligations that other writers will foist upon you. It means siloing yourself in silence. Ryan's advice, quoted earlier in this book, is calm, counterintuitive, and considerably cheaper than an MFA:

> Let's not share. Really. Go off in your own direction way too far, get lost, test the metal of your work in your own acids. These are experiments you can perform down in that old kind of workshop, where Dad used to hide out from too many other people's claims on him.

Find his "own direction" is certainly what Canadian poet Bruce Taylor did. Taylor has attracted a pair of A.M. Klein Awards, but has laboured mostly in un-networked obscurity, issuing something like a collection a decade, to crickets, since the 1980s. His is an idiosyncratic vision. (He describes "seventeenth-century rain" as "curled / like a great cascading periwig / over the cankered rooftiles of old Delft.") Interviewed once by the CBC, he outlined his day job: "I renovate our big, confusing old house, prepare meals, and drive the kids around. Which is to say, I am a housewife." If CanLit has become a community garden, Taylor's work belongs squarely indoors, in the cellar, pickled in the brine of its own stubborn intelligence for future consumption.

Writers like Taylor know that they can extract very nearly all the society they require from literature. They are adult enough to recognize that writing is a selfish, solitary activity, and that it's the quality of their work, not their capacity for kibitzing, that ultimately secures a meaningful, long-term readership. They might have a few literary friends or a social media account; they might not. But if writing well is their aim, they will tend to resent claims on their time. And they will tend to prize a commodity more precious than community: privacy.

Asked recently which three writers she would invite to a "literary dinner party," the prose stylist Fran Lebowitz offered the definitive desert island list: "None. I would never do it. My idea of a great literary dinner party is Fran, eating alone, reading a book. That's my idea of a literary dinner party." If that's too clever for you, try Stephen Dedalus in James Joyce's *A Portrait of the Artist as a Young Man*, who offers up a handy model for being a writer:

> I will try to express myself in some mode of life or art as freely as I can and as wholly as I can, using for my defense the only arms I allow myself to use—dialogue, community, and workshopping.

I'm kidding, of course. Actually, the weapons with which Stephen proposed to arm himself were "silence, exile, and cunning." You probably wouldn't have enjoyed his company.

(*The Walrus*, 2017)

Alan Moore and Brian Bolland's
The Killing Joke

On first glance, the film *Batman: The Killing Joke*—which swings through theaters on July 25 for just two days before going to DVD—looks like it should've been consigned to afternoon television, with its choppy animation. But this new Batman feature isn't for kids. *The Killing Joke* explains the origins of the Joker, Batman's arch-nemesis, and plumbs beneath the face paint for a pathology. It's sourced from a specific pool of graphic novels that were authored by one of two men—Frank Miller or Alan Moore—between 1986 and 1988. Their mission: to make superhero comics visible to adults by dialing up the darkness.

    The dial, of course, got stuck. Acclaimed works like Miller's *The Dark Knight Returns* (1986) and *Batman: Year One* (1987) as well as Moore's *Watchmen* (1987) and *Batman: The Killing Joke* (1988) introduced a gloom that never quite lifted. They recast spandexed superheroes as violent vigilantes, and lowered them into atmospheres fraught with gravity, like the Cold War. "Miller and Moore are often credited with helping the superhero genre grow up," wrote Jeet Heer recently in a smart piece for *The New Republic*, "although their idea of maturity at times seemed mainly to mean including explicit scenes of torture and rape."

    But it's wrong to tie the thoughtful Moore too closely to the reactionary Miller. Moore's celebrated series *V for Vendetta* posted a warning about Thatcherism and supplied the Occupy movement with a face. He turned a repudiated horror comic, *Swamp Thing*, into a repudiation of Reaganism. In 1988, he went so far as to form the publishing imprint Mad Love so that he could bring out a comic protesting homophobic English legislation. Compared to the rest of his work, then, *The Killing Joke* marked a regression. The last of the much-lauded graphic novels of the late eighties, it exemplified traits that continue to bedevil the superhero genre today—misogyny, nihilism, and sadism for the sake of fanboys.

"*The Killing Joke* was not a project instigated by Alan," writes the artist Brian Bolland in the afterword to the 2008 edition, "nor was it, as far as I know, a labour of love for him." This is an unsurprising revelation. By the late eighties, Moore, arguably the biggest name in comics, had stretched the concept of men in spandex as far as it could go.

His twelve-issue series *Watchmen* was looking a lot like the genre's *Citizen Kane*. Moore seemed to have consolidated everything that had come before, from Golden Age propaganda to pulpy fifties horror, demonstrating effortless facility with the medium and its history, while reversing superhero cliches. "I'm not a Republic serial villain," says the villain toward the end of *Watchmen*, in his Antarctic lair. (He's been cornered by the heroes, who assume they've foiled his plot.) "Do you seriously think I'd explain my masterstroke if there remained the slightest chance of you affecting its outcome?" Unbeknownst to the heroes, he's already wiped out New York.

In the superhero movies of today, violence is a non-event. Cities are routinely incinerated, their faceless occupants vaporized out of frame. But the obliteration of a major American city at the end of *Watchmen* was moving precisely because the previous 11 issues had acquainted readers with its citizens. Moore wisely reserved plenty of panels for the non-superpowered civilian, who doesn't keep spandex under her clothes. Then, at the start of issue 12, the illustrator, Dave Gibbons, broke the nine-panel grid, the book's dominant style, and used whole pages to pan across piled corpses. The images were devastating; form exploded to accommodate content's blast radius.

The Killing Joke dispensed with such thoughtfulness. Batman's nemesis, it turns out, was a struggling comedian who lost his pregnant wife the very same day he plunged into a vat at the local chemical plant—conveniently located next to the local playing-card company. ("All it takes is one bad day to reduce the sanest man alive to lunacy," explains the Joker.) Running parallel to this over-determined origin is a present-day plot in which the Joker conspires to illustrate the "random injustice" of life. He shoots the character Batgirl in the spine, then trusses her father up in bondage gear, taunting him with photographs of his naked, paralyzed daughter. When the time came for his editor to sign off on the maiming, Moore recalled him saying, "Yeah, okay, cripple the bitch." Later, Moore admitted, "It was probably one of the areas where they should've reined me in, but they didn't."

You can trace the easy nihilism of many contemporary comics and movies—from *Spawn* to *Kick-Ass*—to cynical products like *The Killing Joke*. It's the nihilism of a third-rate Nietzsche, the kind of starter-kit philosophy that beguiles adolescents. That Batman eventually gets his man and restores order is beside the point. Whether drawn by Bolland or played by Heath Ledger, the Joker is the real draw of the story. Post-Moore, he became postmodern, the personification of moral relativism, of pure chaos. Post-9/11, he became an opiate; as the critic Stephen Metcalf suggested in *Slate* in the wake of the Aurora shooting, the "charismatic malevolence" of characters like the Joker has become dangerously addictive in American culture.

Bolland, for his part, banged out a series of irresistible illustrations, including the iconic cover: a close-up of the Joker aiming a camera at the reader. The implication is that the reader occupies the position of the naked, crippled Batgirl. It's the sort of iconography that's best quarantined in the common room, next to *Scarface* and *Fight Club* posters. Nevertheless, *The Killing Joke* attracted industry awards and admirers. Tim Burton and Christopher Nolan's cinematic Jokers, played by Nicholson and Ledger, respectively, sprang like paper dolls from the pattern set by Moore. "I loved *The Killing Joke*," Burton said. "It's my favourite. It's the first comic I ever loved."

But read between the panels, and it's hard not to feel the pressure of an unvoiced word balloon, inflated near to bursting: Moore's own exhaustion with the arid genre he had helped terraform. Eventually, he disavowed *The Killing Joke*. "Brian [Bolland] did a wonderful job on the art but I don't think it's a very good book," Moore told Barry Kavanagh in 2000. "It's not saying anything very interesting."

In the nineties, Moore laboured over intricate graphic novels for adults, about anything other than superheroes. He researched Victorian England and explored a conspiracy theory about Jack the Ripper and the Royal Family. He relocated Alice, Wendy, and Dorothy (of Wonderland, Neverland, and Oz) to an Austrian hotel on the cusp of World War I, and crafted an epic, controversial tome of erotica. When he returned to men in tights, he made a point of directing his energies to more innocent characters like Tom Strong, who radiated the warmth of the Golden Age of comics.

Moore had innovated once again; "kids' stuff" was no longer a knock against quality.

Moore's disavowal, however, hasn't exactly dissuaded paying customers. To meet demand, over 300 theaters have been added to the two-day showing of *The Killing Joke*, bringing the total count to 1,000 screens. Meanwhile, the graphic novel has already enjoyed the deluxe treatment; the twentieth-anniversary edition comes swaddled in an introduction, afterword, rough sketches, and other dissertation aids. That's the real joke, and it's a killer: the man who helped create the conditions for cynical blockbusters like *The Killing Joke* was the first to reject the product—and did so decades ago. It turns out the superhero genre's greatest hero was also in some ways its greatest villain.

(*The Atlantic*, 2016)

Toni Morrison's Assertion that "All Good Art is Political!"

Donald Trump's victory over Hillary Clinton ran a current through the liberal electorate, jolting many of us into all kinds of activity. Some have shared primers on how to reboot a faith in democracy or pickle our ideals against the coming winter. Others are organizing demonstrations or calling to restore civics to syllabi. Support for journalism has accordioned like an EKG. Even children are drafting correspondence to the Commander-in-Chief. Such twitches in the corpus of liberal democracy have made for fortifying stuff, especially at a time when white nationalist zombies are on the rise and taking jobs in the White House.

But what about the artists? wondered some of us. What role should they play in the resistance? The morning after the election, Dan Piepenbring took to *The Paris Review* blog to rally creative types:

> We owe it to ourselves to do the work. I want to encourage you. If you aspire to write, put aside all the niceties and sureties about what art should be and write something that makes the scales fall from our eyes.

Vox, for its part, ran a piece titled, "6 writers on why we need art now." *The Huffington Post* went with "Dear Artists: We Need You More Than Ever." "It's the poet's job to offer us a way out," Richard Blanco told *Time*, "a glimmer of hope, something that gets toward another space, another place—a healthier place."

A running theme was rolling up the sleeves of one's paint-smudged smock. For example, several of the pieces repurposed an old Toni Morrison quote, circa the re-election of George W. Bush: "This is *precisely* the time when artists go to work." Productivity was also on the mind of art critic Jerry Saltz, over at *New York* magazine: "They may not know it yet, but Trump's victory is a crucible of possibility for a new generation, who will do what artists have always done in times like these: go back to work." You could practically hear the unbroken spines of Idea Journals being cracked all across the nation.

Many of these responses are powered by the belief that art gets shit done—that it's good for us, socially useful, disruptive. "[A]rt is, in part, how civilizations heal, provoke and change minds," wrote Katherine Brooks in the *Huffington Post*. This is a fine idea, and surely felt good to indulge after an election that left many feeling powerless. But it's an idea that ought to come with an age limit: stop consuming after university. Those who make bold claims for the utility of paintings or poems risk reducing art to an omega-3 supplement. Such claims mostly serve to cast their claimants as virtuous and right-thinking. In venerating art, we're usually just venerating ourselves.

"All good art is political!" insists Morrison. "There is none that isn't." Shakespeare is political, she argues, because he wrote about kings. But it's hard to extract a clear agenda from the *Henriad* or to detect a party platform behind *King Lear*. Plus, no play that corrals such complicated, far-ranging voices as Falstaff or the Fool can be said to occupy an obvious political position. This is why no one rushes to label *Henry IV* or *King Lear* "political art."

Political art is art that's especially driven by an agenda or ideology. It has specific designs on its audience, and as a result, it's hard to do well; we remember outliers like W. B. Yeats's "Easter 1916" or Pablo Picasso's *Guernica* (1937) or Marvin Gaye's "Inner City Blues" (1971) less because of their political goals than because of their aesthetic achievements—their memorable forms, original metaphors, and mesmerizing grooves. It's an awful, adult truth, but the degree to which one's earnest message is on the right side of history isn't enough to redeem a clichéd image or rote expression. "Don't think what you have to say is important," says the critic William Logan. "The way you say it is what's important. What you have to say is rubbish."

When blinding style (the way you say it) defers to blunt didacticism (the rubbish), the result is such stuff as John Lennon's *Sometime in New York City* (1972), a hectoring protest album, date-stamped by indignation and largely devoid of wit or nuance. And the blunter a piece of political art gets, the more bludgeoned we tend to feel. This is why urging artists to get political is so perilous; most of them are apt to produce sledgehammers.

For the record, I applaud the cast of *Hamilton* for calling out Vice-President Elect Mike Pence when he attended a recent performance. But the cast made its stand only *after* the production was over, during the curtain call, as Pence made his way for the exit. The actors didn't improvise a new scene about a hotel developer trolling the founding fathers on Twitter. They used their platform, as the beneficiaries of a Broadway hit, to deliver a direct message under the glare of house lights. When it comes to politics, this is probably the most useful thing the few artists famous enough to command our attention can do: leverage the glow of celebrity to illuminate liberal concerns.

Less famous artists, who don't have the ear of a Pence, can still sign petitions or stuff envelopes or knock on doors for the Democratic Party. But they would do well to resist overestimating the power their art possesses. In *The Paris Review*, Piepenbring urges us to "Forget the tired axioms about showing and telling, about sense of place—any possible obstruction—and write to destroy complacency, to rattle people, to help people, first and foremost yourself."

And yet artists have been self-righteously contriving to "rattle" the poor masses and "destroy complacency" since the dawn of Dada, with ever-diminishing returns. (See the Brechtians, who thought that dosing theatregoers with a dollop of alienation would make them more critical. Or the language poets, who thought that dynamiting the subject-verb-object construction would bring down capitalism.) As for helping people, there are probably more practical ways to support those who feel threatened by the prospect of a Muslim registry than toiling over your novel at Yaddo.

But nudging artists to call up their congressman isn't as exciting as urging them to call on their muse. Saltz insists that art is "galvanizing or clarifying or (believe it or not) empowering," and that the Trump calamity is a "kind of call to action that will yield things not yet fathomed or decanted," even if some of us "keep posting pictures of food and stay immersed in the culture of celebrity and complacency." (But what's wrong with posting pictures of food? And why does the writer feel he needs both "fathomed" *and* "decanted?") He continues:

> More important, the shift or clusterfuck under way may jar professionalized artists from being part and parcel of the career machine and return them and all of us to our rightful outsider gypsy position—aristocratic bohemians with highly calibrated bullshit detectors. After all, why should art want to serve consensus? What is interesting, or exciting, or urgent about consensus?

The wariness of "professionalism," the contempt for something called "the career machine," the celebration of "gypsy" outsiders—this is the sort of prose that produces raised fists in undergraduates, Pink Floyd fans, devotees of Objectivism, and, well, Donald Trump supporters.

Can we call "bullshit" on those who make a fetish of "highly calibrated bullshit detectors?" Can we agree that the election has already done enough to romanticize the outsider, that mythic figure who supposedly transcends the system, the mainstream, and other such straw-stuffed structures of conformity? It might not be "exciting," as Saltz would prefer it, but we could do worse than busying ourselves with the boring task of building some consensus. Whether that involves "aristocratic bohemians" is up to them.

In the meantime, let's stop calling for artists to get to work, or heal us, or rattle us, or whatever. Those who decline to create political art, *pace* Morrison, aren't necessarily voting for the status quo. Changing minds is a big job, and many of our greatest artists have already failed at it (if beautifully, memorably). After all, an electorate that can easily possess a copy of George Orwell's *Nineteen Eighty-Four* nevertheless decided that it still needed to elect a Big Brother.

(*The Walrus*, 2016)

Criticism's Overinvestment in Fanboy Concerns

F ANBOYS ARE LOATHSOME, as every right-thinking person is supposed to believe. Overinvested in their enthusiasms, they can't countenance their flaws. Enthusiasms, here, means superheroes and sci-fi. But many subcultures are afflicted by some version of the fanboy. From Leafs fans to Tarantino devotees, some of us are always prepared to root for whatever product is put out on the field. Affection is a priori.

"The final *Rogue One* trailer dropped this morning, and it was in a word; awesome," wrote one fan, a few months back. "Not going to mince words, but this last trailer has me more excited than I was [for] *The Force Awakens*. Yeah, I said it. This last trailer was the stuff of magic." Perhaps unsurprisingly, reactions to the actual movie, now out, have been mixed. But then back in 1998, the very sight of the Lucasfilm logo at the start of the trailer for *The Phantom Menace,* now widely regarded as a disaster, drew the fanboy's approval and cheers.

The fanboy's natural orientation is rapturous anticipation, but he can also be aggrieved, even pre-emptively defensive. Earlier this year, many recoiled from the prospect of *Rogue One*'s female lead, and some Trump supporters are now boycotting the film. Fans who hadn't yet set eyes on *Batman v Superman* nevertheless attacked those critics who'd panned it. Critics of *Suicide Squad* found themselves the target of guerrilla warfare, waged under cover of comments section. Fanboys now routinely swell the spaces below the professional critic's byline, whose authority no longer impresses.

Some rebels have even contrived to bring down the Death Star of film criticism, the reviews aggregator site Rotten Tomatoes.

Over the last year, critics have expended an armory's worth of intellectual firepower on fanboy concerns, while squeezing off small, easy shots at the figure of the fanboy himself. Reviewing *Suicide Squad*, *The New Republic* sneered at "fanboy wankery." *The Chicago Tribune* mocked some fanboy's blog review by quoting from it. ("He rilly rilly liked [*Suicide Squad*], calling it 'insane'...") Even the conservative *National Review*, which had the poor taste to admire *Batman v Superman*, suggested that fanboys comprise a child-like "mob," too immature to appreciate such sophisticated product. (My earlier piece on *The Killing Joke* couldn't resist rattling off a round.)

But it was possibly David Edelstein, writing about *Suicide Squad* for *New York*, who betrayed the reason behind all this superiority: envy. "How early will the fanboys who flock to see *Suicide Squad*—smug in the knowledge that they've won the day, that Hollywood is now desperate to cater to their tastes above all others'—admit that they're watching the year's most muddled piece of storytelling?"

If the fanboy has "won the day," as Edelstein suggests, then surely one of the losers is the critic, who used to steer cultural conversations, but now enjoys far less power than the paying customer. Consider the case of *Ghostbusters*. After some misogynists rejected, sight unseen, Paul Feig's all-female reboot, Hollywood appeared to panic and proposed an all-male panacea, featuring Channing Tatum.

The rise of the angry, overindulged fanboy, however, isn't simply the fault of studios (which will always endeavour to sate their audiences) or social media (which often dispenses soapboxes to bad people). Critics and culture writers have also played a role in empowering the very fanboys they decry.

The fanboy has an origin story. He made his network debut on May 9, 1991, when *The Simpsons* introduced Jeffrey Albertson, a comic shop owner. Sometimes called "Comic Book Guy," Albertson presented as lonely, acerbic, and overweight, bundled from behind by ponytail. He came to be supplanted by more positive representations, including the *Dungeons and Dragons* enthusiasts on Judd Apatow's beloved, short-lived show *Freaks and Geeks* and the young physicists on the popular sitcom *The Big Bang Theory*.

The sudden visibility of the fanboy—and fangirl—marked the culmination of a larger shift that began back in the 1970s, with the rise of the direct market and, by extension, comic shops and conventions. These spaces enabled comic collectors, Trekkies, connoisseurs of sci-fi, and other breeds of marginalized geek to assemble and find sanctuary. By the late 1980s, marketers had begun to take notice, anticipating the big-budget conventions of today—chief among them, San Diego's annual Comic-Con, where studios screen trailers and court large concentrations of fanboy. Like my favourite superhero Tom Strong, reared in a high-gravity chamber by Victorian scientists, the fanboy is a product of social pressures. Hollywood's scrutiny has only strengthened him.

Meanwhile, adult-oriented comics like *Maus*—Art Spiegelman's holocaust memoir in which Jews are represented as mice—were drawing attention from mainstream journalists and critics. Fanboy concerns found their way onto curricula, into canons. Academics like Slavoj Žižek meditated fashionably on *The Matrix*. *Time* magazine counted *Watchmen* among the one hundred best novels of all time. All of a sudden, the fanboy, once cloistered in a subculture, found himself living in a world that privileged his concerns.

But these days, as *Salon*'s Andrew O'Hehir has suggested, critics "can get overly invested" in "spectacles" like *Suicide Squad*. Everything from the latest episode of *Game of Thrones* to the trailer for *Rogue One* gets its exegesis. The murky politics of *Star Wars* are plumbed. Great reserves of knowledge about method acting are brought to bear on the matter of Jared Leto's Joker. Once upon a time, the serious critic viewed comics and other fanboy concerns—narrowly, through slits in a spandex mask—as kids' stuff. His more enlightened heirs, however, have overcorrected. They tend to assume that the slightest superhero product requires their reflection. If "hardcore fanboys" occupy "airless lairs," to repurpose a phrase from *Slate*'s film critic Dana Stevens, they are nevertheless well oxygenated by the attention of a lot of very smart people.

You can argue that this is simply the state of things, that film critics have to respond to the output of Hollywood, to the movies people are talking about. But critics can be more than simply reactive arms of the culture industry. Critics can also help guide and shape taste by virtue of what they elect to write about—or don't. "As long as we are paying attention, or at least buying tickets, the system is working to its own satisfaction," wrote *New York Times* film critic A.O. Scott in his review of *Batman v Superman*. Sadly, Scott followed this excellent point by filing opinions about *Star Trek Beyond* and *Suicide Squad*—by continuing to pay attention! But critics could absent themselves from the "system" easily enough by electing not to file reviews of superhero movies, or to file fewer of them. They could leave the fanboy to his concerns and pursue other cultural conversations.

Yet they often don't. Leon Wieseltier offers a hint as to why. In his review of Scott's book *Better Living Through Criticism*, Wieseltier sees a critic with an "aversion to philosophical and aesthetic commitment," a critic who refuses to make choices, who "honors the heights but gladly descends from them." You can apply Wieseltier's words to many of us, who no longer aspire to be prescriptive. It's fashionable—preferable—to be seen to abhor hierarchies, to take a pass on passing judgment. Low culture, high culture—it's all just texts, as they say in the graduate seminar, where many critics and culture writers incubate. Texts to convert into takes.

Let's be clear: the racist trolls who chased *Ghostbusters* actress Leslie Jones off Twitter ought to be banished to the undersides of bridges. The dude who threatens to rape and kill a film critic for insufficiently praising a Batman movie ought to be handcuffed and hauled off. But these aren't true fanboys. The true fanboy would have too much brand loyalty to reject *Rogue One* because it has a female lead. He wouldn't boycott the movie because its screenwriter expressed an anti-Trump sentiment. The true fanboy is relatively harmless, and no more insufferable than the average person who feels moved to inflict her opinion on others' feeds.

If anything, the fanboy's monk-like devotion to certain artifacts and iconic characters represents a kind of aesthetic commitment that many critics and culture writers now lack. Defending films and other cultural products you haven't experienced, of course, is silly. But fanboys are expressing a form of faith. "[T]he most iconic and popular superhero that comic book fans have never read," says the blurb on my reissue of *Miracleman*. Legends breed in the lacunae of a fanboy's knowledge. He is clerical, not critical.

In any case, he isn't really the problem. Not too long ago, I asked *Slate*'s Stephen Metcalf if contemporary critics, animated by "a strain of fashionable and aggressive anti-elitism," have become overinvested in pop culture. "We have lost the university and the popular press as automatic transmitters of unpopular culture," he replied. "We've seen the giants of modernism cut down to size, as it were, because difficulty is (so it's said) the strategy of the weak."

Many of us have excused ourselves from the inconvenient task of reckoning with challenging works of art and explicating them for a general audience. Plus, fanboy concerns make for such easy pickings. (As John Oliver recently observed, complaining about superhero movies is "the most Internet thing imaginable.") But it might be time for a few of our more successful mainstream critics to own their frustrations and have the courage to abandon the superhero beat—or at least cut back on their coverage of men in tights. It might be time to plant their feet, Avengers-style, and take a stand.

(*The Walrus*, 2016)

Criticism's Overanalysis
of Pop Culture

A FEW WEEKS AGO, *Slate*'s *Culture Gabfest* turned its considerable attention to the new Lorde album, *Melodrama*. The podcast is the finest of its kind, in which several talking heads (each well stocked with opinions) stake out a position on some cultural product or occasion. The *Gabfest*'s three critics, led by Stephen Metcalf, have wandered the Whitney Museum, marked the death of Philip Seymour Hoffman, and leaned into the swerves in philosopher Robert Nozick's thinking.

The discussion of a twenty-year-old's pop album should've been par for the podcast. Still, it was hard not to feel that my favourite pundits, who had been joined by *Slate*'s music critic Carl Wilson, were overanalyzing the text at hand. When Dana Stevens, an otherwise thoughtful film reviewer, sincerely wondered, "How does [*Melodrama*] fall in the pantheon of breakup albums, or would you deny that it is one?", the music critic took pains to deny. "I think it's kind of a heartbreak album," he said, with a slight note of hesitance, as if this were rich, unsettled turf to tussle over. Perhaps the "breakup" and "heartbreak" binary is as consequential a distinction in pop criticism as "ode" and "elegy" in poetry. Perhaps these very smart adults needed finer hairs to split.

Let me hasten to add: I've been consulting the *Culture Gabfest* religiously since it began a decade ago. I love the spectacle of pop culture critics being brainy—provided they top up their thoughts with a foamy dollop of wit and style.

But the trend these days is to tread heavily; increasingly, pop culture critics are bringing more brains to bear upon their modest subjects than seems required. The result often reads like a parody of criticism, freighted with gravity as if filed from Krypton. Here's *The New York Times*'s Jon Caramanica on boy-band alumnus Harry Styles:

> And so the self-titled solo debut of Harry Styles, one of [One Direction's] two breakout stars—the other being Zayn Malik—is both an answer to his past and a template for his future. Mr. Malik, who makes mildly sludgy pop-R&B, got to market first, and also seems at least tangentially interested in the market. Mr. Styles would like to be excluded from that narrative. So goes this sometimes great, sometimes foggy album, which is almost bold in its resistance to contemporary pop music aesthetics.

If you didn't know any better, you'd assume Caramanica was talking about John Coltrane seizing control of the "narrative" by parting ways with the Miles Davis Quintet. So seriously does he take his aspiring man-boy—fomenting a "resistance" to "aesthetics," no less—you can practically hear his highbrow furrowing. Even when he means to wink, Caramanica comes on dry and grave. "First post-boy-band albums," he explains, "are also where symbols of maturity are dangled: Mr. Styles would like you to know he has been debauched, or something like it."

Perhaps this is what Northrop Frye sounded like when faced with having to close read yet another post-boy-band, symbol-rich resurrection myth. In any case, Mr. Caramanica would like you to know he has been critical, or something like it.

There's a long history of first-rate minds taking the seemingly second rate very seriously. Roland Barthes' classic monograph *Mythologies* (1957) was one of the first attempts to flush out into the open the meaning of such ephemera as soap, detergent, and wrestling. Later,

Pauline Kael threw her byline behind lurid Brian De Palma thrillers. Greil Marcus detected great depths in Elvis's performances, and duly dragged them. I worshipped Elvis and, for a time, Marcus's 1975 book *Mystery Train*, which contains passages like this one:

> Elvis has survived the contradictions of his career, perhaps because there is so much room and so much mystery in Herman Melville's most telling comment on this country: "The Declaration of Independence makes a difference."

That would've struck me as pretty cool when I was younger—not for what it revealed about Elvis, which was not very much, but for the sheer moxie of muscling the King of Rock and Roll and the author of *Moby-Dick* into the same weighty sentence. That was a move on par with a lip curl.

In time, however, I came to prefer the froth-fine touch of writers like Clive James, Troy Patterson, Fran Lebowitz, and Anthony Lane. Here's the latter on Wonder Woman's digs:

> The name of the island is true to myth, which suggests that someone at DC Comics has been knuckling down to Herodotus and the Greek tragedians. In "Prometheus Bound," written in the fifth century B.C., we are told that Themiscyra is the home of the Amazons, "who loathe all men." In the movie, directed by Patty Jenkins, the islanders don't get much of a chance to work on their loathing, because men are blissfully absent and, by definition, superfluous. The women are thus free to practice their homely skills, such as leaning sideways from the saddle of a galloping horse until their heads are on a level with their stirrups and then, from this comfortable position, loosing off an arrow at the target.

The scholarspeak cut by the colloquial ("knuckling down to Herodotus"); the light way with a logician's weighty turn ("thus"); the eye for unexposed clichés (that tendency of action heroes to go horizontal to horse); the stylist's apt, unimpeachable phrasing ("loosing off an arrow")—Lane is too serious about what he's doing to take his subject too seriously. Compared to this, Marcus, peering solemnly down the decades at Melville, has lost perspective.

And yet, after the Culture Wars of the 1980s—which razed the Western Canon and blew out the dimensions that defined where a critic could roam—it made for a good career move to lose perspective. By the 2000s, critics were engaged in an escalating arms race to make the most explosive claim on behalf of unfissionable material like Limp Bizkit or *Star Wars* prequels. What's notable about these essays is their tendency to apply more smarts and style than seems warranted by the source material; to overanalyze and out-write.

Consider how Jonah Weiner, in his spirited defence of Limp Bizkit, takes note of frontman Fred Durst's "infelicities on the mic" or "the knuckle sandwich [that] is his emotional lingua franca" or the "critique" that "bubbles up between his lines." Jesse Hassenger, defending the *Star Wars* prequels, also overreaches. "This could turn into what fiction writers might call an imitative fallacy," he writes, "where the prequel trilogy is made intentionally (and unproductively) boring to depict its less immediately exciting subject matter."

But like most things overdone, the trick of overanalyzing isn't hard to master, and can be applied to virtually anything. Because there isn't a knot of allusions to undo in a Carly Rae Jepsen song, the contemporary critic (Barthes's knowing heir) tends to pore over the object's sociological aspects and ideological missteps—how it's handling gender, say. But why the earnest focus on Carly Rae Jepsen? Because, well, it's easy! It's easy to write about things that don't have a ton of depth to them. It's much harder to scale a Daryl Hine poem than look down upon Scarlett Johansson's *Ghost in the Shell*—which is why many writers have forsworn criticism for culture writing.

Culture writing caricatures the outward trappings of criticism (the seriousness, the lingo) but largely waves off aesthetic judgment, and doubles down on the sociology. The result is funhouse prose that warps its subject out of all proportion. Consider the opening of a recent *New Yorker* essay, in which a new Chinese boy band is said to "renovate the form." Renovate the form! That's a small phrase, but a conspicuous one, meant to confer the gravitas that attaches to heroic couplets and wonder cabinets, I suppose.

Or consider, again, Caramanica who elevates a Taylor Swift song about her love life with the word "metanarrative" and describes Swift herself as a "transgressor." Or Jody Rosen's 4400-word defense of schlock, in which he insists that "schlock is too important a tradition not to take seriously and that taking it seriously means making astute judgments about that tradition."

You can plot all this on a curve, beginning with figures like Marcus, that founding Freud of pop overanalysis—pop culture criticism has reached peak seriousness.

None of this, I should point out, is meant to advance some silly value system pitting high art against pop culture; I'll take the John Travolta vehicle *Blow Out* over Antonioni's *Blow-Up* any day. The point is to judge the critic, not the cultural product. Perhaps there's someone out there capable of making an album by that "transgressor" Swift sound as subversive and lyrically substantial as Patti Smith's *Horses*. But a critic like Caramanica or Rosen probably won't be the one to do it. You just don't trust them to know the difference. They treat every pop album the same way—as automatically worthy of scholarly scrutiny.

That said, if what you're working with is the Carly Rae Jepsen Songbook, aren't your critical responses going to be somewhat limited, even predetermined? Aren't you likely to either inflate the object's worth, grabbing for all the gravitas you can, or put a pin to it? And if it's the latter, aren't you apt to conclude, as some killjoy at *The New Republic* recently did, that Jepsen's music "reduces the experience of teenage girls to fantasy instead of taking them on their own terms as actors in this world"? (What was the critic expecting from the co-author of the delightful "Call Me Maybe"? A Kathy Acker cut-up?) Moreover, if the assigned text is an exploitative dating show like *The Bachelorette*, you're apt to discover, as a critic at *The Atlantic* recently did, that *The Bachelorette* is, well, an exploitative dating show!

It's not that these pundits are off base in taking shots at teen pop and reality TV; their critiques are accurate enough. It's that they've brought their phonebook-thick *Norton Anthology of Theory and Criticism* to a pillow fight. And if a critic can't tell that their ambitions are disproportionate to their airy subjects, then they have no business toying with trifles.

(*The Walrus*, 2017)

Authors' Injunctions to Read Widely

THE CLICHÉS THAT WRITERS often share—"show, don't tell," "write what you know"—are harmless enough. Like popcorn, they cut a light and fluffy figure and probably got their start as a kernel of truth. Plus, everybody knows not to take them too seriously. When a writer urges you to "write every day" or "always keep a notebook," you can safely assume that plenty of first-rate talents have broken with these bromides.

But there's one tip that doesn't seem optional, one tip that's practically scripture, as if hunter-gatherers discovered it on clay tablets long ago and transmitted it, via oral tradition, down to your MFA instructor. "Read widely," says Joyce Carol Oates. "Read widely," says Stephen King. "Read widely," says the Google hive mind in deafening, choral unison.

What does "read widely" mean? Perhaps it speaks to the importance of a balanced diet—a comedy of manners today, a concrete poem tomorrow. Or maybe it means toggling fashionably between high and low, between Mina Loy poems and Mini-Wheats boxes. Or maybe it means testing a spectrum of texts, like paint chips, against your monochromatic taste. Or expanding your bandwidth just enough to capture some pirate-radio clamour—to touch the fringe of something fringey and count yourself catholic. As injunctions go, "read widely" goes pretty wide.

Which is part of the problem. At its most obnoxious, the command to "read widely" reflects the more-is-more ethos that courses, like an energy drink, through our literary culture. My Twitter feed is full of writers and critics who relentlessly strive to be up on their field, logging every literary debut like librarians, returning from writing conferences with shareable JPEGs of their book-engorged tote bags, or lighting out for yet another reading, the stacks on the book table like some mountain range, the promise of a horizon. Here's hapless omnivore Aleksandar Hemon, a novelist and critic who will eat anything: "I read compulsively—preferably a book of my choice, but anything would do. I've read, with great interest, nutritional information on cereal boxes. I regularly read wedding announcements in *The New York Times*."

But most writing isn't worth consuming. (That includes cereal boxes and *New York Times* wedding announcements.) And most people urging you to read widely probably have a hard time ranging outside their comfort zones. There's no doubt that, in the political realm, we need more connection with those we disagree with. But for the most part, "read widely" belongs to a class of expression that's good to be heard saying (as in: we need "more dialogue" or we need "to have a national conversation about sheet cake"). In my experience, only a minority of writers like to chase their Leslie Jamison with some Conrad Black, or their Yvor Winters with some Roxane Gay. Many can barely metabolize a Stephen Marche tweet without declaring a stomach ache, and Marche is a reasonable guy who can write a good sentence.

The real problem with telling young writers to fan out across genres and forms is that it doesn't help them find a voice. If anything, it's anti-voice. Learning the craft of writing isn't about hopping texts like hyperlinks. It's about devotion and obsession. It's about lingering too long in some beloved book's language, about steeping yourself in someone else's style until your consciousness changes colour. It's Tolkien phases and Plath crushes. It's going embarrassingly, unfashionably all in. (And, eventually, all out.)

To read widely—to flit from book to book, writer to writer—is to flaunt an open mind while never stopping long enough to fill it up. Consider instead what poet-critic Christian Wiman says about the consumption of poetry: "Seamus Heaney has noted that if a person has a single poem in his head, one that he returns to and through which, even in small ways, he understands his life better, this constitutes a devotion to the art. It is enough." Devotion to art, in other words, is a devotion to individual works—and not many, at that.

The most useful writing advice, like a doctor's script, is always specific. It doesn't widen, it narrows. "Those sentences that begin with the word 'Although,'" writes Joseph Epstein, "or those sentences requiring a 'however' somewhere in their middle, are almost always dead on arrival." That's thrillingly precise. So, too, is critic Stephen Metcalf's urgent warning to avoid overuse of em-dashes and, especially, semi-colons. Epstein and Metcalf, in other words, aren't giving permission. They are shutting down otherwise tempting avenues. The greatest teachers I ever had always held firm opinions about the books you should bother with and about how to read and write. You didn't have to agree with them to be energized by the charge they threw off. The charge was the point.

The call to "read widely" is a failure to make judgments. It disperses our attention across an ever-increasing black hole of mostly undeserving books. Whatever else you do, you should not be reading the many, many new releases of middling poetry and fiction that will be vying for your attention over the next year or so out of some obligation to submit your ear to a variety of voices. Leave that to the editors of Canada's few newspaper book sections, which often resemble arm's-length marketing departments for publishers. Leave that to the dubious figure of the "arts journalist."

Instead, shutter your ear against mediocrity. To fall in love with language, don't fan out. Fall down a rabbit hole. Cynthia Ozick wanted to be Henry James. Nicholson Baker has a whole book about his obsession with John Updike. For a period in high school, all I could countenance was David Foster Wallace. Before that, William Gibson. Lately, I've found myself falling into an Alan Furst phase. This doesn't mean I plan to seek out other writers of historical thrillers. They aren't Furst, after all. There isn't any more room in that rabbit hole. As another poet-critic, Michael Hofmann, puts it:

Both one's likes and the basis on which one likes them can only be exceptions. They are personal, they are absolute, and they are nonnegotiable. And there are not very many of them. They even preclude, at times, the least curiosity or desire to add to their number.

If you want to become a writer, here's my advice: bury yourself in an enthusiasm until it becomes oppressive, then tunnel your way clear of it. Repeat.

(*The Walrus*, 2017)

Seth Abramson's Very, Very, Very Long Bio

It was Lyz Lenz's profile of Seth Abramson's journalism, over at *Columbia Journalism Review*, that sent me to his website in the first place. Abramson had risen to something like fame in the Trump era, threading tweets and minting books: three volumes since 2018, based on other journalists' reporting. But he'd had other lives, too—as lawyer, professor, and pundit—and I wanted to refresh my memory. For a time, he'd been a fixture in the poetry world. He'd even written about responses to a mildly viral book review of mine once—though "written" seems insufficient; Abramson was already pulling threads together, assembling links to the responses my hapless review had spawned.

But whatever you think about her subject—and for all her apparently deft knife work and analysis—Lenz fails to summon the one truly and unambiguously towering fact about the poet-journalist-pundit: Abramson's website's very, very, very long bio.

In fact, the bio is so long it comes with its own summary—the way academic papers come frontloaded with abstracts. "Over a quarter-century career in higher education, publishing, criminal investigation, journalism, and the law," the summary begins, and then, deep breath, "Seth Abramson (MA, MFA, JD, Ph.D.) has worked for Harvard University, Dartmouth College, Georgetown University, Wesleyan University, University of Iowa, University of Wisconsin-Madison, the Institute of Art and Design at New England College, and the Nashua Trial Unit of the New Hampshire Public Defender."

That's only the summary's first sentence. The whole thing—summary and full bio—runs to nearly 2400 words. It's so big it throws a shadow. It's longer than this essay, and piles up endless facts, affiliations, dates, degrees, publications, and accolades. ("He buries you in text," observes Lenz.) It's tempting to psychoanalyze the thing, which I won't do. But if, as good old Roland Barthes observed, "it is language which speaks, not the author," then Abramson's hopelessly human bio is speaking a mile a minute, anxious to impress, and wary of leaving out that single proof point that might win you over.

Author bios are seemingly minor texts. Afterthoughts. They point out a few publications, maybe an award or two. They might tell you where the author teaches (if she's faculty somewhere) or in which periodicals she's appeared (if she's a journalist, say). They'll often end by noting where the author lives, pinning her to the globe. On dust jackets and Twitter profiles, bios have a haiku's worth of space in which to work. (On personal websites, they have more room to roam—or run amok.)

But these minor texts have major ambitions. They not only strive to say something meaningful about their subjects; they strive to become *inseparable* from their subjects. "I used to steal birds, but now I'm a newspaper man," says Fox, in Wes Anderson's stop-motion film *Fantastic Mr. Fox*. "Oh, sure," responds the real-estate agent, a weasel. "I've seen your byline." A bio often arrives at the end of its essay or poem, if you've scrolled that far, to put a face on all the words.

A bio, we might say, is an act of creation. Mythmaking, even. Take the filmmaker Peter Bogdanovich, who wrote about movies in the early 1960s, before he became a director. By the time *Pieces of Time*, a collection of his writing, appeared in 1973, he'd made *The Last Picture Show* and *What's Up, Doc?* Thus the bio on the dust jacket's back flap could reasonably declare, "Peter Bogdanovich at twenty-one was writing monographs on film for The Museum of Modern Art. Now in his early thirties, Mr. Bogdanovich is at work making movies as well as writing about them." There's a bildungsroman buried in those two sentences, tracing the arc of a rising star, from early success to bulb-spangled marquee. We're meant to be blinded by the brilliant fact of a wunderkind.

More often, though, a writer is a nobody, and his bio, the first front in a war on your indifference. I recall being a young poet, slowly amassing publications like armaments, and thinking, yes, finally, I can declare that my poems have graced *The Fiddlehead* or *Grain* or some other esteemed Canadian literary journal you've likely never heard of. Nowadays, an aspiring writer can pin the Twitter handles of magazines (badges conferring cultural capital) to their profile pages.

Bios aspire to be weighty—to lend weight. They cling to the bottoms of our poems and essays, and pull, anchoring the sort of hot air that might otherwise drift off into oblivion.

Many bios simply want to blend in. Others want to be noticed or have a point to make. I admire the American Gothic strain of boilerplate, where a towering writer stands shoulder to shoulder with a spouse and affirms said spouse's accomplishments. A Stephen King bio ends: "He lives in Bangor, Maine, with his wife, novelist Tabitha King." The bestselling horror maestro is sharing the spotlight, here: shining the halogen on the other novelist in the household.

The most conspicuously opaque bio is surely Anne Carson's: "Anne Carson was born in Canada and teaches ancient Greek for a living." Carson, a poet and classicist, was fast becoming a cultural superstar around the time her books started bearing that bio; her gesture at the material need to make a living doubles as sly comment on the fate of virtually every poet and classicist *not* named "Anne Carson." Moreover, saying you were born in anything bigger than a city is like saying you were born in the Milky Way. Carson, you're meant to gather, is somewhere out there—like Pynchon or the yeti. It's a bio that winks, but it's a mythmaker, too, as obfuscating as an obelisk.

Put another way, the Carson copy exposes the politics of bios. The most privileged writers, the ones whose reputations have come to precede their proof points, have almost always reached the point where they have little use for dangling their accomplishments.

These are the celebrities who have outpaced the modest boilerplate the rest of us proles require.

Their bios have the luxury of relaxing, of letting in the pets and spouses.

Too much comedy, on the other hand, can signal youth and insecurity. Sci-fi novelist Neal Stephenson's third book—and first big hit—*Snow Crash* appends a long, jokey bio with groaners on the order of, "Mr. Stephenson now resides in a comfortable home in the western hemisphere and spends all of his time trying to retrofit an office into its generally dark, unlevel, and asbestos-laden basement so that he can attempt to write more novels."

This is the equivalent of writing in Comic Sans. Several novels later, at the back of another Stephenson paperback, the bio is sober, prosaic: "Neal Stephenson is the author of seven previous novels. He lives in Seattle, Washington." The weight of commercial success has compressed the bio, squeezed out the gags. Heavyweights need merely tally their outputs.

If you must be funny, you'd better be brief. The first page of my *Fran Lebowitz Reader* notes crisply, "Fran Lebowitz still lives in New York City, as she does not believe that she would be allowed to live anywhere else." Here is the meta-bio in all its grating glory, poking fun at the convention of trying to fix a writer to some geography.

But Lebowitz's single, epigrammatic sentence hints at another, darker meaning. After all, the humorist, who suffers from an infamous case of writer's blockade, has barely written anything in decades. What exactly, her bio suggests, is there to say, really?

Perhaps it's best to keep bios brief: a book, if you have one, the place where you dwell, and get out of there. You're definitely better off not mentioning that prize you won ten years ago; great writers should have prizes to burn. (Whatever you do, don't mention nominations.) Every word you add is potentially a brick removed—from your reputation and from the reader's sense of a self-assured, well-mortared talent.

Bios make, but also break. And betray. Personally, I like when magazines have their own format, and take a blue pencil to the byline I send them. I like to see myself cut down. It's never a good idea to talk too much about yourself.

(*Lit Hub*, 2021)

Prose Poetry's Pitfalls

Poetry, said W. H. Auden, is "memorable speech." It's a reasonable definition: broad enough to include a lot of flora and fauna, but strict enough to put up fencing. You should be able to say a poem, and your head should want to hold on to it. Rhyme and meter can help with this. So, too, can a vivid image. "The stars are not wanted now; put out every one. / Pack up the moon and dismantle the sun." That's Auden, and just try to forget it.

There are always outliers, of course—"concrete poems," where clusters of words are shunted into shapes and pictures, or "sound poems," where a poet uses their voice to honk out patterns of noise. But most civilians know a poem when they see one. A poem strikes us as inevitable: it can be no other way, employ no other words. This is an illusion, of course, but the poem pulls it off because it's already pressed itself upon our memories. Auden's every move—the way the sound of "pack" pays off "put"; the way the stock cosmic props are redeemed by the strangeness of "dismantle"—lays down ruts in the mind. We're duly reassured we're dealing with the real thing.

It's the insiders—the poets, the tenured—who like to "problematize" poetry and wield their whatabouts. The "prose poem" is one of the most abiding whatabouts. It remains an outlier, a problem. "A prose poem is a poem without line breaks," writes Jeremy Noel-Tod in the introduction to his recent anthology, *The Penguin Book of the Prose Poem* (2019). Blame the French, who revel in unravelling categories. Aloysius Bertrand, in the nineteenth century, was the first to compose a block of text and call it poetry. Other beloved disturbers of shit, like Baudelaire and Rimbaud, later took up the idea. Prose poetry didn't catch on in North America for another century or so. Even then, it remained controversial. When Mark Strand's book of prose poems *The Monument* was up for a Pulitzer in 1979, one of the judges, Louis Simpson, dissented. *The Monument*, felt Simpson, just wasn't poetry. "If a prize intended for playing the violin were awarded to a trumpet player," he reportedly said, "everyone would see immediately how absurd and unacceptable this was."

Noel-Tod, a lecturer at the University of East Anglia, declares that prose poetry is "the defining poetic invention of modernity" and marvels that the form is "suddenly everywhere." He's probably right about its popularity. A book of the stuff, by Eve Joseph, just scooped up Canada's $65,000 Griffin Poetry Prize. Other twenty-first-century attempts have drawn acclaim: Claudia Rankine's book-length meditation on race, *Citizen: An American Lyric*, and Patricia Lockwood's viral "Rape Joke." Plenty of legacy brands have dabbled in the form, too: Elizabeth Bishop, say, and Seamus Heaney. Noel-Tod's anthology covers a spectrum, including translations. Front-loaded with contemporary examples, the book runs backward, irising out toward the middle of the nineteenth century.

But all this history and activity does nothing to make the form, for skeptics, convincing rather than contrived. Here, in full, is "The Mysterious Arrival of an Unusual Letter" by Strand:

> It had been a long day at the office and a long ride back to the small apartment where I lived. When I got there I flicked on the light and saw on the table an envelope with my name on it. Where was the clock? Where was the calendar? The handwriting was my father's, but he had been dead for forty years. As one might, I began to think that maybe, just maybe, he was alive, living a secret life somewhere nearby. How else to explain the envelope? To steady myself, I sat down, opened it, and pulled out the letter. "Dear Son," was the way it began. "Dear Son" and then nothing.

Isn't this just postcard fiction? A prose vignette? A plain old short story? (Strand himself seemed content with the modest term "prose piece.") You could place those ten sentences at the start of one of Paul Auster's postmodern thrillers and no one would be the wiser. A prose poem, we might conclude, is a stretch of prose willed into being something else by sheer force of naming. It's an act of alchemy. It's a leap of faith. It's Genesis 1:3—let there be poem.

Perhaps feeling the pressure, Noel-Tod has packed his introduction with an impressive compilation of definitions and justifications. He seems to have read everything anyone has ever had to say or write about the oxymoron, going back centuries. He doesn't quarrel with any of it; if someone's had a thought about the form, Noel-Tod is happy to log it. It's as if piling up enough statements by enough eyewitnesses will prove this yeti is a legit species that can be tagged and taught. It's not a bad approach; the form needs all the help it can get.

One of Noel-Tod's witnesses declares that the prose poem "is the circle we draw around our interactions with the world." Another says it "resonates with 'the absences that it accommodates.'" These soft-focus definitions should give us pause. Sonnets, villanelles, ballads, heroic couplets—a critic can be crisp about such things because they have apprehensible contours. The advocates for the prose poem, however, tend to lapse into a fatal fuzziness that betrays the emptiness of the form they're plumping for.

Put another way: if you accept that Strand's brief story is a poem, then everything is a poem—and nothing, too. Prose poetry is the original trolling.

Central to Noel-Tod's introduction is the assumption that the prose poem's lack of boundaries is a good thing:

> Without line breaks, the prose poem is free—like this paragraph—to extend across and down the page as far as the printer's margins will allow. And it is in this freedom that we can locate the distinctive feeling to which the prose poem gives form: expansiveness.

Indeed, Noel-Tod argues, the prose poem has a "genius for expansiveness." But then you could say the same thing about other expansive phenomena, like forest fires, cancer, and man-spreaders on public transit. Why is expansiveness a plus? "The prose poem," Noel-Tod writes, "drives the reading mind beyond the city limits." Is the prose poem really a chauffeur for the "reading mind"? Are city limits still the threshold to the unknown that Noel-Tod seems to think they are? Beyond many city limits, one finds suburban sprawl, maybe a Boston Pizza. Unsurprisingly, once we're past his introduction—and its utopian talk of "mind-expanding revelations"—we find a conspicuous uniformity of voice and style. Here's the work of one poet in the Penguin book:

> A text, resting on a table, having been turned to a page of illustrated finches years before. (The page was torn out years before.) And beside it, the tumbler of water. And beside themselves, the finches. And where the page was torn, an edge. An absence. A muted singing.

And another:

> To light a lamp is to hide darkness in the same closet as sleep, along with silence, desire, and yesterday's obsessions. To read a book is to marry two solitudes, the way a conversation erases and erects, words prepare for wordlessness, a cloud for its own absence, and snow undresses spring.

And another:

> Imprecise, as a world seen through cloth, ease of the friend that follows. Agony internal to the shape. The tinier holes through which a quality refines. A private lack, a riveting in some riveting act.

And another:

> Because I refuse to accept the opposition of night and day I must pit other, subtler periodicities against the emptiness of being an adult. Their traces inside my body attempt precariously, like any sign, to produce understanding, but though nothing may come of that, the grass is growing. Can words play my parts and also find their own way to the house next door as rays converge and solve their differences?

On and on, for pages on end, the reader's mind going blank, fogging up in the face of so much hot air. When prose poems don't sound like Strand's piece—that is, like straight-up exposition—they tend to sound like the excerpts above: ponderous, imprecise, and indistinguishable. Dispensing with Noel-Tod's "city limits" has left his poets free all right—free to be slack, vague, clichéd, and repetitious.

As the book winds down, and as the reader approaches the nineteenth century, the clichés shift, and the poems fill up with darkness, stars, flowers, and moons. Surely one reason for the enduring appeal of the prose poem is that it offers the neophyte a shortcut to poetic profundity. What could be more alluring than a form that absolves the poet of holding a beat or sticking a rhyme? The poet becomes a consciousness ranging forth, so breathlessly inspired, so seized by their line of thought, they can't even pause to break a line. (To wit: I made up an excerpt above, the first one, in a few minutes. I felt duly mystical.)

The barrier to writing poetry, let alone the prosy kind, is already enticingly low. Nearly every attempt to stretch the definition of poetry has generally loosened what it once required of its practitioners. Free verse ditched ABAB. Language poetry, syntax. "[P]rose," Noel-Tod cheerfully points out, "is a mode of writing that allows the stylist plenty of slack." Here, the editor betrays the mistaken belief that more rope—more freedom—means better art. In fact, if you want to ruin an artist, give them a blank cheque, too much time, and no limits. See Orson Welles, Fran Lebowitz, and Guns N' Roses. "No verse is free for the man who wants to do a good job," warned T. S. Eliot, the guy who helped make free verse cool.

There *is* some good stuff in the Penguin book, but it's strewn, star-like, across a lot of void. Blink and you'll miss Laura Kasischke's brief piece about a father's Alzheimer's, which is one of a scant few examples to use repetition for a more compelling reason than to make its author sound oracular. There are mild gags, anecdotes with well-earned twists, and the odd poignant item: Jane Monson's "Via Negativa," about a mother felled by an epileptic attack, or Czesław Miłosz's "Christopher Robin," in which Winnie the Pooh contemplates aging and death, "matters too difficult for a bear of little brain." These are neither straight-up prose vignettes, like the Strand, nor expansive clouds of dry ice, like so much else in the book. They have a sense of style, economy. They resist the prose poem's worst impulses.

Eliot considered the prose poem "an aberration which is only justified by absolute success." Patricia Lockwood's "Rape Joke" is one such success, but hardly an exemplar of the sort of thing the Penguin book makes compact with. Using anaphora—most of its paragraphs start with "The rape joke . . ."—Lockwood's speaker recounts a rape:

> The rape joke is that come on, you should have seen it coming. This rape joke is practically writing itself.
>
> The rape joke is that you were facedown. The rape joke is you were wearing a pretty green necklace that your sister had made for you. Later you cut that necklace up. The mattress felt a specific way, and your mouth felt a specific way opening against it, as if you were speaking, but you know you were not. As if your mouth were open ten years into the future, reciting a poem called Rape Joke.
>
> The rape joke is that time is different, becomes more horrible and more habitable, and accommodates your need to go deeper into it. Just like the body, which more than a concrete form is a capacity . . .

And so on. It's a moving, controlled performance, every word in its place, every paragraph paying off. Its precision and music—"more horrible and more habitable"—set it damningly apart from so many of its peers. It's one of a few exceptions that prove the unruliness all around.

A more ruthless editor might've made a stark choice and printed the finest forty prose poems in the language. A top forty. A statement. But focusing the reader on atypical outliers by great individual talents is not the MO of Noel-Tod, nor is it that of most anthologists, who are in the business of bringing the good news about a form, a school, an era. Anthologies tend to serve the interests of professors, who have ground to cover, and not those of readers, who can only be wowed one great poem at a time. Bulk surveys prioritize a topic—the prose poem, the Renaissance, war—over individual genius. Preoccupied with forests, anthologists inevitably miss the trees.

Indeed, the Penguin book marshals plenty of examples by poets, like Elizabeth Bishop, not necessarily known for their prose poems. For poets like Adrienne Rich and John Ashbery, the prose poem seems to have dangled a deceptive freedom. For others, it seems to have been a fad, a fondue kit, something to try one's hand at. Major talents will often dabble in a form to dispense with it; in Bishop's wake, you'll find a litter of clothes tried on briefly. Yet who would prefer Seamus Heaney's "Fiddleheads" to even a stanza of "The Harvest Bow"? Here's the former, in its entirety:

Fiddlehead ferns are a delicacy where? Japan? Estonia? Ireland long ago?

I say Japan because when I think of those delicious things I think of my friend Toraiwa, and the surprise I felt when he asked me about the erotic. He said it belonged in poetry and he wanted more of it.

So here they are, Toraiwa, frilled, infolded, tenderized, in a little steaming basket, just for you.

And here's the final stanza of "The Harvest Bow":

> The end of art is peace
> Could be the motto of this frail device
> That I have pinned up on our deal dresser—
> Like a drawn snare
> Slipped lately by the spirit of the corn
> Yet burnished by its passage, and still warm.

The former is charming, sure, but slight, like a well-turned inscription. The latter, on the other hand, is less perishable, more musical. Masterful. The half rhymes that bind the lines ("peace/device," "dresser/snare," and "corn/warm"), the pulsing iambs, the warm alliteration ("burnished by")—all of these elements, carefully deployed, give the passage lift and life. More importantly, they encourage the mind to memorize.

Eliot came to characterize his own attempt at prose poetry, "Hysteria," as "a kind of note for a poem, but not . . . a poem." Noel-Tod has included it anyway. Some of the entries in the Penguin book might seem new to readers, but that's probably because they've been B-listers in their authors' bodies of work. They should've been forgotten, but these underdogs, believes Noel-Tod, form "an alternative history of modern poetry and an experimental tradition that is shaping its future." It's a pretty thought. It conjures up a past when the adjective "alternative" still meant something cool. It gives otherwise dull blocks of unmemorable text an edge.

(*The Walrus*, 2019)

Lyric Poetry's Pitfalls

TEN YEARS AGO, I STOPPED writing lyric poetry. I had a couple of slim, well-received collections to my name, and my poetry occasionally appeared in a magazine with pedigree, like *Poetry*. One time, an editor at *The New Yorker* even mailed a personalized, encouraging rejection on letterhead. (They rebuffed poems by paper in the good old days.) Still, the cupboard was no longer stocked with stanzas. Perhaps I needed a break, a sabbatical.

A good lyric poem, after all, takes toil. Sometimes a poem will fall out of the sky fully formed like a meteorite, but such cosmic events, though real, are rare. A good lyric poem also takes a toll. Immediately upon finishing your first-person meditation on grandpa's box of old photos or that first fallen leaf of the season, you face a void. You have to start over.

And the longueurs between lyric poems can be long. Elizabeth Bishop published a very slim body of poems in her lifetime. (Famously, she fussed with "The Moose" for twenty years.) The Canadian poet Bruce Taylor seems to average one book of poems a decade. Christian Wiman has written eloquently about a period of poetic silence. ("Whatever connection I had long experienced between word and world," recalls Wiman, "whatever charge in the former I had relied on to let me feel the latter, went dead.")

Only slightly more troubling than this void is the apparent ease with which others can appear to pump out product. Nothing is easier to counterfeit than a lyric poem. You don't need facility with a fretboard, and you don't need to know your way around a camera or a palette. You don't even need stationery—just memory, really. The barrier to attempting lyric poetry is so low it's basically asphalt. Platforms for the stuff are plentiful, and rotten poems, furred with hyperlinks, abound. What's more, there's no critical mass of unsparing critics to help readers sort through the glut. When I would see what was being venerated, I almost always felt discouraged. So, I put a pin in poetry. I'd been composing lines since the 1990s, and anyway, I told myself, I wanted to focus on reviews and essays.

Four years of avoiding the void went by. But in 2017, I stumbled on a workaround: I would write poetry but in the service of a story. I would write a long-ish narrative in heroic couplets. (I'd been admiring Nabokov's kayfabe verse at the start of his novel-in-endnotes *Pale Fire.*) A long-ish narrative meant I wouldn't have to start over every morning. On waking, there would already be poetry to work on because there would be a story to advance. And the heroic couplets meant I would always have a rhyme scheme to complete. (Free verse is an abyss of options; a rhyming couplet, a rope bridge across the darkness.)

The workaround worked. In 2020, my first verse novel, *Forgotten Work*, appeared—and drew the most readers I'd ever had. Last summer, a second book set in the same futuristic world, *The Full-Moon Whaling Chronicles*, came out. Each book busied me for about three years. And each morning when my iPhone went off, there was something to do: a character to describe, a scene to set, a couplet to complete. Take that, void.

What's more, abandoning the short poem liberated me from my own consciousness—and from the *de rigueur* ruts and rote moves of the lyric poet thinking about grandpa's photos or fallen leaves. No self-expression for me; I had a plot to unpack and characters to develop.

To wit: at one point in *Full-Moon*, twenty-year-old Kaye finds herself astride a kind of bike-cum-boat called a "Humpback." She's zooming through Tokyo circa 2070. Climate change has left the city flooded but strangely functional:

> Soon, she came to crest
> The onramp, Tokyo before her, endless
> Towers ringed with water as if Venice
> Had exploded skyward, buildings taking
> Leave of what our eyes can take in, making
> Their canals seem modest, more like moats.
> Street-level Tokyo required boats,
> But elevated roadways were amassed
> Around the buildings' waists: spaghetti cast
> In concrete.

I would never have gotten to an image like "spaghetti cast / In concrete" or the idea of Venice exploding skyward if I'd stuck with lyric poetry. My cli-fi conceit had demanded cleverness.

Elsewhere, inspired by Alan Moore's revisionist work on the comic book *Swamp Thing*, I place Kaye amid a youth subculture whose enthusiasts implant themselves with plant life:

> A pop-up masque had spread across
> The Wood. She'd spotted Floras filmed with moss
> And ivy. Forking branches topped some heads
> Like antlers. Thick vines fell in ropey dreads
> Across bark-roughened backs. The leaves of leeks
> Stood still on pallid scalps. One "he/him's" cheeks
> Had broken into baby's breath, the girl
> Beside him ballerina-ed with a twirl
> Of large, translucent petals at her tiny
> Waist: a tutu. Heavies went for spiny
> Implants: cactus shit.

The needs of narrative—and a fantastical narrative to boot—unlocked all manner of peculiar language ("pop-up masque," "ballerina-ed") and unanticipated metaphor ("ropey dreads," "tutu"). Over the course of writing two science-fiction verse novels totaling about 600 pages, I felt myself leveling up—and leaving lyric poetry behind.

The needs of narrative also kept me moving and helped me avoid certain sand traps—the selfie-stickiness, the passages that start to skew purple. A professor of mine once pointed out that the beautiful closing paragraph of James Joyce's short story "The Dead," the final number in his collection *Dubliners*, works in part because Joyce has shown restraint: he's saved the poetry—"the snow falling faintly through the universe" bit—for the end of the book. Lyrical moments, I learned then, have to be earned. (My meditation on love in *The Full-Moon Whaling Chronicles* arrives on page 364, just before the epilogue.)

I still read the odd lyric poem. I'm always here for an amazing new Bruce Taylor piece, whenever he deigns to deliver one. And I always inspect with great interest the latest products by A.E. Stallings, Daniel Brown, Michael Lista, Christian Wiman, Luke Hathaway, Carmine Starnino, Robyn Sarah, Mark Callanan, Alexandra Oliver, Evan Jones, Matthew Tierney, and a handful of others.

But the resources of poetry—rhyme, meter, metaphor, simile—seem to me wasted on most of the page-long poems that fatten all those unread literary journals boxed in your garage or that dwell on the other end of the hyperlink in your feed. Verse novels—oriented outward, with the aim of entertaining their readers—have the potential to reach a readership that doesn't typically mess with poetry.

"Poetry is not a turning loose of emotion," writes T.S. Eliot in one of his most iconic essays, "Tradition and Individual Talent," from 1919, "but an escape from emotion; it is not the expression of personality, but an escape from personality." My eyes had rolled over this line many, many times, but I'd never really understood it until I embarked on my verse novel adventure. Bang out hundreds of pages of rhyming couplets about something other than your identity or your perceptions, and you, too, will likely fall out of love with lyric poetry. You will certainly fall out of yourself. You might even land somewhere new.

(*The Millions*, 2024)

Mourn

Fandom Before the Internet

IN THE EARLY DECADES OF the twentieth century, a great civilization of Jewish wits occupied Vienna's coffeehouses. Some, like the journalist Alfred Polgar, achieved renown; others, like the romantically unproductive Peter Altenberg, cult status. An anti-Semitic quota system prevented many of these writers from becoming university faculty; they were forced to thrive amid clinking cups and noisy conversation. (Altenberg even had his mail directed to his preferred haunt, Café Central.) The coming of the Second World War, however, eventually emptied the coffeehouses. Vienna's Jewish writers were dispersed and, in some cases, forgotten.

One of the great fans of these now-obscure writers was the Australian critic Clive James, who absorbed much of his enthusiasm for the coffeehouse wits from the pianist Alfred Brendel. As James tells it,

> Brendel carries on his person their best sayings, individually typed out on slips of paper. Away from the piano, Brendel's fingertips are usually wrapped in strips of Elastoplast. (So would mine be, if they were worth ten million dollars each.) When you see those bits of paper being hauled from his pockets by his plastered fingers, you realize you are in the presence of a true enthusiast.

It's a memorable anecdote, in part because of Brendel's commitment to remembering, in part because of his monk-like faith in print media. Nowadays, an enthusiast talking up his heroes to an innocent would probably produce a smartphone.

The internet certainly gives the illusion of being a great enabler of enthusiasm. There's no lack of links to email to nonbelievers, no shortage of fan sites or chat rooms in which those who share a very specific fetish can organize. All manner of button lets you share or retweet at will. (No slips of paper need change plastered hands.) Platforms like YouTube permit lay-archivists to post grey literature that would otherwise be inaccessible, like the reclusive Canadian singer Mary Margaret O'Hara's lone Christmas original.

But if it's the perfect time to be an obscure work of art, it's also end-times for Brendel's breed of cult enthusiast; our information-deluged era has rendered his ascetic devotion obsolete. It's not just that the champions of the obscure have been spoiled by the ease with which they can express their fandom; it's that their most important function, keeping a torch lit for the lesser known, has been taken over by the web.

Not so long ago, the obsessive fan had no easy way to instantly preserve and share the obscure object of his enthusiasm. The writer with a pet interest pitched it to editors and hoped it landed. The amateur, in possession of no editors' ears, founded fan clubs and mimeographed fanzines. The music aficionado patronized record stores, the bibliophile, estate sales. Bins were combed through, library stacks dragged. Fandom demanded physical effort, and effort ran on passion. Writing about the obscure Canadian poet Charles Bruce, the Montreal-based poet-critic Carmine Starnino notes,

> I certainly had no clue of his existence until my friend Michael Harris picked up *The Mulgrave Road* (for ten cents!) during a Saturday morning visit to a Westmount estate sale. He invited me over to his home that afternoon. He was excited ...

Harris proceeds to read a poem from Bruce's forgotten classic of Canadian poetry: contraband salvaged from the void. (See the comic-strip essay, "Charles Bruce's Poems," earlier in this volume for another view of this moment.)

Fandom also required memory—the analogue kind you keep be-tween your ears. The obsessive fan of yesteryear couldn't count on an archive of linked computers, coupled to a search algorithm as intelligent as the one devised by Sergey Brin and Larry Page. Maverick reputations like Weldon Kees (poet), Monte Hellman (filmmaker), Karen Dalton (folky), and Nick Drake (ditto) survived because they were internalized by devotees—as opposed to externalized on YouTube or personal blogs.

For example, the work of the late musician Dennis Wilson was long coveted by an elect group who knew that he was so much more than simply The Beach Boys' reckless also-ran drummer. The only one who'd ever really surfed, Wilson wrote raw, impressionistic songs that Beach Boys albums couldn't quite metabolize. "We didn't know what we had," said bandmate Al Jardine regretfully, decades later. As the band pursued an increasingly kitschy incarnation of itself, Wilson stockpiled his unwanted work: off-brand ballads and rockers that took unexpected turns, his damaged voice riding a widescreen orchestral swell like driftwood.

Some of the songs appeared on Wilson's one solo album, 1977's *Pacific Ocean Blue*, which went out of print for years. (A 1991 CD became a collector's item.) Some of the best songs weren't even released. They had to hole up in the minds of monks. "I heard [the instrumental track] 'Holy Man' only once when we did a rough mix of it in March of 1976," recalls one of Wilson's sound engineers, John Hanlon. "Then it sat in my head for thirty-one years. I couldn't hear it anywhere else. They hadn't done any vocals, but it was such a magical melody that I would've done anything just to hear the track one more time."

To supplement memory, the obsessive fan of yesteryear was forced to covet and seek out used editions, bootlegs, grainy video, hearsay, rumour, word of mouth, brittle clippings, Brendel's slips of paper, cassette tape, and other ephemera. But "forced" suggests his poverty was a bad thing. In fact, lack of content correlates to deeper commitment. The obsessive fan slaked his thirst with droplets of data, spaced out across months, even years. Yes, I know, I sound like a wartime propagandist. But lack of content—an intolerable proposition in the Age of Scrolling, when one post displaces the next by flick of thumb—taught frugality and toughened consumers of culture into cacti. They would've been scandalized by the hyperlinks that geyser out of online essays.

Don't get me wrong; it's lovely to type a name into a search bar and call up content about some little-known figure you care about. A deserving artist or work shouldn't be the preserve of a few. But the dedicated, discerning obsessive understood the irreplaceable value of physical effort, of combing the inhospitable world. If you took Richard Teleky's creative writing classes in the 1990s, you would've felt obliged to look up many neglected but deserving books, including Paula Fox's *Desperate Characters*. A slim, cleanly executed novel that takes place over the course of a weekend, it concerns a Brooklyn couple trying to find a cat. (The wife is bitten at the start of the novel and spends the length of it worried about rabies.)

The book disappeared for years, but then Jonathan Franzen, Fox's most famous fan, campaigned to get it brought back into print. (Kurt Cobain and Courtney Love did something similar in 1993, using newly acquired power to persuade Geffen Records to reissue albums by the neglected English band the Raincoats.) Anyway, during the dark age of *Desperate Characters*, Teleky did his part; he bought up used copies, whenever he stumbled on them in stores, and made them gifts. That was how, in a chilly vacuum without AbeBooks, Teleky attended to his torch-work.

"25 years ago I tore this Richard Wilbur poem out of the *New Yorker* because I loved it so much," began a recent tweet by the poetry critic Kamran Javadizadeh. Below the tweet, Javadizadeh had attached a photo of the magazine page. The page was frayed, only vaguely rectangular, and deeply wrinkled; fine tributaries of shadow ran through and rippled the poem's words. What's more, a pair of rents, in the bottom righthand corner, had partially obscured Wilbur's name. In short, the page looked like papyrus torn from a codex by some misfit Benedictine. But the poem, "For C.," was still there, still singing behind the wrinkles.

The tweet itself—an ironic home for so tattered a thing—had drawn over five hundred likes. But the likes paled in comparison to the love. Javadizadeh, after all, had kept the page for a quarter of a century. He had clearly cherished this piece of paper. And the paper, in turn, had nourished him.

I've held onto a lot of paper over the years. I still have the first issue of *Poetry* magazine I ever bought—the April 2004 issue—which singlehandedly introduced me to four poets I would come to adore: Christian Wiman, Kay Ryan, Samuel Menashe, and A. E. Stallings. I still have a xerox of an essay by Ryan, which I made at the York University library, a bound volume of the bygone magazine *Parnassus* splayed flat on the photocopier. I still have the 2005 issue of *Bookforum* that was devoted to Thomas Pynchon. I still have dozens of issues of MOJO magazine, going back over twenty years. They form stacks on the floor of my bedroom and occupy bins in my shed. The Al Jardine quote, above, comes from a MOJO—from the very article that introduced me to Dennis Wilson's work.

Occasionally, I revisit online articles. I do! But sometimes the content goes missing. Sometimes paywalls drop like the door of a citadel; or a revamped website, blasé about its own past, distorts an article's formatting. Paper is surely the better medium to remember by. It's tactile—it's palpable. Its words are really there, composed of ink. (No battery is required to maintain their shape.) Plus, print is portable. An old number of a magazine can be borne away like a Bible.

It can even *become* your Bible. I spent years tracking down the work of cult artists showcased in the February 2000 issue of MOJO. That single edition—with longform features on Big Star, Fred Neil, and The La's—fired my browsing for the better part of two decades. It was the multipage sidebar that transfixed me: dozens of capsule summaries of obscurities like Liam Hayes (a reclusive songwriter from Chicago) and James Booker (once described by Dr. John as "the best black, gay, one-eyed junkie piano genius New Orleans has ever produced").

Obviously, more info about these artists existed *somewhere* in the world. But the internet circa 2000 CE contained exponentially less content than it does today. Hayes and Booker effectively didn't exist outside of MOJO. Those capsule summaries were gospel.

If anything, the hardship that came with seeking out artists like Hayes was part of the pleasure of listening to them. Hayes was the auteur behind a near-mythical Chicago band called Plush. The music of Plush made compact with the carefully arranged work of Brian Wilson, Jimmy Webb, and other soft-pop maestros who have little to do with our current zeitgeist. To wit: Plush's 2002 album *Fed* was painstakingly recorded on analogue tape and arranged by the guy who did the strings for Earth, Wind & Fire. (It's a record that wasn't of its time because it was for *all* time.) *Fed* cost so much to make, though, that it struggled to find US distribution. A Japanese label took up the cause, and Chicago's Reckless Records resolved to stock the pricey import, which is how I came by my copy. Listening to *Fed*—a masterpiece that relatively few people knew about in 2002—felt strange, like I was hoarding the only extant copy of a lost Beatles album.

As for Hayes, he remains a figure out of time. The preamble to a 2018 interview describes the songwriter's "extremely offline" life:

> No Twitter account, no Facebook, not even text or emails. You wanna interview Hayes? You gotta know someone who knows someone ... type up some interview questions, send them on over and wait for scanned, type-written pages to show up.

Like a Liam Hayes record, the auteur's attention was a hard-won commodity; the obsessive artist demanded obsession from his fans. You couldn't casually enjoy Hayes's work; you were, by default, a diehard. (Even his most recent album, 2018's *Mirage Garage*, came out on cassette initially—a middle finger to our digital moment.) Now, of course, you can easily download Hayes's music to your preferred device.

Perhaps I'm a pair of binoculars away from birding with Franzen. Perhaps we should be happy to see the work of neglected but deserving artists digitized and made widely available. But there's something to lament in the obsolete figure of the obsessive fan, who made the best of his barbarian epoch. We should mourn the monk-like devotees of Wilson, Fox, Hayes, and others, who carried the fragile reputations of their charges this far, far enough to see them uploaded forever—so long as the links don't break.

(*The Walrus*, 2016; *On Browsing*, 2022)

Bygone Phenomena Like Innate Talent, Quiet Ambition, and Deference to Authority

I GREW UP IN A SUBURB OF Toronto during the 1980s, which is to say, Before Internet. What it meant to be a writer was mostly limited to what the television had to say on the matter. Kathleen Turner's pulp novelist in *Romancing the Stone* offered one example—but Turner is already famous and bestselling when the movie begins. How had she *become* bestselling? The TV was mute; Turner's artistic development—her bildungsroman—wasn't pertinent to the plot.

My house was a twenty-minute walk from the subway that might've taken me someplace else—a bookstore stocked with *Paris Reviews*, say. But Kipling Station marked the furthest west stop on the line. And anyway, subways were for Saturdays with the family. The local mall grudgingly kept a Coles, stocked with calendars, Dean Koontz, and the spinner rack of comic books in the basement, which squeaked when turned.

When it came to accounts of the writing life, I had to content myself with Roald Dahl's essay, "Lucky Break—How I Became a Writer," which you stumbled on towards the end of his short story collection, *The Wonderful Story of Henry Sugar and Six More*. The essay was meant to introduce Dahl's first published story, about his time as a pilot with the RAF. I suspect many kids simply passed over the essay, the better to get to fighter planes. But I must've reread it a dozen times.

And yet I didn't remember much about the essay when I revisited it recently, for the first time in something like twenty years. I did recall the "lucky break" of the title: the famous writer C. S. Forester has sought out the young Dahl, who has only lately returned from World War Two. Up to this point, Dahl hasn't published anything—has had, if we're to believe him, "no thoughts of becoming a writer." Forester, for his part, is after fodder; he's looking to convert somebody's war-time experience into magazine content. The two have lunch, and Dahl, bored with his job at Washington's British Embassy, agrees to help. He goes home, jots down some memories, sends them off, and promptly forgets about the ask.

But when Forester gets back to him by letter, Dahl discovers the material he supplied the famous writer is no good, which is to say *too* good. "You were meant to give me notes," writes Forester, "not a finished story. I'm bowled over. Your piece is marvelous. It is the work of a gifted writer. I didn't touch a word of it." Forester has already forwarded Dahl's piece along to an agent who, in turn, has already placed it with the *Saturday Evening Post*. The check, minus commission, is enclosed. "Did you know you were a writer?" Forester asks.

I still buy Dahl's account of how he stumbled into writing. But I'm not sure I ever bought his innocence, his obliviousness. Years after I first read "Lucky Break," my first publisher would tell me—would tell anyone who would listen—that one has to *allow* oneself to be lucky. (This was Barry Callaghan, the son of Morley Callaghan, who knows from lucky breaks; he lives in a house in Rosedale, one of Toronto's most affluent neighbourhoods.) Even as a kid, I sensed that the young Dahl had sensed an opportunity. "Just for fun, when it was finished, I gave it a title," he says of the "notes" he whipped up for Forester. "I called it 'A Piece of Cake.'" Clearly, Dahl was adding some icing.

I don't doubt that Dahl *wasn't* aggressively pursuing a writing career, if only because I can relate: my first published poems were passed along by a teacher of mine to Callaghan's magazine *Exile* without my knowing it—a lucky break of more modest proportions. Plus, I too have been slightly blasé about my "career," such as it is, only to be kick-started by the kindness of others. I have depended on unprompted encouragement: an email out of the blue, say, from an editor. Indeed, I might have forgotten about Dahl's essay if Kim Jernigan hadn't written, with a gig.

Even then, I nearly backed out. Revisit a book from my youth and record something about the trip, about who I'd been, how far I'd come? As commissions go, here was catnip in a poisoned chalice. A writer will prefer himself to most other subject matter, even if he knows almost nothing about himself. (It's usually to his advantage to beg off the autobiography.) Still, if I internalized anything from Dahl's essay, I would like to think it was the Englishman's strange, seemingly incongruous mix of ambition and ambivalence.

Other parts of the essay I had forgotten? Dahl's banal bullet-list of a writer's must-haves ("You should have a lively imagination," "You must have stamina"), and his description of his notebook, which I used to marvel at. Here was the Ur-text in which Dahl had trapped the fleeting, one-to-two-sentence ideas for his books and stories, which might have disappeared altogether had he not pinned them to a page. Ideas for books and stories did that, apparently—they sprang away. You might even have to pull over to the side of the road, produce a fingertip, and record an idea in the dust on your car, as Dahl tells us he once did.

Is it cruelly redundant to describe the attitude of a children's author towards his precious ideas as, well, precious? To be sure, Dahl's books do well; he was likely preserving gold in that dust. Still, it now seems to me that writers—whether of stories, poems, or essays—ought to learn to be careless with ideas, and that ideas, if they're any good, had better learn to survive in writer's minds, at least for the length of a road trip. And anyway, ideas are what amateurs have. They get turned into patents and internet start-ups. Writers are in the business of bottling good sentences, one at a time.

If Dahl's essay has a precious commodity, in the sense of something rare and valuable, it's of mid-century vintage: a matter-of-factness that my generation would mistake for cynicism, maybe even elitism. "You should be able to write well," he observes at one point. "By that I mean you should be able to make a scene come alive in the reader's mind. Not everybody has this ability. It is a gift, and you either have it or you don't." This wouldn't have struck me as extraordinary when I first read it, as a kid. Nowadays, it's hard to imagine a writer of Dahl's stature—especially one whose business is the delicate matter of sparking the tinder of adolescent imaginations—suggesting in print that talent isn't distributed equitably.

Moreover, Dahl's practical suggestion, that writers need day jobs to subsidize their work, predates the epoch of writers' colonies, government grants, and entitlement. But then even Forester's question—"Did you know you were a writer?"—would be unheard of today. No one accidentally discovers that they're a writer anymore; they simply *decide* they are a writer, and then invite you to their reading.

Any meathead with a graduate degree could make meat pie out of the Englishman who wrote "Lucky Break"; they would point out that Dahl (white, straight, male, and privileged) had the luxury to let lucky breaks happen. Fair enough. But we deconstruct Dahl at our own peril. In an age of relentless self-promotion and brand-building, the narrator of "Lucky Break" offers an almost-alien alternative to what it means to be a writer: secretly hungry, but outwardly modest, quietly ambitious, but deferential to authority (the authority of good editors and good fortune). He cheerfully offers up an unrepeatable path to publication, and it's his cheerful hopelessness, or studied haplessness, that's worth cherishing.

(*Canadian Notes & Queries*, 2015)

My Academic Hopes

Back when I was a Ph.D. candidate, I used to debate the worth of stylish critical prose with a professor of mine. I liked the kind of critic like Hugh Kenner who, having quoted somebody else's use of the word "Aristotelian," couldn't help but point out the word's resemblance to a "porcupine of tongued consonants." I thought metaphors like that pretty sharp.

My professor, however, didn't like critics who seemed to be trying to out-write their subjects. Put another way, I thought critical prose an opportunity for "porcupines of tongued consonants" and other showy metaphors. She thought prose should simply show the proofs. When she came to the part of my dissertation where I had it that Pound "hijacked" the poetic image, she duly circled the verb: too colourful.

"I am in blood / Stepp'd in so far that, should I wade no more, / Returning were as tedious as go o'er." That was Macbeth's colourful way of saying there was no point turning back. In other words, I waded forward and finished the dissertation. But scholarship wasn't in my future, on the far shore—and it wasn't just the lack of academic jobs. Reading the brief, bracing introduction to Michael Hofmann's first book of reviews and essays, *Behind the Lines*—reading it while working on a dissertation—confirmed what I had long suspected: I wasn't a scholar.

"Seeking to direct opinion, making my contribution to debate, was much more to my liking than the 'contribution to knowledge' that was required for a Ph.D.," writes Hofmann, who eventually put aside his own scholarly ambitions for scrappy reviewing.

I was always prepared to drop everything if a book came through the post with a little review slip—whereas I never gave much for libraries, and the larger the less. I relished what seemed to me the freedom of reviewing, and the multiple address...even if it did mean the end of any academic hopes I might have entertained.

My sober, rigorous professor might have found that unnecessarily flashy: try not to take note of the alliteration of "libraries," "larger," and "less," the internal rhyme of "less," "relished," and "address."

But Hofmann's confession stuck, though not simply because of style; he seemed to be writing about me. To be sure, I plugged away at my dissertation—I had come too far not to. But I had little interest in turning chapters into chum for peer-reviewed journals. I liked pitching reviews to *Poetry* magazine or working on a piece for the now-defunct *Books in Canada*, even though these non-academic publications weren't going to advance a scholarly career. What's more, I needed to make money. When it came time to defend my dissertation and lay claim to a doctorate, I had to take the day off from work; I had long since left academia for a job in communications.

Opinionated writers with an excess of flair—or, in my case, a tendency to overwrite—often make their happiest home outside the ivory tower, on more hardscrabble turf, where something like a marketplace reasserts itself, and readers must be won over. (No, I don't own any Ayn Rand, swear.) Hofmann's book was proof that an enthusiastic non-specialist could cadge together a work of critical art from many disparate commissions and occasions.

And the book's introduction affirmed the value of deceptively provisional book reviews. "A lot of the articulacy and the connections and the nerves that might have gone on poems," says Hofmann, "have gone on these pieces." Such thinking was helpful back when I used to worry over whether I should waste a promising metaphor on some critical prose—back when I thought writers, like the comic character Spawn, possessed a finite supply of power, and so had better deploy it wisely. (I still think, perhaps irrationally, that writers had better hoard their best lines—but Hofmann taught me that reviews are at least a worthwhile home for the lines.)

A healthier job market might have held me in academia. But Hofmann would've still had my number. "[F]irst impressions, followed by bags of technique"—that's how he describes his critical process. And to my mind, his ratio of impression to technique (content to form, idea to style) sounded about right. The person who brings "bags of technique" to an argument or even a banal point—the word "Aristotelian" is a mouthful; scholarship isn't my thing—probably isn't a scholar. Such a person is happiest polishing their pitches to dazzle some editor, and their prose to dazzle the rest of us. (They belong in a street fight, not the stacks.)

Perhaps it's too showy or colourful to equate Hofmann's introduction, as encountered in my second-hand copy of *Behind the Lines*, with light in a void. But it had traveled years to illuminate at least one reader.

(*Partisan*, 2015)

Elise Partridge (1958–2015)

When it comes to poets, we like to hold a torch for firebrands who flared out early—see Sylvia Plath, John Keats, and Hart Crane. In-depth profiles of living practitioners often favour the conspicuously youthful, such as Patricia Lockwood and Ocean Vuong.

Elise Partridge, however, was no longer a young woman when she published her first collection of poems in 2002. She had dared to take her time and, worse, become middle-aged. Then, a little over a decade after making her debut, Partridge's career was clipped short by colon cancer. She died in 2015.

Fortunately, the body of work she left behind has been given a second life by *New York Review Books*. *The If Borderlands* brings together the three volumes Partridge published with smaller Canadian presses (an American-born poet, she lived for years in British Columbia), plus some uncollected work. It's an astonishing book that should secure Partridge some readers outside the mossy parapets of the poetry world. Like all great poets, she deployed words in unusual and memorable ways. But she always aspired to be clear, even entertaining.

Partridge's public life as an acclaimed poet was sonnet length. In the late seventies, she was a student of future US Poet Laureate Robert Pinsky, who took one of her pieces for *The New Republic*, where he was an editor. But Partridge wouldn't publish a collection of her own for a few more decades. She was forty-four years old when Montreal-based Véhicule Press—the publisher of the book you're holding—brought out her 2002 debut, *Fielder's Choice*. It was a perfect collection; time had burned away the juvenilia and fostered mature, accomplished poems.

Time, however, was already a problem; Partridge had been diagnosed, the year before, with breast cancer. She would see the publication of only one more book in her lifetime—2008's *Chameleon Hours*, which was reviewed in the *Washington Post* and included poems that appeared in *The New Yorker*. A third book, *The Exiles' Gallery*, came out mere months after her death in 2015.

It didn't matter to Partridge that the audience for contemporary poetry had largely retired to the creative writing workshop; she wrote about everyday subjects for non-academic readers—and she wrote ambitiously, with style and energy, as if she had the ear of the culture. Unsurprisingly, mortality was one of Partridge's prominent subjects. Take this excerpt from "Cancer Surgery," where she takes inventory of her hospital room and makes banal details (gauze, a get-well balloon) seem alien:

> Dark again.
> Red digits blink: morphine drip.
> Chest a gauzy snowpatch, itchy with tape.
> A silver balloon sways on the updraft—
> messenger from some festivity
> too far to imagine, ocean-trench creature
> bobbing dopily where goggle-eyed fish ghost by.
> How did I land here,
> shot down like a migrating bird
> who had other latitudes in mind?

Like Plath, Partridge, at her darkest, was blazingly vivid. Her poetry seemed made of magnifying glass, under which swam brilliant images and metaphors. One of her most moving poems, "Last Days"—about a pregnant friend with cancer, who stayed alive long enough to give birth to a daughter—imagines the fetus as a "handsbreadth girl / (five-month spindle Buddha, / her brain's coral byways / travelled by your voice)...." The friend passed away before she could ever glimpse the daughter she'd carried. "Her shivering two red pounds— / you never got to cup them," Partridge wrote.

Partridge was too much an authentic talent not to seize on—and wring the music and metaphor out of—such harrowing subject matter. She belongs in the company of John Updike, whose excellent last book of poems, *Endpoint*, was quickly committed to paper as he was dying of cancer. Clive James, too, produced some of his most memorable lines in a fit of farewell. (See my essay, "Clive James's *Poetry Notebook*," which appears earlier in this volume.)

Partridge, it should be said, wrote about much more than her illness. *The If Borderlands* includes poignant autobiography, elegies for abandoned objects, and more. An extraordinary feminist poem, "My Last Duchess (The Manservant)," reimagines Robert Browning's "My Last Duchess" from the perspective of the help, rather than the callous duke who narrated the original. Then there are the exquisite recollections of childhood, like "The Artists' House," which somehow hack into the worm's-eye view of children encountering the world for the first time: "Inside, Ruth's whole family hung on the walls. / In the study Uncle Clint, / unfinished, clutched a glove, a blob of white. / The house wore forest twilight…."

In the choppy wake of Partridge's passing, notable writers took to social media to record their grief. *The If Borderlands* now provides her brief, brilliant career with a less ephemeral monument. The title is especially germane; it references a poem about counterfactuals, in which a "niece doesn't die, / one massacre's forestalled." Like Partridge railing against fate, some of us might bargain for more of her, wondering what could have been. But that would be a mistake. The poems Partridge left behind are right here, to be read now.

(ELLE, 2017)

Rishma Dunlop (1956–2016)

For a couple of years as a graduate student, I worked for Rishma Dunlop. Overflowing with projects—this was her natural mode—she needed something like an assistant. Mildly impoverished, I needed the income. Another professor put us in touch.

Our arrangement would have to be unofficial, of course; I already had my teaching assignment. Grad programs tend to discourage their students from taking on extra work. Read, teach, thesis—repeat.

But right here was the sort of policy that Rishma would've rolled her eyes at. (She rolled them often.) Even at our first meeting, I sensed we shared a truth: it's the extracurricular work, the work no one asks a writer to do, that matters most. Her own grad thesis—a creative piece—had been a first for her program. She would continue to probe the edges of what was possible, in any given situation, for the rest of her career as a poet and educator.

I helped Rishma with a couple things during that brief, abbreviated career: editing poems for some journal or project; administrative stuff. I didn't share her taste, exactly; she had patience for poets I couldn't quite admire. But she possessed the right kind of impatience—for bureaucracy, for a certain self-defeating strain of Canadian reticence. Her scrappy energy rubbed off easily. Students adored her.

We tended to meet over a lovely meal at some restaurant I couldn't really afford. Rishma tended to foot the bill. An impresario at heart, she always had several things on the go, which put a conspiratorial edge on our meetings. It's still hard to believe she's no longer around, no longer hatching some beautiful, stylish project.

(*Journal of the Motherhood Initiative*, 2017)

Harold Bloom (1930–2019)

When I was younger—back when I decided I was the sort of person who should try to read poetry given that I was writing so much of it—I bought something called *The Best of the Best American Poetry: 1988–1997*. *The Best American Poetry* is compiled annually by a guest editor who is recruited to riffle through the previous year's magazines (the ones that make room for poems) and assemble the better specimens. (For more on this series, see my essay, "The *Best American* Anthologies' Boosterism," earlier in this volume.)

The book I bought, however, represented a further, finer culling. It sifted only its predecessors: the first 10 volumes in the series. Here, then, were poems that had survived a double gauntlet. Not only was the chaff long gone but much of the wheat, too.

Actually, *The Best of the Best* sifted *nine* volumes. Yale professor, cultural arbiter, and professional lightning rod Harold Bloom—who edited *The Best of the Best* and died this week at the age of eighty-nine—took no poems from the 1996 edition and took pains to say so. "I failed to discover more than an authentic poem or two in it," writes Bloom in his introduction. "The series editor, David Lehman, kindly suggested some possibilities, but the poets involved had done better work elsewhere in these volumes."

The 1996 volume was edited by Adrienne Rich, the celebrated poet and feminist, but Bloom had no bandwidth for it. Rich's picks, he felt, were evidence of the collapsing standards he'd tried to buttress with his 1994 book *The Western Canon*. "That 1996 anthology is one of the provocations for this essay," he wrote, "since it seems to me a monumental representation of the enemies of the aesthetic who are in the act of overwhelming us. It is of a badness not to be believed, because it follows the criteria now operative: what matters most are the race, gender, sexual orientation, ethnic origin, and political purpose of the would-be poet." The essay rattled me like a rocket blast. It was as if I'd suddenly discovered I was living in a war zone. Apparently, a bloody conflict, The Culture Wars, had been raging all around me.

I didn't know then just how conductive a lightning rod this Harold Bloom was. (Naomi Wolf, a former student of Bloom's, had yet to accuse him of sexual harassment.) But his sentences were electric. Some of them, anyway. His intro begins with an epigraph: "They have the numbers; we, the heights." Bloom then gestures at it the way he might a quote on a chalkboard. "My epigraph is from Thucydides," he tells us, "and is spoken by the Spartan commander at Thermopylae." He goes on to unpack the metaphor:

> Culturally, we are at Thermopylae: the multi-culturalists, the hordes of camp-followers afflicted by the French diseases, the mock-feminists, the commissars, the gender-and-power freaks, the hosts of new historicists and old materialists—all stand below us. They will surge up and we may be overcome; our universities are already travesties, and our journalists parody our professors of "cultural studies."

What must David Lehman, poetry cheerleader and custodian of the *Best American Poetry* brand, have made of these sentences, when he first read them? I certainly didn't love the language of "freaks" and "diseases." (These days, it makes me wince.)

But Bloom could be stirring, too. "For just a little while longer," he continues, "we hold the heights, the realm of the aesthetic. There are still authentic poems being written in the United States." Who wouldn't want to "hold the heights"—at least in the late nineties, when it was easier to be an aesthete? Who doesn't want "authentic poems"?

I couldn't help but like the graveness of Bloom's intro. The gravity of it. "My charge," he explains, "was to select 75 poems out of 750, and not to look outside the volumes of this series...I have made a heap of all the best I could find, where I was instructed to search." Bloom's precision, here, is subversive, irascible, and irresistible. It's as if the rigorous aesthete can't fully endorse the gig he's reluctantly signed on to because the end product can't possibly include all the poems *he* would like you to read. A lot glances off the undergraduate mind, which can be as flimsy and flexible as a tin roof. But sometimes it finds itself electrified.

It's easy enough to dismiss Bloom or fire off a dart tipped with the word "problematic." The canon he championed was often male, mostly white, and far from what the hall monitors mean by "inclusive." In the aforementioned intro alone, he refers to the "Saturnalia" of the sixties and dismisses a *Times* writer who compares Prince to Mozart. Bloom exiled himself from his colleagues at Yale and came to occupy a department of one. There was no lawn he couldn't chase you off of. (See his feelings about *Harry Potter*.) Plus, there's the Wolf stuff.

But even these days, it's hard to quarrel with Bloom's bullshit detector, which took a pragmatic view of the limits of literature. "The Resenters prate of power, as they do of race and gender: these are careerist stratagems and have nothing to do with the insulted and injured, whose lives will not be improved by our reading the bad verses of those who assert that they are the oppressed." You need to hold your nose through the caps on "Resenters" and the verb "prate," but the professor has a point.

Perhaps Bloom could feel the way he felt because, as other remembrances make clear, he really *did* seem to have read everything. He could certainly make you feel, rightly, that nothing is more important than reading the right poem. "Nevertheless, there are poems here that should be perpetuated for future generations," he declares in that twenty-year-old intro, and you believe him. Which poems count as "right," or should be perpetuated, of course, will never be resolved. (I, for one, think he's wrong about many of his pet interests, from Hart Crane to John Ashbery.) But the example of Bloom's resolve, if not the contents of his thoughts, still delivers its charge.

(*Slate*, 2019)

Phil Spector (1939–2021)

A FEW YEARS AGO, I wrote a verse novel called *Forgotten Work* about an obscure band and its obsessive fans. The band's chief songwriter, one James Gordon, is an autocrat. He flogs his bandmates through endless sessions in pursuit of perfection. He pulls a gun on them and commits perfectly great takes to the sort of flames that specialize in erasing masterpieces. The bulk of the book is set in the future; Gordon has vanished, and a cult following (kitted out with smarteyes and flying scows, natch) is searching for any trace of the auteur.

But Gordon himself is hardly science fiction. I modelled him, in part, on the music producer Phil Spector, who died in prison on January 16, 2021, at the age of eighty-one, from COVID complications.

Spector was rock's Ur-autocrat. In the early sixties, in LA's Gold Star Studios, he conjured the iconic sound of the girl group: cavernous, awash in echo, and clattery with castanets. But "conjured" is wrong; Spector's so-called "Wall of Sound" was a feat of brute masonry. The young, imperious producer—glassed in by his iconic shades and abetted by crack arranger Jack Nitzsche—would drive the best session musicians in LA through take after take. (Soon, the musicians stopped sounding like themselves and started sounding like the widescreen music in Spector's mind.) Spector produced some of the most thrilling music of the sixties. But he also abused his wife, Ronnie Spector—who sang lead on the Ronettes' deathless "Be My Baby"—and would pull firearms on future clients Leonard Cohen and Dee Dee Ramone.

When "River Deep – Mountain High"—a bombastic Ike and Tina Turner single that employed two drummers—failed to top the charts in 1966, the producer retired from pop in protest. Although he'd return for brief periods, to oversee albums by John Lennon, George Harrison, and others, Spector became a recluse, befogged by myth, substance use, and mental health problems. Decades later in 2003, he would shoot Lana Clarkson, a veteran cult movie actress, at the so-called "Pyrenees Castle," Spector's mansion in Alhambra, California. (He claimed she'd "kissed the gun.") After an initial mistrial, he would finally be found guilty in 2009 and sentenced to nineteen years in prison.

It's sadly telling that it takes no less than a murder to decisively tarnish an auteur; spousal abuse alone hasn't especially ruffled the legends of Lennon, say, or Miles Davis. Perhaps we write off volatility and violence as the necessary lashings of the authentic artist's stormy personality.

In any case, before the unruly fact of Clarkson's killing, it was easy to romanticize Spector. It was easy to view his penchant for guns in the studio as an intense affectation, a signifier of all-or-nothing aesthetic commitment, like the "Back to Mono" button he boasted on his lapel. Plus, he hadn't recorded much in decades. Unfinished albums like doo-wop singer Dion's *Born to Be with You*, which Spector produced in 1974, had become cult items. The tantalizing prospect of sessions with a different Dion—Celine, she of the Wail of Sound—had come to naught. A brief spell in the early 2000s, with the English band Starsailor, yielded but two tracks.

The fruits of these late, crumbling efforts could hardly hold a castanet to "Be My Baby" or "You've Lost that Lovin' Feelin'," completed decades before. Still, the aura of an auteur, sitting on a stockpile of unexpressed genius, managed to cling. In a 2003 *Guardian* article about Spector's work with Starsailor, published not long after his arrest, the aura was as palpable as dry ice:

> The four Wigan lads were whisked by limo to Spector's house in LA's Alhambra, overlooking the poorer, Mexican district. Visitors are scrutinised by security cameras during

the long walk up the driveway. [James Stelfox, bassist for Starsailor] tells of a vast "castle" inhabited by signed pictures of Monroe, the Beatles and Sinatra.

Spector made his entrance in a curly wig, huge built-up heels and one of a collection of identical suits with "PS" embroidered on the label. If this was designed to impress Starsailor, Spector needn't have bothered. They were "in awe" of him, if also "shaking and nervous", but were immediately put at ease by his enthusiasm.

Starsailor would eventually fire Spector, who seemed to toggle between different moods, "day to day." Nevertheless, Stelfox was unequivocal: "We've got two tracks out of Phil Spector, which is more than anyone else has managed in twenty-three years…What a privilege."

When artists withdraw to castles, fandom fills the void. Obsessives like Spector—or the filmmaker Stanley Kubrick or the novelist Thomas Pynchon—tend to attract obsessives of their own, fans who find rich soil in stretches of artistic silence. Indeed, there's a strange pleasure in plowing the antimatter that great artists couldn't bring themselves to seed (perhaps, in part, because there's no shortage of less-than-great artists who dependably—desperately—bring work to market or, at least, the internet).

I love to think about the famously unfinished novel *Exterior Signs of Wealth*, by Fran Lebowitz, a writer who's committed very few words to print since her heyday in the seventies. Or the unwritten masterpieces of A.M. Klein, who turned away from poetry after composing his finest poem, "Portrait of the Poet as Landscape"; who, having reached his peak, almost immediately retreated down the slope. Or the lost Pynchon novel about Japanese monster movies, once mentioned in a *Washington Post* article. Or that album Spector never made with Celine Dion.

These fantastical works, if ever realized, would likely disappoint; their authors are ultimately—hopelessly—human. "No sleep, depression, mood changes, mood swings, hard to live with, hard to concentrate, just hard—a hard time getting through life," said Spector, in a court deposition. "I've been called a genius and I think a genius is not there all the time and has borderline insanity." He'd been taking medication for manic depression for the better part of a decade, he told the court.

It's tempting to project, to imagine that reclusive artists are stewing over something great, some work of art that wants a wine cellar—that wants time—to come into its own. It's easy, too, to reframe mental health problems as romantic madness. But the example of Spector—sleepless, unable to concentrate, and, finally, violent—exposes the limits of fandom. It reveals the way we can work ourselves into a lather in aid of washing off a hero's sins. Sure, you could wander the producer's castle in awe, as Starsailor did. But you could lose your life there, too. Fandom prefers to meet vivid heroes, not faded specters.

(Previously unpublished, 2021)

Peter Van Toorn (1944–2021)

"God, how they'll love me when I'm dead," Orson Welles once told his acolyte Peter Bogdanovich. To myth-seeking minds, Peter Van Toorn, who died on October 6, 2021 at the age of seventy-seven, was something like Canadian poetry's Welles: a romantic, difficult talent, popularly known for a single masterpiece and then a supposed lifelong slide into obscurity.

Van Toorn was born in Holland in 1944 and came to Canada as a child. He studied at McGill University under poets like F.R. Scott and Louis Dudek. (Northrop Frye described Van Toorn's work as "the product of an unusually intelligent mind.") He eventually taught at Concordia University and, later, John Abbott College. Van Toorn edited a couple of anthologies and took several runs at what would turn out to be his life work; his early books—*Leeway Grass* (1970) and *In Guildenstern County* (1973)—were eventually absorbed into the monumental *Mountain Tea*, which was nominated for Canada's Governor General's Award for Poetry in 1984.

Fizzing with ideas and formal bravura, *Mountain Tea* suggested a poet who could pull off anything: free verse, sonnets, translations. Even now, the book confounds categorization. At his freest, Van Toorn broke his lines thoughtfully and lay alliterative traps, triggering the reader's delight:

> Even so,
> not counting wind in the pines,
> wind in the brakeslams,
> there's hardly any

to go by. Go
by, put arms around, smoke on, ride off, bounce
on a blanket about.

Conversely, he could storm inside a sonnet by Rimbaud and make fresh mischief:

With rips in my pockets big enough to
put my fists through, my coat in great shape too,
I made for the mountains, Muse, true to you.
Jesus, the dreams of love I'd wake up to!
Skies I wore for hats!

Like the album *Charlie Parker with Strings*, Van Toorn's masterpiece cut chaos with classicism.

In time, *Mountain Tea* fell out of print, and Van Toorn, into neglect. Montreal's Véhicule Press reissued the book in 2003. "I believe it is fair to say that Canadian poetry will not come of age until it is ready to rediscover and rehabilitate the work of Peter Van Toorn," declared the poet David Solway in the introduction. The reissue drew interest. Zachariah Wells, Michael Lista, and others wrote about *Mountain Tea*. A younger generation made its pilgrimages—by phone, on foot.

In my verse novel *Forgotten Work*, a cult following casts about for a lost band named "Mountain Tea." Perhaps Van Toorn himself sensed he was doomed to be a cult item. In the early 1970s, irritated by the anti-aesthetic impulses of Canadian editors and critics, he contemplated an anthology called *Mainstream*, going so far as to pull together a manuscript of neglected Canadian poetry. Publishers balked, and Van Toorn scrapped the book. Another project, an essay collection called *Handy Handles*, came to naught.

Orson Welles, too, abandoned many projects. Still, he managed to complete a number of post-*Citizen Kane* pictures, some of which were wonderful. Van Toorn never published another book after *Mountain Tea*.

(Published as an unattributed obituary in PN *Review*, 2021)

Ed Piskor (1982-2024)

In one episode of the popular YouTube show *Cartoonist Kayfabe*, the late Ed Piskor is flipping through the fourth issue of *Love and Rockets*, the iconic comic series by the Hernandez brothers—when suddenly Piskor pauses. "This is definitely the issue," he says, off screen, "where I realize, like, you will never make comics like this, you do not have the experience that the bros have, so you better just figure out how to make your own kind of comic, cuz it's impossible to even approximate this if you don't have a lot of tools that, that these dudes just *have*, you know—through life, through experience, whatever."

"It is mind boggling," agrees Piskor's friend, the cartoonist Jim Rugg, also off screen.

Piskor, who co-hosted the daily show with Rugg, was a maverick cartoonist and unflagging missionary for the medium of comics. He was the Quentin Tarantino of T-squares: an overheated fusion of fan and artist, throwing off light and energy with every utterance. And his superpower was awe. "Good luck," he'd often say ruefully, confronted by another artist's impossible-to-pull-off drawing. His pale, narrow index finger was always darting into the shot (you came to know the character of each co-host's hand) to point at a perfectly inked swoop of line or an inspired feat of economy. (Sometimes, the enthusiastic Piskor leaned in so close to the art he obscured it.) He would marvel at artists who'd found simple solutions to convey, say, a complicated setting—then joke about his own tendency to draw every pill bottle in the pharmacy.

But Piskor's self-effacing awe was always infectious, never defeatist. He often signed off from videos by declaring that he was fired up and ready to get back to the drawing board.

A lot of us were ready to get back to our boards. *Cartoonist Kayfabe* was approaching 100,000 subscribers when Piskor died by apparent suicide. (There had been sexual misconduct allegations, followed by an online mob.) The show, which covered comics new and old, was COVID-era comfort food. It inspired a devout fandom, including a mix of professionals and aspirants. It also rebooted dormant passions and lapsed dabblers; as I noted earlier in this book, *Cartoonist Kayfabe* got me drawing again after a quarter-century hiatus. I came to adopt Piskor's preferred brand of marker. I came to steal his solution for "s" from his charmingly scrappy, hand-lettered font.

Piskor's own comics were the product of a roving, ravenous fandom. Like Tarantino, who authored cinematic love letters to kung fu, blaxploitation, the spaghetti western, and other genres, Piskor transmuted hero-worship into original work, trying his ink-stained hand at beloved styles and subjects. He crafted large-scale histories of hip-hop and the X-Men: two loves of his life. (The first volume of *X-Men: Grand Design* reproduces pages Piskor drew as a kid on lined notebook paper.) His black-and-white horror series, *Red Room*, channeled a passion for outlaw comics. His last completed work, *Switchblade Shorties*, was doled out on Instagram every twenty-four hours: a paean to the daily strips of yesteryear.

Piskor retained a soft spot for the assembly line comics of his youth, but he was a hands-on auteur at heart. He wrote, lettered, penciled, inked, and coloured his comics. His models were indie cartoonists like Robert Crumb, Daniel Clowes, Jaime and Gilbert Hernandez, and others operating outside of the Marvel-DC dyad, which very nearly amounted to a monopoly at one point. These independent cartoonists, Piskor's heroes, held onto their rights—and tended to handle the whole production themselves.

X-Men: Grand Design surely confounded twenty-first century fanboys. A devotee of practical, pre-digital methods, Piskor favoured flat colours, dot screens, grimy yellow caption boxes, hipster-hatching wormholed in from the 1970s, and off-white paper implying newsprint. (He'd conquered YouTube, but skewed analogue.) At one point, he depicts a scene from the childhood of Charles Xavier, who will later lead the X-Men as wheelchair-bound Professor X. The young Charles has discovered he can read minds and that his new stepbrother is violent. Piskor draws Charles's thoughts, which include an image of the stepbrother stabbing Charles. But here's the cool part: Piskor replaces each of Charles's eyes with an "X." It's a punk-rock choice; the X-eyes, off-model for a self-serious Marvel comic, allude to Charles's future as an X-Man—but also to the cartooning conventions of the past, to a shared tradition of convenient shorthand.

Put another way: Piskor drawing Marvel characters was like Sid Vicious covering "My Way."

With his trademark Pirates hat, gaze-blotting sunglasses, and YouTube ubiquity, the Pittsburgh cartoonist cut a conspicuous, polarizing figure. In one episode of *Cartoonist Kayfabe*, Piskor and Rugg review a *Wonder Woman* comic made by Gilbert Hernandez. The comic, like Piskor's X-Men lark, was a brilliantly counterintuitive pairing of indie cartoonist and corporate property. But Hernandez still faced hurdles from DC editorial in getting access to the characters. Piskor, natch, goes off:

> If an artist like Gilbert Hernandez *deigns* to make a comic with your ridiculous dreck that you have out on the stands on a monthly basis, and you don't let him do what he wants, that is a fault of you the editor, the publisher. Fuck your trademarks or whatever. This guy can put a brand new coat of paint on something that has languished for a million years, you know. This stuff is *dead*.

Piskor had little patience for comics made by so-called "jobbers"—artists labouring for the benefit of corporations that are more invested in protecting IP than producing compelling panels. With DIY heroes like the Hernandez brothers in mind, he was a vocal, pugilistic partisan for creator rights.

He also worked hard. He was constantly updating us on the pages he'd gotten done, constantly talking through new ways to shave time off his process, constantly metabolizing. The example of his hustle was a threat to excuse-making. When he went to Japan, he returned home lugging two dozen volumes of storyboards for Miyazaki movies. "These are more important to me than the movies," he said on his show, placing his hands, almost protectively, on a shot-filling tableful of covers, "because as I understand it, the man is thinking on paper." Later, thumbing through one of the Miyazaki books, Piskor says,

> What I've been doing is, I'm laying out my new *Red Room* comics, and before breakfast, I'll sit down with these and just, like, look at the compositions, and just see…what's possible with the picture plane. It's just a good treat for your eyeballs before you engage in this same kind of practice of laying out your stuff.

Piskor was an easy target for the heat-seeking hatred of envious peers. He was also human. I've left the drama surrounding his death in parentheticals because I'm not an investigative journalist. (Anyway, the cartoonist Katie Skelly handled it all elegantly in her obituary for *The Comics Journal*.)

My interest is the man steeping his mind in another man's storyboards before breakfast.

I fell down the *Cartoonist Kayfabe* rabbit hole shortly after finishing work on a verse novel a few years back. It takes an enormous effort just to write a plain old novel; it takes a kind of madness to compose one in rhyming couplets. But the spine-warping labour of drawing comics day in and day out for years on end requires superhuman focus—the sort that can laser through steel.

What irradiated spider-bite produces such persistence? (I know, I know, I'm mixing my Super- and Spiderman metaphors.) Piskor clearly drew inspiration and nourishment from the work ethic of others. He has cited the example of Robert Crumb filling sketchbooks and "living on the page." He has cited his friend and fellow Pittsburgh cartoonist, Tom Scioli, who used to ink comics on the bus. The trick, as Piskor often suggested, was to get off your phone and chain yourself to your desk.

Skelly's obituary records an apocryphal story:

> In his teenage years, Piskor suffered a near-fatal bout of colitis resulting in a case of intestinal bleeding that saw him hospitalized for a month. Believing the incident to be caused by the anxiety he faced in school, Piskor claimed to have convinced his parents to allow him to be self-homeschooled for the rest of his high school career following his recovery. His new, unorthodox schedule granted him longer pockets of time in which to study the likes of Jack Kirby, Chris Claremont, Jim Lee, Rob Liefeld and the canon of superhero comics.

Because I have the first volume of *X-Men: Grand Design* still open to Professor X's childhood, I can't help but see something of Piskor in the young, bald Charles sitting on the floor of his room, next to a stack of books (panel three, page 11). I also can't help but be floored. Piskor has filled the background of this narrow, almost throwaway panel with unnecessarily splendid detail: spines on a bookcase, drawers on a dresser, panels on a door, and so on.

Perhaps Piskor, if he were still with us, would take himself to task for drawing all the pill bottles in the pharmacy once again. Perhaps he would chalk it up to "graphomania," a term that often came up on *Cartoonist Kayfabe*. Perhaps there's a simpler, less time-consuming solution to suggesting a child's bedroom.

Nevertheless, and to borrow a line from Piskor, this is definitely the panel where I realize I will never make comics like this. Also: time to get back to the drawing board.

(Previously unpublished, 2025)

Peter Bogdanovich (1939–2022)

Late in his little-remembered picture *They All Laughed* (1981), the director Peter Bogdanovich places his camera at the top of a flight of courthouse steps. A man and woman, laden with luggage, ascend the steps, pass the camera, and move out of shot. Next, a cab pulls up, and releases John Ritter. Ritter, playing a private eye, nearly forgets to pay his fare, he's in that much of a hurry. He takes the courthouse steps in several strides, but this time, the camera swivels, following him inside. Finally, Bogdanovich cuts—to a bird's-eye view of Ritter in the courthouse lobby—and you can be forgiven if you've forgotten you've been looking at a single piece of film, unbroken; forgetting is the point of long, immersive takes.

After the bird's-eye-view shot, Bogdanovich cuts to Ritter's pained face in close-up. As his actor swivels about, Bogdanovich cuts to what Ritter's eyeballing. Different hallways. Different paths his quarry might've taken.

"I really love the way it was shot," said the director Wes Anderson, when he discussed the scene with Bogdanovich for the film's twenty-fifth-anniversary DVD. Anderson liked how the scene gave the impression of precision, of a filmmaker in command of his medium. Clearly, the man who'd made *They All Laughed* knew how the footage would fit together.

"I like movies where I feel the director, the storyteller, is taking me somewhere," Bogdanovich replied. "I have faith that he's got a strong grip on me, and he's taking me somewhere."

Bogdanovich might as well have been talking about himself. The late poet and critic Clive James once described him as "[e]xtraordinarily concerned in his films with the integrity of his technique and the burden of what he was saying with it." What a refreshing, nourishing thought for our post-truth moment—that being clear is a burden we ought to be concerned about!

Bogdanovich—who passed away on January 6, 2022 and whose most acclaimed pictures include *The Last Picture Show* (1971) and *Paper Moon* (1973)—started making films in the late sixties. But his heart was in the thirties and forties, the Golden Age of Hollywood. Like his heroes Howard Hawks and John Ford, he was obsessed with the most efficient way to put a story over. He strove for long, unbroken takes, avoided shooting a lot of coverage, was conservative with close-ups, and kept dialogue to a minimum. Above all, he wanted to be in control of his message.

Being in control has never been a particularly good look for an artist. Entertainment that grips us—the "gripping read"—tends to be associated with the baser outputs of Hollywood and genre fiction. The desire for control can feel obsessive, even paranoid. Think of Phil Spector, pushing his session musicians through take after take in search of his Wall of Sound, while micromanaging every detail of the life of his spouse, the singer Ronnie Spector, down to her shoes. Too much craft can seem too controlling, too conscientious. We like our artists a little rumpled.

So, as virtues go, control is underrated. And yet when it's present, we feel it. See, for instance, Stanley Kubrick's trademark tracking shots, which are so distinctive we might as well be peering through the director's very pupils. Even behind a stormier surface—a Jackson Pollock canvas, say, or a Sylvia Plath poem, or a David Lynch film—we sense a presiding intelligence: an adult in the room, even if the room has been upended by gale-force winds. The work may look messy and yield many different meanings. But the adult knew what they were doing. We have something like Bogdanovich's "faith" that we're in good hands.

The absence of control, too, is almost always felt. The rebels who really *do* lose control—who submit to psychedelics or chance techniques, scissoring the page and setting the ribbons aswirl—usually go too far. They might have had some high-minded goal of unseating the authorial "I" or toppling capitalism, but the results aren't always fun to endure. See language poetry. See the hot mess at the open mic.

Or see social media, which allows anyone to be a *creator*, a ghastly noun that seems to mean a writer without an editor: a self-publisher, really. (We used to frown on self-publishing.) Controlling the message is devilishly hard when you're typing at the tempo of, say, Twitter. I'm not even thinking about the ill-advised tweets that capsize careers. I'm thinking about run-of-the-mill tweets that betray their authors' ulterior motives: boasts disguised as "professional news," or pleas for attention that come suspended in the jello of jokes. I'm thinking about tweets that don't have a handle on their tone, that don't come with a properly functioning guidance system.

That hastily launched missives so often go awry isn't surprising. It's always been the case that writing is hard work. It's such a feat when you think about it. Every sentence—every word—presents a fork. Make the wrong choice and you wind up at a dead end, maybe with a mob after you, the villagers armed with gardening implements or, worse, memes. You have to be constantly vigilant as a writer. You have to have a strong grip while exercising the lightest touch.

Consider an *Atlantic* essay by Caitlin Flanagan—a close reading of Meghan and Harry's exile and, specifically, their blockbuster interview with Oprah a few years ago. (It was such a blockbuster that none of the participants needed surnames.) Flanagan is good on Meghan, but hilariously precise when it comes to Harry:

> When Harry was allowed into the conversation, he sat beside his wife looking like he'd been shot from a cannon. Before he met Meghan, he was a prince of Europe—almost a crown prince—a young man whose life was part of a continuation from Excalibur to Afghanistan, where he fought with valor in the manner of Prince Hal finding within himself Henry

> V. Now, however, he is like Antonio: tempest-tossed and thrown up upon the wide beaches of the brave new world.

Where to start here? There's the obvious excellence of the details: the explosive simile ("looking like he'd been shot from a cannon"), the pocket history ("from Excalibur to Afghanistan"), and the samples from Shakespeare ("tempest-tossed," "brave new world").

But there's something else, too, a sense of calm, of cool—general as Joyce's snow—in Flanagan's prose. Nowhere does she commit to a definitive opinion about Harry; her essay isn't a "take." A take, of course, is internet-speak for a very, very specific thesis. It's a narrow position, a small patch of turf: "What Homer Gets Wrong about Sirens." It's a little like the prosaic, bare-bones '55 Chevy in the road movie *Two-Lane Blacktop*, which has been stripped of aesthetic luxuries and rebuilt for street-racing: it has to get somewhere, and very quickly.

Flanagan obviously has opinions. (She has written about private schools, HR departments, an Instagram influencer, that Woody Allen memoir, Melania Trump, the perils of *Rudolph the Red-Nosed Reindeer*, and so on.) But she doesn't write takes, and anyway she's too smart to come out and say, "Harry is in over his head, and quite possibly unhappy, and the podcast thing is doomed, and the chicken coop he now keeps with Meghan is probably problematic." That would be no fun for us. Flanagan takes her time and marshals her resources; she has to be subtle if she wants to hold the reader.

Take that opening—"When Harry was allowed into the conversation"—and note the passive construction, how carefully and quietly it brings poor Harry to heel. Or take the sentences that follow on from Flanagan's initial sketch:

> Once, he led men into battle, as his forebears had done for generations. Now he is a Californian with a Spotify deal, charged with thinking up some podcasts, which could be a heavy lift. For Harry, the situation is evolving.

Flanagan knows she doesn't have to do much more than set the facts beside each other, so long as she uses words with maximum polarity: there was a leader of "men" who had "forebears"; here is a "Californian with a Spotify deal." The choice of that word "charged" is especially savvy, yet more proof of an unhorsed prince no longer holding the reins. So, too, is the qualification, "which *could* be a heavy lift" (italics mine, obviously; Flanagan rarely mallets a point). The paragraph's ironic last line, in very precisely chosen present tense—"For Harry, the situation is evolving"—is far more damning than any conclusion Flanagan herself might've drawn out and left at our feet.

It's a relief to read prose that's the product of a sure hand, that doesn't *seem* to have strong designs on us. Flanagan can be ruthless, but she also knows the windmill-power of a wink. She knows a daub of irony, here and there, does way more work than indignation. She is so obviously in control of her writing.

The same can be said of Bogdanovich, who was not just a great director, but a stylish writer, too, one who left behind a heap of essays, monographs, and full-length books. A savvy interviewer, he pressed his heroes on points of craft, but left the right quotes uncommented on. Here's the director John Ford, holding forth in a 1964 profile Bogdanovich filed for *Esquire*:

> "Producers don't know anything about making pictures," [Ford] said earnestly. "And that's why I shoot my films so they can only be cut one way." He puffed on his cigar. "They get to the cutting room and they say, 'Well, let's stick a close-up in here.'" Ford paused. "But there isn't one. I didn't shoot it."

Ford was famous for the practice of "cutting in the camera"— basically, filming only what he needed. The dearth of footage forced his editors to work with puzzle pieces that fit together only one way. Cutting in the camera was control by other means. It pre-thwarted the potential whims of the studio brass.

Inspired by the example of craftsmen like Ford, Bogdanovich came close to losing his job over a fight scene in *The Last Picture Show*, his most celebrated movie. (Bogdanovich had refrained from filming a master shot, which would've provided coverage.) Nevertheless, Bogdanovich remained committed to the bygone practice, and used it throughout the filming of *They All Laughed*, nearly a decade later. "We cut it in the camera more than any picture I've ever done except maybe *Saint Jack*," he told Anderson in that DVD interview. "There's nothing left out. It was shot exactly the way it's cut." You can hear the pride in Bogdanovich's voice.

You can hear it, too, in the many audio commentary tracks he recorded for the DVDs of his movies—celebrated comedies like *What's Up, Doc?* (1972) and lesser-known items like *The Cat's Meow* (2001). Bogdanovich was always pointing out the long takes he managed to pull off, his hard-won use of deep-focus cinematography, his ability to advance the plot without a word of dialogue, and other old-school feats of restraint, economy, and clarity.

Perhaps Bogdanovich's greatest moment as a director—his *monument*—is the long take in *The Last Picture* Show in which Ben Johnson (playing town patriarch "Sam the Lion") delivers an aching monologue about an old affair to young Timothy Bottoms (playing a high school senior). Johnson and Bottoms have been fishing some overcast water, and as Johnson dilates on his lost love—and as the camera zooms slowly in, creeping up on the sort of close-up Bogdanovich was careful not to overuse—sunlight breaks through the clouds and gilds Johnson. It's an extraordinary moment of good fortune, a moment you could never plan for, as if the gods of cinema had approved the shot.

Then, disaster. Bogdanovich zooms out to bring Bottoms back into the frame, for Bottoms's character has a question to ask about marriage. But during the filming of the scene, Bottoms forgot his line! Bogdanovich had to cut away so that his young actor could be fed the line, which you hear over a shot of the water. Then the film cuts back to Johnson as he resumes his monologue, which he duly nails.

It's heartrending stuff—for the viewer, who is moved by Johnson's words, but also for Bogdanovich, who didn't want to have to splice a random shot of water into the middle of a tour de force. And yet it *is* a tour de force: a perfect performance (Johnson went on to win an Oscar that year) embedded in a *near*-perfect shot.

It's a collaboration between exquisite craft, sunny serendipity, and whatever trickster deity loots the minds of actors at the worst possible moment. It's a reminder that a director, as Bogdanovich's mentor Orson Welles once said, is a person "who presides over accidents," a person who should want to go "fishing for accidents." It's a reminder that even great artists sometimes need to get a grip—and let go.

(*The Yale Review*, 2022)

ACKNOWLEDGMENTS

Variations of these essays first appeared in *Air Mail*, *The Atlantic*, *Canadian Notes & Queries*, ELLE, *Flavorwire*, *Journal of the Motherhood Initiative*, *Lit Hub*, *The Millions*, *The National Post*, *The New Republic*, *Partisan*, *PN Review*, *Slate*, *The Walrus*, and *The Yale Review*. My thanks to the editors, including especially Ash Carter, Chloe Schama, Meghan O'Rourke, Lenika Cruz, Michael Schmidt, Katy Waldman, Jonny Diamond, and Sam Adams.

A different version of "Fandom Before the Internet" first appeared in *The Walrus*, then wound up in my book *On Browsing* (Biblioasis, 2022). Thanks to Dan Wells, Biblioasis's publisher, for letting me reprint it here.

Dan also greenlighted an ongoing comic-strip, *The Pigheaded Soul*, for his magazine *Canadian Notes & Queries*, yielding the strips in this book. (Some of these were in the pipeline and haven't appeared in CNQ yet, so I will have to draw you new ones, Dan.)

The *Cartoonist Kayfabe* channel on YouTube, hosted by Ed Piskor and Jim Rugg, inspired me to start drawing again—after twenty-five years away from the drawing board. My friend Mitch Brewer has been a source of inspiration, too, encouraging me as he's received pictures of my panels, one text at a time. Comic fans should check out Mitch's very funny and accomplished superhero series *Blood Force*.

Thanks to Michael Lista, Evan Jones, Rick Ramdeen, and Bobby Lotz—and, more recently, Ira Wells, Stephen Marche, and Jordan Michael Smith—for ongoing and invigorating conversations, usually over drinks. Michael and I co-edited the short-lived, sharp-tongued website *Partisan*, where a couple of these pieces first appeared. I'm particularly thankful for his friendship and fearless example.

I remain indebted to my editor, the poet-critic Carmine Starnino, who commissioned a number of these essays for *The Walrus*, sharpened the vision for *Fan Mail*, and kept me (mostly) calm. I remain a founding member of his fan club.

And I remain grateful for my brilliant wife Christie—and for her extraordinary love and patience as I worked on these essays over the course of the last decade.

INDEX

Abramson, Seth 227-228
Amis, Kingsley 72-76, 123
  The Alteration 72-76
Amis, Martin 32, 123, 198
Anderson, Wes 28-29, 31, 228, 279, 284
  Fantastic Mr. Fox (2009) 228
Auden, W.H. 92, 96, 232

Ballard, J.G. 57-60, 123-125
  Concrete Island 57-60
  Crash 57, 59
  High-Rise 57, 59, 60
  The Drowned World 60, 123-125
Beach Boys, The 61-64, 126, 249
  Pet Sounds 61-64, 188
  Smile 26, 63
  Today! 62
Beatles, The 15, 62, 63, 160, 161, 172, 196, 252, 270
  Let It Be 160
  Rubber Soul 62
  Sgt. Pepper's Lonely Hearts Club Band 63
Best American series, The 165-169, 265-267
Bishop, Elizabeth 35, 175, 233, 238, 240
Bloom, Harold 18, 71, 147, 265-267
  The Western Canon 265
Bogdanovich, Peter 17-18, 28-31, 32, 50, 102, 228, 272, 279-280, 283-285
  At Long Last Love (1975) 30
  Paper Moon (1973) 28, 280
  Pieces of Time 228

  Saint Jack (1979) 284
  She's Funny That Way (2014) 28-29, 31
  Targets (1968) 29-30
  The Cat's Meow (2001) 284
  The Last Picture Show (1971) 28, 30, 228, 280, 284-285
  They All Laughed (1981) 30, 279
  What's Up, Doc? (1972) 28, 228, 284
Bolaño, Roberto 15, 175
  The Savage Detectives 115, 175, 177, 182
Booker, James 251-252
Brown, Daniel 71, 81, 243
Brunetti, Ivan 150-151
Byron, George Gordon, Lord, 81, 105, 106-107
  Don Juan 81, 106-107, 115

Callow, Simon 47-52
  Hello Americans 47
  The Road to Xanadu 47
  One-Man Band 47, 50-52
  Being an Actor 48-49
Capote, Truman 108, 112
Carson, Anne 107, 108, 112, 176, 229
  Red Doc> 108
Corman, Roger 29, 127

Dahl, Roald 254-257
  "Lucky Break—How I Became a Writer" 254-257
De Palma, Brian 18, 37-40
  Dressed to Kill (1980) 37-40

Carrie (1976) 38
Scarface (1983) 38
Sisters (1973) 38
Body Double (1984) 39
Blow Out (1981) 148, 221
Dexys Midnight Runners 148-149
Too-Rye-Ay 148-149
Disch, Thomas 80, 147
 The Castle of Indolence: On Poetry, Poets, and Poetasters 147
Dunlop, Rishma 264
Dylan, Bob 172, 196, 197-198

Eliot, T.S. 55, 71, 85, 92-94, 194, 236, 237, 239, 243
 The Waste Land 78, 81
 "Tradition and the Individual Talent" 93, 243
Eugenides, Jeffrey
 The Virgin Suicides 180-183

Fermor, Patrick Leigh 23-27
 A Time of Gifts 23, 24, 26
 Between the Woods and the Water 23
 The Broken Road 24-26, 27
 A Time of Silence 27
Finnegan, William 146-147
 Barbarian Days: A Surfing Life 146-147
Flanagan, Caitlin 281-283
Ford, John 18, 29, 102, 280, 283-284
 The Searchers (1956) 18, 28, 30, 151
Fox, Paula 113, 250, 253
 Desperate Characters 113, 250
Frost, Robert 18, 35, 36, 71, 77, 78, 90, 92, 105

Galassi, Jonathan 175-179
 Muse 175-179
Gerhard 15, 85, 86-87
Gibson, William 14, 17, 60, 75, 116-122, 225
 "Burning Chrome" 116
 Burning Chrome 122
 Count Zero 118
 "Johnny Mnemonic" 116, 117-118, 119-122
 Neuromancer 116-117, 119, 122
 Pattern Recognition 119
 Peripheral, The 121-122
 Virtual Light 118, 119
Goldsmith, Kenneth 170-174
 "The Body of Michael Brown" 170-174
 Seven American Deaths and Disasters 172
Guns N' Roses 27, 61, 236
 Chinese Democracy 61
Guriel, Jason 104, 135-137, 138-140, 141-145
 "Charles Bruce's Poems" 65-66
 "Christopher Lehmann-Haupt's Blurb for Gravity's Rainbow" 113-115
 "Jason Guriel's Childhood Comic Store" 138-140
 "Randall Jarrell's Pigheaded Soul" 41-42
 Forgotten Work 17, 79, 81, 82, 241, 268, 273
 Full-Moon Whaling Chronicles, The 17, 241, 243
 On Browsing 17, 141, 253, 287

Hawks, Howard 29, 100-102, 280
 Bringing Up Baby (1938) 100-102

Hayes, Liam 251-253
Heaney, Seamus 224, 233, 238-239
  "Fiddleheads" 238
  "The Harvest Bow" 239
Hellman, Monte 126-128, 249
  Two-Lane Blacktop (1971) 126-128, 282
Hernandez, Jaime & Gilbert 274-276
  Love and Rockets 18, 274
Hitchcock, Alfred 18, 29, 38, 40
  Psycho (1960) 37, 38
  Rear Window (1954) 38
  Vertigo (1958) 38
Hitchens, Christopher 68, 81, 105, 111, 123, 125, 130, 162, 198
Hofmann, Michael 225-226, 258-260
  Behind the Lines 258-260
Hopkins, Gerard Manley 35
  "Spring" 35

James, Clive 11, 18, 30, 32-36, 68, 103, 198, 219, 247, 263, 279-280
  Cultural Amnesia 11, 34, 35, 115
  "Japanese Maple" 32-33
  Poetry Notebook: Reflections on the Intensity of Language 34-36
Jarrell, Randall 41-42, 192
Joyce, James 87, 202, 243, 282
  Ulysses 87, 111, 115
  Portrait of the Artist as a Young Man 202
  "The Dead" 243, 282

Kenner, Hugh 258
Kubrick, Stanley 13, 60, 270, 280
  A Clockwork Orange (1971) 60

Lane, Anthony 219, 220
Lebowitz, Fran 201-202, 219, 230, 236, 270
  Exterior Signs of Wealth 270
  The Fran Lebowitz Reader 230
Linklater, Richard 24, 127
  Before Midnight (2013) 24
Lista, Michael 243, 273
Lockwood, Patricia 36, 261
  "Rape Joke" 233, 237-238
Lowell, Robert 34, 35
  "A Quaker Graveyard in Nantucket" 34
Lynch, David 13, 185, 187, 193, 280
  Blue Velvet (1986) 193
  Eraserhead (1977) 13

Melville, Herman 114-115, 219
  Moby-Dick 114-115, 219
Metcalf, Stephen 151, 205, 216, 217, 225
Moore, Alan 86, 87, 203-206, 242
  Swamp Thing 203, 242
  Miracleman 216
  The Killing Joke 203-206
  Watchmen 203-204, 214
  V for Vendetta 59, 76, 203
Morrison, Toni 208
My Bloody Valentine 15, 27

Nabokov, Vladimir 17, 77-79, 178, 241
  Lolita 109, 183
  Pale Fire 17, 77-79, 81, 82, 241
  The Original of Laura 26
Noel-Tod, Jeremy 232-239
  The Penguin Book of the Prose Poem (ed.) 232-239

Orwell, George 72, 74, 75, 211
  Nineteen Eighty-Four 72, 75, 211

Paglia, Camille 187
Parker, Dorothy 77, 146, 159, 192, 198
  The Portable Dorothy Parker 146
Partridge, Elise 261-263
  The If Borderlands 261-263
  Fielder's Choice 261
  Chameleon Hours 262
  The Exiles' Gallery 262
  "Cancer Surgery" 262
  "Last Days" 262
  "The Artists' House" 263
Patterson, Troy 55, 219
Piskor, Ed 18, 42, 132-133, 135-136, 274-278, 287
  X-Men: Grand Design 275-276, 278
Pound, Ezra 36, 80, 105, 109-110, 176, 258
  The Cantos 78, 88
Proulx, E. Annie 16, 166
Pynchon, Thomas 111, 113-115, 229, 251, 270
  Gravity's Rainbow 100, 113-115
Patterson, Troy 55, 219

Replacements, The 160, 190
Robbins, Michael 160-164
  The Second Sex 160-163
  "Alien vs. Predator" 160-161
  Alien vs. Predator 160, 164
Ryan, Kay 16-17, 18, 71, 81, 89-99, 107, 200-201, 251
  "I Go to AWP" 18, 89-90, 201

"Notes on the Danger of Notebooks" 95
Synthesizing Gravity: Selected Prose 91-99, 115

Scioli, Tom 132-134, 137, 149-150, 277-278
  American Barbarian 137
  I Am Stan 132-134
  Jack Kirby: The Epic Life of the King of Comics 132
  Godzilla Masterpiece Theatre 149-150
Seidel, Frederick 36, 161, 163
Seth 86, 136, 146
  Clyde Fans 84
Sim, Dave 15, 83-87
  Cerebus 15, 83-88
Skelly, Katie 277-278
Smith, Stevie 18, 96-97
Spector, Phil 18, 62, 268-271, 280
  "Be My Baby" 64, 268, 269
  "River Deep - Mountain High" 268
Stallings, A.E. 71, 129-131, 243, 251
  This Afterlife: Selected Poems 129-131
  "Silence" 129
  Archaic Smile 130
  Olives 130
  "Another Bedtime Story" 130
  "Scissors" 131
Starnino, Carmine 65, 243, 248, 287-288
Stein, Gertrude 95, 105
Stillman, Whit 53-56
  Metropolitan (1990) 53, 54, 55-56
  Barcelona (1994) 53, 55, 56

The Last Days of Disco (1998) 53, 55, 56
Damsels in Distress (2011) 56

Tapper, Jake 103
Tarantino, Quentin 38, 148, 212, 274, 275
Taylor, Bruce 201, 240, 243
Thammavongsa, Souvankham 200

Van Toorn, Peter 272-273
　Mountain Tea 84, 272-273

Wallace, David Foster 16, 27, 157-158, 184-189, 192-193, 194, 225
　The Pale King 27
　Infinite Jest 115, 184, 185, 188
　A Supposedly Fun Thing I'll Never Do Again 185
　"E Unibus Pluram: Television and US Fiction" 185-186
Welles, Orson 29, 43-46, 47-52, 102, 236, 272, 273, 285
　Chimes at Midnight (1965) 50, 51
　Citizen Kane (1941) 18, 30, 43, 44, 47, 52, 144, 204, 273
　Macbeth (1948) 48
　Mr. Arkadin, or Confidential Report (1955) 43-46, 50
　Othello (1952) 50-51
　Other Side of the Wind, The (2018) 26, 31
　Trial, The (1962) 50, 51
Wilson, Carl 156-159, 194, 217
　Let's Talk About Love: Why Other People Have Such Bad Taste 156-159, 194
Wilson, Brian 18, 61-64, 252
Wilson, Dennis 126-128
　Pacific Ocean Blue 249, 251
Wilson, Edmund 32, 191
Wiman, Christian 16-17, 34, 67-71, 251
　Hammer is the Prayer: Selected Poems 67, 69-71
　"In Praise of Rareness" 67
　"Poštolka (Prague)" 69-70

Yeats, William Butler 172-174, 208

Žižek, Slavoj 32, 111, 214